Acclaim for James E. McWilliams's

JUST FOOD

WHERE LOCAVORES GET IT WRONG AND HOW WE CAN TRULY EAT RESPONSIBLY

"Terrific.... For anyone who's interested in how we're going to feed the earth's burgeoning population in ways that sustain and replenish resources instead of stripping them away.... And it's going to make some people, especially ranchers and politicians, uneasy."
—Kim Pierce, *Dallas Morning News*

"Environmental responsibility is the main subject of *Just Food*.... As everyone who reads him knows, McWilliams doesn't shy from breaking locavores and generally right-minded food people of many of their most cherished assumptions, even if he shares many of their practices."
—Corby Kummer, TheAtlantic.com

"*Just Food* is a passionate, informed take on the current food craze.... McWilliams delights in pointing out that a lot of what seems intuitively correct about food turns out not to be so.... Even when you disagree, McWilliams has challenged the accepted wisdom and given you something to think about."
—Russ Parsons, *Los Angeles Times*

"Forceful, analytic.... Before Alice Waters and Michael Pollan, the ethical question about food was how to keep people from starving. McWilliams revisits this problem to great effect.... He offers a sustained analysis of the unsexy things we can do to make agriculture better and never loses sight of the fact that farming is, at the end of the day, very hard work."
—Elizabeth Lopatto, Bloomberg.com

"McWilliams has guts. Some of the changes he champions will draw fire from all quarters.... McWilliams forgoes sloganeering in favor of measured logic, but he doesn't downplay the notion that a worldwide food crisis is imminent and that we had better fix things. Soon."
—Mike Shea, *Texas Monthly*

"Important and pressingly relevant.... McWilliams provides some notable perspective on issues from biotechnology to pesticides to agribusiness, arguing that the best efforts of well-meaning American consumers cannot feed a growing world."
—Rebekah Denn, *Christian Science Monitor*

"With wit, clarity, and a highly engaging style, McWilliams brings a voice of reason to the complex debates about sustainable food choices."
—Sarah Murray, author of *Moveable Feasts*

"Rich in research, provocative in conception, and nettlesome to both the right and the left.... McWilliams presents some appealing alternatives to the views of both the agrarian romantics on the left and the agribusiness capitalists on the right."
—*Kirkus Reviews*

"*Just Food* will challenge a lot of what you've read. It will make you think.... McWilliams shatters the romantic, feel-good image of agriculture that foodie culture has promoted.... In the process, he challenges the notion that organic farming is always better for the environment, and that genetically modified crops are always a bad thing."
—Emily Battle, *Fredericksburg Free Lance-Star*

"Surprises abound in *Just Food*—McWilliams stands a lot of popular mantras on their heads with the power of research and rationality.... Bound to be controversial, his argument is sure to come out ahead."
—Steve Ettlinger, author of *Twinkie, Deconstructed*

"*Just Food* encourages eaters to rethink the ethics of eating local. . . . McWilliams does credit the locavore movement for getting Americans to pay attention to where their food comes from and what goes into producing it, but he says it's time to be realistic about its limits."   —Addie Broyles, *Austin American-Statesman*

"Thought-provoking. . . . McWilliams's perspective acts as a welcome foil to folksy, romanticized notions of the food revolution, using sound rhetoric and research to synthesize an examination fit for anyone who takes seriously the debate over a sustainable food system."   —*Publishers Weekly*

"With the world population headed toward 9 billion by 2050, James McWilliams wants more genetically modified organisms and more subsidies to feed people, not cattle. *Just Food* is sure to irritate organic food fundamentalists."   —Forbes.com

"McWilliams is stirring up trouble . . . the kind that makes us all scratch our heads and think harder. . . . McWilliams's biggest—and boldest—statement is that if we really want to reduce the greenhouse gases emitted from our food system, we should all become vegetarians. He has a valid point."
—Meridith Ford Goldman, *Atlanta Journal-Constitution*

"McWilliams makes a strong case against eating only organic food and for the potential benefits of genetically modified foods. He also explains why grass-fed beef can be bad for the environment."
—Christina Gillham, Newsweek.com

"McWilliams looks toward a time when politics leave the dinner table and dinner is no longer a minefield to be traversed but 'just food' on our plates and nothing more."
—Marya Zanders, *Daily Iowegian*

"In the wake of all this fuss over food miles...McWilliams's argument has me thinking more about how I shop for food....McWilliams does offer solutions." —Lauren Salkeld, Epicurious.com

"Provocative....If you want to fire up people's emotions, tell them what they should or shouldn't eat." —Grant Butler, *Oregonian*

"McWilliams makes it clear, as diplomatically as possible, that the idea of using organic methods to feed the world's population is a pipe dream....He shows a healthy sense of realism by stopping short of advocating vegetarianism for all, settling instead for urging us at least to reduce our consumption of protein from land animals." —Jacob Sullum, *Wall Street Journal*

"Balanced and rational....Having once been on the side of the locavore himself, McWilliams does an admirable job of addressing the arguments any locavore reading his book might have." —Nisha Tuli, *Winnipeg Free Press*

"*Just Food* is a great step forward in establishing accuracy in agriculture. Confused omnivores need to read this book before their next meal." —Raoul Adamchak, author of *Tomorrow's Table: Organic Farming, Genetics, and the Future of Food*

"A solid, comprehensive analysis of our global food system." —Moe Beitiks, Inhabitat.com

"Someone needed to give Michael Pollan a noogie....McWilliams goes to great lengths to emphasize that he generally appreciates the intent of well-meaning locavores....However, 'buy local' is just too simplistic to really work....McWilliams expounds upon finding less ideologically driven alternatives to the way food is produced to better help the environment." —Chuck Robinson, *The Packer*

JUST FOOD

JUST FOOD

WHERE LOCAVORES GET IT WRONG
AND HOW WE CAN TRULY
EAT RESPONSIBLY

JAMES E. McWILLIAMS

BACK BAY BOOKS
Little, Brown and Company
New York Boston London

Back Bay Books / Little, Brown and Company
Hachette Book Group
237 Park Avenue, New York, NY 10017
www.hachettebookgroup.com

Originally published in hardcover by Little, Brown and Company, August 2009
First Back Bay paperback edition, June 2010

Back Bay Books is an imprint of Little, Brown and Company. The Back Bay Books
name and logo are trademarks of Hachette Book Group, Inc.

Library of Congress Cataloging-in-Publication Data
McWilliams, James E.
    Just food : where locavores get it wrong and how we can truly eat responsibly /
James E. McWilliams.
        p. cm.
    Includes bibliographical references and index.
    ISBN 978-0-316-03374-9 (hc) / 978-0-316-03375-6 (pb)
  1. Food habits—Moral and ethical aspects.   2. Food preferences—Moral and ethical
aspects.   3. Food industry and trade—Moral and ethical aspects.   4. Natural
foods.   5. Organic living.   6. Environmental ethics.   I. Title.
    GT2850.M375 2009
    394.1'2—dc22   2009015514

10 9 8 7 6 5 4 3 2 1

RRD-IN

Printed in the United States of America

To Ceci

Contents

JUST FOOD

Introduction:
From the Golden Age to the Golden Mean
of Food Production

He who has food has many problems.—Byzantine Proverb

Approximately 500 million years ago large clumps of sand and mud formed sedimentary rocks that trapped microscopic plants and animals. This geologic mash eventually decomposed into fossil fuels. For better or worse, these fuels would later serve the endlessly proliferating wants and needs of advanced human civilization. About fifty years ago scientists began to document the environmental problems caused by burning these fuels to power modern life, global warming being the most notable of them. At the turn of the twenty-first century, environmentalists tied this vast history into a tight knot by showing how conventional food production was responsible for a large portion of the greenhouse gas fouling today's atmosphere. Omnivores, the developed world learned, had a dilemma. We were killing the environment, and thus ourselves and our future, with a diet addicted to fossil fuels.

The most powerful response to this problem has been to produce and consume locally grown food, in other words, to become a "locavore." What has happened since this locavore revolution started has been nothing short of spectacular. Millions of consumers in advanced societies the world over now demand that their food be locally sourced. The phrases "food miles" and "local farmers' market" fall off the environmentalist's tongue as inspired pearls of environmental wisdom. Organizations of environmentally concerned members eating "100-mile diets" have bloomed across North America and Europe. "Slow food" is gaining on fast food as a conventional culinary ethic. In a matter of years, the idea of eating locally produced food has come to seem so indisputably sensible that it's almost a moral obligation to book a seat on the bandwagon headed for the closest sustainable farm.

This revolution—brimming with buzzwords such as "sustainability," "agroecology," "foodshed," and "carbon footprint"—has resonated far and wide. Best-selling locavore writers have accomplished the seemingly impossible task of getting Americans to ponder where their food comes from, an achievement that must be celebrated. After all, we recently couldn't have cared less about the source of our food, but today Alice Waters is a household name. Michael Pollan is our unofficial farmer-in-chief. Wendell Berry is the agricultural romantic's poet laureate. Many consumers now turn up their noses at tomatoes that are not heirloom, cows that do not eat native grass, and pigs that do not frolic across a verdant free range. The Golden Arches are the avatar of evil, and chicken nuggets are on par with crack cocaine as a substance to avoid. All in all, it's very real progress. Locavores, and their ceaseless emphasis on fresh, local, sustainable food, are to be thanked for fueling an upsurge in ecological awareness about food and the more hopeful facets of its production.

But for all the deserved accolades, the locavore approach to reforming our broken food system has serious limits—limits that our exuberant acceptance of eating local has obscured. Although these limitations are many, the one I'm particularly concerned with is this: *Eating local is not, in and of itself, a viable answer to sustainable food production on a global level.* In fact, it's a relatively small step toward that critically important goal. As an environmental historian and the author of several books dealing with agriculture, I've become increasingly convinced (somewhat against my will) of this point.

Current popular assessments of our food issues repeatedly and passionately insist that the problem of sustainable production can be solved though a primary emphasis on localism. The underlying premise is that agribusiness has undermined the environmental balance of small-scale food production and all we have to do is restore it by "relocalizing" the food system—that is, taking it back to the way it once was. Most of my friends, as well as many of the writers, thinkers, and activists I most admire, strongly advocate this position.

My own research, however, has taught me something different. In the most general terms, it's taught me that "the omnivore's dilemma" is too complicated to be managed through a primary reliance on food grown in proximity to where we live. Such an emphasis, in fact, can in many cases be detrimental to the environment. By no means do I deny that localism has benefits, nor do I deny that agribusiness is generally irresponsible. But I am nonetheless insisting that there are more productive, creative, and global ways to think about the complicated problem of eating an ethical diet. There are alternatives to the local alternative.

My goal here is not to write a reactionary tract against the locavore movement. Instead, it is to step back, survey the broader landscape of food production and consumption, and—with all due respect to the locavore ethos (and I have a lot of it)—grapple honestly with questions that locavores have yet sufficiently to confront: How can we, both collectively and as individual consumers, achieve a sustainable *global* diet? How can the world keep growing in population, feed itself, and at the same time preserve its natural resources for future generations? How can we produce an abundance of safe food while minimizing dangerous environmental costs?

Too often environmentalists brush aside such "feed the world" questions as traps intended to promote the productive strengths of factory farming. They point to that infamous agricultural experiment undertaken between 1945 and the 1980s called the Green Revolution and, with justification, highlight the environmental degradation and corporate consolidation that the revolution required to feed the masses a steady diet of rice and wheat. But who ever said that farmers growing food for the world should abandon the quest for—as the agricultural ecologist Gordon Conway puts it—a *doubly* Green Revolution? Who ever said that agribusiness, at least as it currently operates, has a monopoly on the quest to feed the world? For that matter, who ever said local was necessarily equivalent to sustainable, much less the only antidote to the excesses of the Green Revolution?[1]

These kinds of questions have driven my research. I've tackled them knowing full well that my answers will inevitably generate controversy. It hasn't taken me long to learn that challenging ideas about food is not unlike challenging ideas about religion. A systematic examination of what's required to produce food responsibly for billions of people necessarily demands that we confront issues which elicit emotional responses. Regrettably, our current culinary discourse has been pushed to extreme ends of the spectrum. There's agribusiness on the one hand and there's the local farmer on the other. But somewhere in the middle there's a golden mean of producing food that allows the conscientious consumer to eat an ethical diet in a globalizing world. Ambitious as the goal may be, the golden mean is what I'm seeking to pin down in the chapters ahead.

When it comes to food, there are plenty of big issues for environmentally concerned consumers to explore. In addition to the concept of food miles, there are genetically modified foods, farm-raised fish (aquaculture), a reassessment of organic crops, liberalized but regulated trade policies, and sustainable ranching—all key issues that remain central to taking environmentally responsible food production beyond the local context. These issues are thoroughly discussed in the pages ahead and, I hope, productively reconceptualized to offer a vision of global food production that makes sustainability and commercial viability overriding and complementary priorities.

The track record for rationally discussing controversial matters of food and agriculture isn't encouraging. As a rule these issues have been cynically politicized before being explored as legitimate responses to our broken food system. Because the food wars, like any war, need their weapons, these very general ways of thinking about food production and consumption have entered the court of public opinion as cannon shots of contention rather than opportunities to find common ground. Something about food fosters radical dichotomies. We instinctively feel an overwhelming desire to take sides: organic or conventional, fair or free trade, "pure" or genetically engineered food, wild or farm-raised fish. Like most things in life, though, the sensible answer lies somewhere between the extremes, somewhere in that dull but respectable place called the pragmatic center. To be a centrist when it comes to food is, unfortunately, to be a radical.

The fact that we've avoided that center—short-changed complexity for extremism—is unfortunate for the cause of sustainable food production and ethical consumption. It's my sincere hope that this book can expand the dialogue about sustainable food without causing yet another tawdry food fight between radicalized perspectives and opposing interest groups, for if there's one thing conspicuously missing from our public discussion of food and the environment, it's nuance.

In the most general terms, then, my mission in the following pages is to transform what have been culinary-ideological weapons into building blocks for a model of sustainable global food production. What emerges will hardly offer a pat or complete answer to one of the twenty-first century's defining challenges. Nevertheless, through a balanced presentation of the most recent and thoughtful work on food production and the environment, as well as a much-needed historical perspective gutted of myth and nostalgia, I will make a case. This case, if all goes well, will help the omnivore, herbivore, and locavore make food choices that are environmentally just while at the same time reminding us that until we help make basic changes in how the world approaches food, our options are, somewhat tragically, limited in scope.

THE FACT THAT I aim to offer a balanced account should not imply that my analysis lacks passion or conviction. Underscoring every proposal I highlight in the following pages are precise, and surely controversial, views about nature and agriculture that I should make clear from the start.

The more I thought, read, and wrote about such divisive matters as biotechnology, aquaculture, factory farming, and the organic revolution, the more it became clear to me that each issue, in one way or another, has been distorted by a popular misunderstanding of agriculture. This misunderstanding ultimately boils down to the misleading allure of a lost golden age of food production—a golden age of ecological purity, in which the earth was in balance, humans collectively respected the environment, biodiversity flourished, family farms nurtured morality, and ecological harmony prevailed.

Thing is, there was no golden age. The perpetuation of this myth is a cheap but very powerful rhetorical strategy to burden the modern environmentalist with a false standard of pastoral innocence. Our contemporary failings as producers and consumers are routinely dramatized as a shameful fall from grace. The problem with this scenario is that we humans have always abused the environment, often without mercy. Romantics can bellow into the wilderness for an enormous shift in human perspective, but the genie of exploitation is out of the bottle. For over 10,000 years humans have systematically manipulated nature to our advantage by making plants and animals do our bidding. I honestly don't believe that this basic relationship will ever change. My proposals will, for better or worse, reflect this opinion.

I'm not being cynical on this point, just realistic. Writers who insist otherwise, who believe that achieving truly responsible food production requires rediscovering some long-lost harmonious environmental relationship, are agricultural idealists who do not know their history. These agrarian populists are complicit in what Julie Guthman, the author of the incisive book *Agrarian Dreams*, aptly calls a "stunning erasure" of the past. A hopeless romance with some wilderness of the imagination has shielded them (and us) from the harsh essence that's at the core of agricultural practice. The inspiring poet Wendell Berry can declare himself bound "for ground of my own where I have planted vines and orchard trees" that in "the heat of the day climbed up into the healing shadow of the woods." But staunch opponents have another take on that healing shadow.[2]

Speaking of agriculture per se—all agriculture—the prominent plant geneticist and microbiologist Nina Fedoroff told me that "agriculture is more devastating ecologically than anything else we could do except pouring concrete on the land." Although obviously overstated, her underlying point makes considerable sense. Her thoughts have been echoed by other scientists, who, drawing on the history of how humans have enslaved nature to satisfy hunger, rightly note that "domestication reinvents the rules of nature," that "cultivated plants are nature's misfits," and that farming is, at its historical essence, the art of strategizing against the natural world.[3]

The opinions of another school of prominent agricultural writers similarly counter the agrarian idealists who labor under the misguided assumption that nature is "the supreme farmer." Richard Manning, the author of *Against the Grain: How Agriculture Has Hijacked Civilization*, is refreshingly candid on this matter. Manning, who writes especially well about preindustrial agriculture, argues that "agriculture created poverty," that "agriculture was simply opportunism," and that "grain is the foundation of civilization, and so, by extension, catastrophe." "I have come to think of agriculture," he explains, "not as farming, but as a dangerous and consuming beast of a social system." Again, Manning is writing not about factory farming but of the essence of farming in general. Victor Davis Hanson, an angry but eloquent former raisin farmer in California, quakes in rage at the notion of romantic agrarianism, insisting that "the quaint family farmstead, the focus for such fantasy, is becoming a caricature, not a reality, in the here and now." His advice is advice I've taken to heart: "Any book about farming must not be romantic or naïve, but brutally honest."[4]

As someone whose agricultural experience consists of gardening, I prefer to take my cues from voices like Hanson's, because not only are their hands dirty with the biology and business of farming, but history bears out their perspective. Indeed, they work and write in the vein of an agricultural history that is shot through with the accounts of hard-bitten men who have yoked their own oxen, dredged their own plows, and balanced their own books, leaving behind not the slightest legacy of romanticism but instead a considerable dose of venom. Frankly, their accounts of agriculture are simply more plausible.

Sober agrarian assessments, perhaps because they're not especially marketable, have gone unappreciated. The new agrarians—those who conceptualize agriculture as a countercultural ideal to industrial modes of production—write often about how we must return to the land and let nature do our farming. But they slight the history underlying their idealism. They ignore those who ran from farming, got out at the first chance, took a job in another sector, never, not for a moment, looked back. The results of sidestepping this bitter view of agriculture would be insignificant if the stakes were not so high. The quest for sustainable methods of global food production cannot wait. What worries me is that well-meaning locavores who have the power to influence thousands of consumers down the primrose path of localism will come to realize that their dreams were unrealistic after it's too late to regroup and pursue more achievable approaches.

The history of agriculture provides ample warning against such a perspective. Too often, however, we're asked to erase the actual history of agricultural practice and the relentless press of population and listen to the disembodied wisdom of the ages. But no matter how rhapsodic one waxes about the process of wresting edible plants and tamed animals from the sprawling vagaries of nature, there's a timeless, unwavering truth espoused by those who worked the land for ages: no matter how responsible agriculture is, it is essentially about achieving the lesser of evils. To work the land is to change the land, to shape it to benefit one species over another, and thus necessarily to tame what is wild. Our task should be to deliver our blows gently. Not very sexy, perhaps not very heartwarming, but this is my view.

I suppose it would have been a lot more fun to have written a book on the sublime virtues of slow food, Chez Panisse, Berkshire pork, or the gustatory pleasures of an heirloom tomato. For sure, it would have been a pleasure to indulge my research abilities in something sensual and fulfilling. But such concerns, given the challenges we face as socially aware consumers, strike me as overly precious. Such idealization of the luxurious—a staple of food writing today—distracts us from the reality of the concrete. So I've chosen to save the romantic rhetoric for the parlors of hobby farmers and seminar rooms of the chattering culinary class.

After all, regular consumers have already been duly flogged, with one sermon after another telling us that we have sinned, that we must repent and restore our agrarian innocence, that we should go back to the land, repair our environmental souls, seek ecological redemption, and do everything but start foraging for nuts and berries and hunting wild boar for sustenance. How else to save humanity? How else to eat a responsible diet? How else to go green? It's an entirely false, if not melodramatic, premise. Real people living and eating in a real world deserve a more sophisticated answer to these myriad questions, all of which make up our shared dilemma.

WHAT FOLLOWS IS in many ways a very personal book. Intensifying my interest in sustainable food is the fact that achieving a responsible diet has long been an ongoing quest for me as an individual. I care deeply about food, and I care even more deeply about the environment. Indeed, I spent a couple of very earnest years riding the locavore bandwagon myself. My conversion to being an emotional and intellectual locavore was the only activist decision I'd made in my life. As my passion started to stir, I could be found haunting local farmers' markets around my hometown, Austin, Texas, bashing "big industrial" and "Frankenfood" at every opportunity, investigating like a Checkpoint Charlie the groceries that crossed the threshold of my kitchen, becoming a tiresome dinner companion, and once, after teaching two history classes on a balmy Texas afternoon, slaughtering my own locally raised, scrap-fed chicken on an oak stump in a friend's backyard. Sure enough, as my knife scored the chicken's fibrous neck, I rejoiced that a genuine movement was afoot and that I, with blood on my oxford shirt, was present at the creation. I had found my cause: saving the environment through the way I ate. Empowerment!

Turns out I wasn't much of an acolyte. I'm a skeptic and a pragmatist at heart, so in less enthralled moments my doubts simmered and eventually boiled over. Something about the "eat local" ethic, heady as it was, began to hit me as not only pragmatically unachievable but simplistically smug. I started to ask questions that got me funny looks down on the chicken farm. Was this all it took to make for an environmentally virtuous diet? A biweekly bike ride to Boggy Creek—a wonderful farm near my home—to buy a box of strawberries? A pound of grass-fed beef handed over the counter by Russ, my butcher at Whole Foods? A quick jerk of the knife across a chicken's carotid artery?

The problems of global warming and environmental degradation were so widespread and complex—so global—that it felt mildly disingenuous to believe that my little noble acts of locavore heroism were anything more than symbolic gestures. Really, wasn't this just checkbook environmentalism (however well intentioned), with me doing little more than salving my conscience by buying overpriced tomatoes and cooking with parsnips when the weather got chilly? The premise of it all began to feel thin.

It's hard to identify exactly when my skepticism became committed doubt, but several random observations nudged me down the path of crankiness. Maybe it was watching one too many times the pretentious woman with the hemp shopping bag declaring "This bag is not plastic!" make her way to market in an SUV the size of my house. Or maybe it was the baffling association between buying local food and dressing as if it were Haight-Ashbury circa 1968 that got me thinking that my sacred farmers' market was a stage set more for posturing than for environmental activism. Maybe it was reading yet another predictable introduction to yet another glossy coffee-table cookbook written by some hotshot chef telling me that I was part of the problem when I purchased food at—gasp—*a supermarket*. Granted, minor disturbances all, but they pushed me to take a closer look at the emperor's clothes.

Self-righteousness might have gotten under my skin, but there were also these sobering numbers I kept reading about. When Christopher Columbus landed in Hispaniola, the world's population stood at 450 million. By the late nineteenth century it had grown to 1.5 billion. Today there are almost 7 billion souls on the face of the earth, and frightening as it is to contemplate, by 2050 there will be 9.5 billion. In the past fifty years the world's population has doubled. We all need food. Not only that, but the populations of India and China—the bulk of the world—are on the verge of being able to eat a modern diet regularly consisting of meat, vegetables, and grain. This is an irrepressible component of globalization—one with potentially severe environmental consequences—that we can no longer afford to ignore.

Nowhere in the locavore canon has there been a serious discussion about this looming demographic catastrophe. You can reliably hear advocates insist that "organic can feed the world," but there is no blueprint for that transition. The conservation biologists Paul and Anne Ehrlich sum up the current relationship between exploding population and shrinking resources in these terms: "The projected 2.5 billion further increase in the human population will almost certainly have a much greater environmental impact than the last 2.5 billion added since 1975. Our species has already plucked the low-hanging resource fruit and converted the richest land to human uses." This fact is, in essence, the elephant in the locavores' room. The world's productive land has already been turned over to exploitation. The low-hanging fruit is gone. Going local, in light of it all, is akin to making sure that everything is fine in our own neighborhood and then turning ourselves into a gated community.[5]

It's little wonder that the manifestos of local production and consumption almost never confront these hard numbers. After all, the figures, so unyielding and alarming, plead with us in their urgency to think beyond an exclusively local perspective. At the least, the diet we strive for must take us beyond the local food activist Vandana Shiva's mantra that "all rules...should promote local production by local farmers, using local resources for local production." But is it viable to feed 9 or 10 billion people through local modes of agricultural production, without long-distance trade? And what if, by some crazy miracle, it were?[6]

What would happen to local traffic patterns if every consumer in Austin made daily trips in their SUVs to visit small local farms to buy locally produced food? What would happen to the nation's water supply if the entire American Southwest insisted upon preindustrial, locally produced food? What would happen, for that matter, in New Delhi, New York, Casablanca, Mexico City, or

Beijing? And how the hell would I get my daily fixes of wine and coffee? The problem and the solution—local, slow, nonindustrial food—eventually struck me as fundamentally incompatible with these logistical (and sensual) concerns. I realize that most locavores are much more flexible when it comes to obeying their founding premise. But still, it is by taking the ideology to its logical extreme that we make its inherent weaknesses most visible.

When I asked myself the demographic questions, no matter how imaginative my answers, no matter how doggedly I pursued alternative options, I kept slamming into realities—the reality of 10 billion people scattered across the globe, of declining soil quality, of limited arable land, of shrinking fresh water supplies, of the Ehrlichs' "already plucked...low-hanging resource fruit." Considering these inescapable global facts, I remained steadfastly unable to envision anything but a food dystopia arising from the universalization of the movement that I had once embraced with religious passion. It might have worked in 1492, but not today. Not on the eve of 10 billion. We need bigger systems.

This is not to dash the hopes of the locavore. It's only to point to what's heretofore been hidden in plain sight: there are very real limits to the locavore vision, limits that cannot realistically be overcome. When I left the locavore bandwagon, I did not completely leave behind its ethic. I simply want to place it in a new perspective, one that acknowledges that there's a world of consumers out there whose concerns about food have little to do with anything that Chez Panisse, Berkeley, or the slow-food movement happens to be celebrating.

Rest assured, I'll control my antielitism. I say this in part because I am pretty much a member of the food elite. For those of us fortunate enough to spend our leisure time fretting over heirloom tomatoes, the world is not just our oyster, it's our Malbec, our Blue Point, and our cave-aged Manchego. And good for us. If you have the leisure time to ponder the subtleties of taste, and if you can afford to travel the world and eat a diet that hews to the earthy wonders of *terroir*, well then, be glad and rejoice. But let's be honest with ourselves: it's a narrow perspective. Most of the world wants food, just food, and if we don't figure out how to produce that food in a sensible and sustainable manner, one that honors future generations, our localized boutique obsessions are going to appear comically misguided (if not downright tragic) to future historians.

And so my journey as a locavore fizzled out on the shoals of common sense and healthy skepticism. Radical locavores continue to brook little deviation from the sacred commandment that local food is virtuous while imported food is irresponsible. But nowadays, the more I talk with advocates of localism, the more I sense their own doubts and frustrations with the idealistic agrarian worldview. Even those located firmly within the locavore movement feel alienated by its expectations. How could they not? The demand that we eat exclusively locally produced, preferably organic food poses an unrealistic hurdle for even the most dedicated, activist-minded foodies. Dreams can be grand, but at some point we must admit their limitations and seek their spirit in more realistic endeavors.

What follows is a mass of information delivered with doses of humor, humility, objectivity, and even a little anger, but it's ultimately the story of how I came to terms with the locavore's dilemma. Readers hoping for a journalistic travelogue of eating adventures had best close the book now. Despite my opinion that food miles are the least of our concerns, I did not circumnavigate the globe to investigate the topics that I'm writing about directly. Instead, I settled in behind my desk in Austin, Texas, made the requisite phone calls, sent the critical e-mails, read the relevant reports, learned the scientific lexicons, did the hard research, and threw down my cards when I thought my hand was good. Thus, what follows is my own answer to what I once took to be my own problem. I'd like to think it's a valid, if imperfect, answer based on a rational vision of the future rather than a romantic obsession with the past. I'd also like to think it has relevance for anyone who cares about the environment and the precarious future of food.

THE FIRST PART of an ancient Byzantine proverb reminds us, "He who has food has many problems." And these problems, I would add, are problems for a reason—they're difficult to solve. What follows is thus not a rigid prescription for sustainable eating. Instead, it's a broader framework for developing an environmentally sensible diet. The most general premises I work from are these: first, sustainability means meeting our present-day needs without denying future generations the right to do the same, and second, the key benchmarks of measuring sustainability involve soil quality, water usage, biodiversity, global warming, chemical emissions, and the conservation of natural space.

I do not provide a top-ten list on how to eat a green diet. I'm no fan of books that reduce everything to a few pat answers for achieving a goal as elusive and complicated as environmentally sustainable food production. And so, rather than insult readers with simplistically prescriptive answers, I instead offer a vision of sustainability that assumes that, as socially conscious consumers, we're prepared to take on more complexity in the quest to achieve an environmentally responsible diet.

As nice as it would be to sum up the essence of what follows in a bumper sticker ("Eat Local!"), I pursue a more varied "portfolio solution." Like any portfolio, there will always be room for improvement, some aspects that perform better than others, maybe even a few superior performers and a couple of duds. But ultimately, as immodest as the goal might be, I hope to provide a new baseline from which environmentally conscious consumers can begin as they refine the endlessly complex act we're too often told should be simple: eating responsibly.

1

Food Miles or Friendly Miles?:
Beyond the "Farm to Fork" Paradigm of Production

Who gets to define "the local"?—MELANIE DuPUIS

No single concept unites the locavore movement more powerfully than food miles—the distance our food travels before we eat it. It's an elegantly simple measure of environmental consciousness, has the benefit of being easy to understand, and requires one and only one basic change in behavior: reduce food miles. Doing so is considered critical to the related tasks of relocalizing the food supply, shrinking the supply chain, minimizing the fossil fuels used to deliver our food, and supporting local farms. At first glance, the argument that minimizing the distance food travels is better for the environment appears to be unassailable. How could anyone possibly object to the intuitively sensible argument that it's always a good idea to buy local food?

As it turns out, there are ample grounds for objection. The concept of food miles, appealing as it may be, is flawed on many levels. To begin to see why, consider an analogy. Suppose you have a friend with a weight problem. This person consumes fries, burgers, lots of processed food, chili dogs, pizza, bacon, sausage, loads of ice cream, and enough beer to float a battleship on. Exercise basically consists of walking from the sofa to the fridge and back. The only redeeming aspect of this person's dismal diet is that he drinks only a single cup of coffee a day, with no sugar and only a splash of half-and-half. Then suppose that one afternoon, after a dreadful visit to the doctor, this person declares that it's high time to get in shape! In a fit of enthusiasm, he announces that he will start his new regime by... *leaving the half-and-half out of his coffee.*

The locavore emphasis on food miles is a lot like this person's emphasis on half-and-half. We're currently captives of an industrialized food system burdened with a catalogue of debilitating problems. Nevertheless, we've collectively chosen to isolate and develop an entire localist ideology around a bit player in the larger drama—the distance our food travels from "farm to fork." Locavores—who, it must be noted, have never really defined "local"—envision their work not only as supporting local culinary and agricultural initiatives, but also as an overt challenge to corporate consolidation, globalization, and in some cases capitalism in general. For whatever reason, the gurus of high cuisine have started to think less about feeding the world a sustainable diet and (to talk the talk here) more about restoring the local "foodshed," rediscovering the "taste of place," "relocalizing" the food system, "reembedding food into local ecologies," and, once and for all, "coming home to eat."

Heady stuff. However, the groundswell of support for what seems to be a perfectly logical approach to reforming our broken food system actually counteracts the sustainable goals responsible consumers want to achieve. Food miles are the half-and-half in our coffee; in reducing them, we make little progress toward the ultimate goal of sustainable production.

Fleshing out this argument requires doing four things. First I'll chart the rise and triumph of the food-mile trend and then explain why it is, paradoxically, only a minor link in the complex chain of food production. Next I'll speculate on the underlying reasons for the concept's popularity, highlighting the political motivations empowering our cultish attraction to the fetish of localism. Third I'll elaborate on how the unintended consequences of perpetuating an "eat local" brand—consequences that can be cynically populist, isolationist, and protectionist—have hollowed out the movement's core and exposed the brand to the most dangerous kind of corporate exploitation. Finally, I'll sketch out another model for thinking about food and transportation, one that allows for extensive trade while stressing the importance of both transportation efficiencies and streamlined processes of production and consumption in order to reduce the energy we expend on food.

I suppose what follows could be interpreted as an attack on the food world's sacred cow. I should thus stress that I'm not attacking locavores for the sake of attacking locavores, but rather because there's a more complex story to tell about food and the distance it travels. Considerable research that never quite hits the media bull's-eye tells us that we must be prepared to think more holistically when it comes to evaluating the carbon footprint left by our food choices. In addition, questioning the food-miles premise introduces what will be a recurring theme of this book: we must be prepared to dissolve entrenched but simplistic dichotomies—in this case the idea that distance is bad, proximity is good—in order to help pave the way to the golden mean. In focusing on food miles at the expense of so many other detrimental factors of production and consumption, we're wasting time, energy, and a heap of good intentions that could very well save future generations from the mess that previous generations have dumped upon us.

1500 Miles

Fifteen hundred miles. If you've heard of food miles, you've heard the figure. Cited more often than any other number as the distance that our food travels from farm gate to dinner plate, "1500 miles" now defines the issue. Do a quick Google search for "1500" and "food miles." You'll be inundated with trite variations on the same theme: "most produce grown in the United States travels 1500 miles before it gets sold"..."the average grocery store's produce travels 1500 miles"..."produce traveled an average of 1500 miles from producer to consumer"..."fresh produce travels over 1500 miles before being consumed." And so on.

Interestingly, although the figure has saturated the locavore literature, it was derived from a small database and a set of flimsy assumptions. As Jane Black recently explained in *Slate*, researchers at the University of Wisconsin's Leopold Center for Sustainable Agriculture examined only thirty-three kinds of vegetables, and they measured the distance they traveled to one city, Chicago, in order to calculate the figure. They relied on "terminal market data" collected by the U.S. Department of Agriculture (USDA) to estimate the flow of food in the United States, even though, as Black writes, "the country's 22 terminal markets handled only 30 percent of the nation's produce." They ignored the fact that the other 70 percent is managed by retailers through their own (likely more efficient) distribution networks. And finally, because terminal market data only list states, researchers assumed that the product was sent from the center of the state, an assumption that works for California but not for states where agricultural production is more condensed geographically.[1]

The fact that this inflammatory number seems to be minimally accurate hardly matters. Perception, after all, is reality. The 1500-mile mark, by virtue of being endlessly repeated, infuses the enlightened discourse of the culinary tastemakers, so much so that it's become the exclusive basis for a relatively new way of conceptualizing how we should eat an environmentally responsible diet. You can't open the food section of a newspaper without being covered in the sap of feel-good stories that repeatedly sermonize over the same lesson: eat local. When you encounter vendors at farmers' markets displaying cardboard signs defending their local produce with the statistic that conventional food comes from "1500!! miles away," there's no point in demanding a footnote. Discussion is preempted. The underlying message is essentially set in stone: food miles are deeply powerful as a proxy for the pervasive belief that it is bad for the environment for food to travel such long distances.[2]

If the 1500 figure fell from the heavens, the underlying concern for its implications developed in the earthly here and now. This is a genuinely important matter—one involving fossil fuel, greenhouse gases, and considerable energy expenditure—and it must be faced head-on. Between 1968 and 1998, the world's population almost doubled. Food production rose 84 percent. Trade in food rose 184 percent. The volume of food crisscrossing national borders has risen fourfold over the past forty years. Commodities now travel greater distances and with more frequency than ever before. If for no other reason than its conspicuousness, this dramatic increase has become the surest symbol of an inefficient, far flung, gas-hogging food system, one that's hooked on fossil fuels, wedded to maximized production, and begging for reform. The argument for reducing food miles seems beyond criticism, rooted in documented reality, easily achievable, and unquestionably just. There's good reason that people treat this freshly minted trend like a timeless creed.

Challenging the localism assumption becomes all the more difficult given that the locavore movement is crowned by the sanctified status of the farmers' market. "Farmers' markets," write a team of agricultural economists, "tend to be one of the first manifestations of a relocalizing food system." The farmers' market owes its meteoric rise to the increasing popularity of food-mile critiques leveled since the 1990s. One important reason that these alternatives to retail consumption have flourished so brilliantly is that they're comfortable venues where consumers can become intimate with the food and the people who grow it.[3]

I'm always impressed with the personal nature of my farmers' market. The supply chain is significantly demystified when Local

Farmer hands over local peaches from a dusty box with his dirt-encrusted hands. We know where the farms are, we know what the farmers look like, we know when they picked their produce, we think we know how they grew it, and we know that big corporate interests have been left out in the cold, all of which lends our decision to pay extra or make extra trips for locally grown food an air of virtue and a sense of environmental altruism. It just *feels* right to buy local produce at the farmers' market, and one reason it feels so good is that we think it is, ipso facto, a small act in the larger drama of saving the planet. It's at the farmers' market that we thumb our nose at 1500.

The lowered food miles that help distinguish the crunchy farmers' market from the tube-lit A&P have—or at least claim to have—the added benefits of ensuring a safer food supply and better-tasting goods. Frankly, I'm skeptical of both assertions, and while I won't go too deeply into the matter, I often wonder if consumers could consistently discern the difference in a blind taste test between farmers' market produce and Wal-Mart produce. I'm equally doubtful, unlike 85 percent of Americans, that a small operation is any better than a large one at keeping food free of dangerous bacteria. In any case, the fourfold increase in farmers' markets between 1990 and the present is, along with the rise of community-supported agriculture, the greenest manifestation we have of the unexamined axiom that local food is better food for the environment.[4]

If ever there were a consensus on an environmental ideal, the supreme virtue of going local with the food supply by shopping at a farmers' market would seem to be it. And this is what makes me suspicious. Shouldn't this very consensus raise red flags? Is it possible that such a seemingly untouchable concept—locally produced food is food produced with less energy—might be too easy an answer to the vast environmental problems infecting our food supply? Could it be that we flock to this idea because of its accessibility and simplicity rather than its inherent ability to actually solve an incredibly complex problem? Answers to these questions are worth pursuing.

LCAs

To say that there's a veritable consensus on the benefits of lowering food miles is not to say that the concept has completely sidestepped criticism. Below the media frenzy lurks a sophisticated strategy of energy evaluation known as a life-cycle assessment (LCA). Because the concept is neither simple nor amenable to a quick sketch in a thirty-second news spot, it has received scant attention in the mainstream press. Nevertheless, LCAs are essential to understanding why a food-miles litmus test is an inadequate measure of our food's environmental impact. They're also essential to achieving a more environmentally streamlined system of food production. What LCAs ultimately uncover are the hidden links in the food-supply chain that are the most environmentally damaging and in turn most in need of repair.

A life-cycle assessment is like a full physical. It's a thorough energy evaluation that takes into consideration as many factors of production and consumption as can reasonably be measured. Transportation is only one factor, and as it turns out, a relatively minor one. This more comprehensive approach to evaluating the carbon footprint of food production began in Denmark in 1993 at the first European Invitational Expert Seminar on Life Cycle Assessment of Food Products. Not a real zinger for the nightly news, but it was there that scientists began to conceptualize food production in the broadest possible terms. They looked not just into transportation distances but also into water usage, harvesting techniques, pesticide application, fertilizer outlays, the amount of carbon absorbed through photosynthesis, disposal of product, packaging, crop drying techniques, storage procedures, nitrogen cycles, climatic conditions, and dozens of less obvious cultivation inputs.

Since then, other analysts of our ever-expanding food system have undertaken similar measurements on the consumption end of the equation. Researchers are now considering, for example, the emissions put out by consumers who buy food several times a week from many different outlets (can't get toilet paper at the farmers' market) and the efficiency of home cooking methods (including what kind of oven is used). The point to these investigations is not to play "gotcha" with the locavores. Instead, it's to identify the most energy-draining stages of consumption. With such hot spots isolated, we can better direct our efforts to reducing their impact—something locavores have ostensibly aimed to do from the outset.

The application of LCAs to food production can yield surprising results for those singularly wedded to the logic of food-mile measurements. A couple of examples reveal how the process typically works to identify the stages of production most in need of repair. A 2003 LCA on the Danish fishing industry concluded that when it comes to flatfish production, the environmental hot spot was not transportation but rather the logistics of the fishing process itself. The upshot, one that an emphasis on food miles would have missed, was the discovery that overall fuel consumption could be reduced by an enormous *fifteen times* if fishers used a seine instead of a beam trawl to catch fish. A seine is a net that hangs vertically in the water, whereas a beam trawl is a net that's weighted to the ocean floor and dragged across it, which requires substantially more energy than a seine. In light of this discovery, anyone opposing the consumption of flatfish shipped around the world on the basis of food miles would be grossly misdirecting his or her efforts. Technically, it would make more sense to ask whether the fish at the counter was caught with a seine or a trawl than to ask how far it traveled.[5]

Other examples of unexpected LCA results abound. With canned mackerel and pickled herring, the hot spots were the processing and disposal (of cans and waste) stages, segments of the supply chain that consumed far more fossil fuel than the transportation of these products across vast global distances.

An LCA study done in 2000 on agricultural energy consumption in Denmark similarly found transportation to be a minor link in the chain. The real energy sink again was with production. Evaluating everything from soil structure and weather conditions to tractor model and driving techniques, scientists found that what mattered most in terms of energy efficiency was the chopping methods used to harvest crops. The report found that on most farms, "if the knife cylinder is replaced by a cutter wheel," a fuel reduction of 29 percent would result. "New cultivation methods," the authors wrote, "may change the whole picture." It is for this reason that Randi Dalgaard, a scientist at Aarhus University in Denmark, notes that "producing food and getting it to consumers involves far more than just transportation. How the food is produced and the sustainability of the processes used is the real issue and it's these areas that need to be addressed."[6]

Life-cycle assessments have been around since the 1970s. Companies traditionally used them to assess durable goods in order to cut costs. Today, however, these studies are focusing more than ever on food, and the intended result is to cut not only costs but energy usage as well. Research projects like the Danish ones described here are quietly mounting a well-documented counterattack to the culturally entrenched belief that eating local is necessarily better for the environment. One study of hamburger production observed that "baking and storage are the most energy consuming stages and transportation the least energy consuming one." An evaluation of shrimp farms in Thailand discovered that energy costs were almost exclusively bound up with the "intrinsic properties of geographical location" rather than the distance the shrimp travel to reach consumers.[7]

Taking a bird's-eye view of these food LCAs, Rich Pirog—who is, ironically, the person who veritably founded food-miles analyses—has shown that production and processing account for 45.6 percent of the fossil fuel usage, restaurant preparation takes up another 15.8 percent, and home preparation sucks up a whopping 25 percent of the overall energy used to produce and consume food made in the United States. Transportation is the *lowest* of all the factors evaluated (at 11 percent), a fact that has led scholars writing in the journal *Environmental Science and Technology* to conclude that "although food is transported long distances in general . . . the GHG [greenhouse gas] emissions associated with food are dominated by the production phase."[8]

Other results have broadened the perspective on food miles. Because of LCAs, we've learned that it is four times more energy-efficient for London consumers to buy grass-fed lamb imported by ship from New Zealand than to buy grain-fed lamb raised locally. This may seem completely ridiculous, but in terms of energy use, the comparative advantage of growing lamb on the other side of the world far outweighs the transportation energy costs. After these findings were published in 2006, the environmental advocates at the Landcare Research organization, a New Zealand institute dedicated to sustainable farming, conceded that "localism is not always the most environmentally sound solution if more emissions are generated at other stages of the product life cycle."[9]

Winter tomatoes that originate in Spain and travel to England obviously cover more miles than British tomatoes to go from farm to fork, but mainly because of the fact that so many British tomatoes are hothouse-grown (which can take up to ten times more energy), Spanish tomatoes are more energy-efficient in the aggregate. German apple juice imported from Brazil, which racks up over 10,000 miles on the odometer, is also less energy-consumptive than apples grown and processed locally. Study after study has shown that local is not necessarily greener.[10]

LCAs also flesh out the food system in ways that highlight the subtleties of transportation, distance, and production. One of the most common points overlooked in the "eat local" trend is the industrial food system's ability to achieve economies of scale. When former North Carolina senator John Edwards was running for the Democratic presidential nomination in 2007, his wife, Elizabeth Edwards, announced to the media, "I live in North Carolina. I'll probably never eat a tangerine again." It was her gesture to the locavore voting block. However, as several economists were quick to confirm, Edwards's remark ignored the benefits of scale economies. They showed that if it had theoretically been possible to buy a local tangerine from a farmer who trucked in that tangerine from sixty miles away, that still would have been more energy-consumptive than buying a tangerine from a larger load trucked in from Florida, sent by rail from California, or even shipped from Spain.[11]

How? What mattered in the Edwards claim was not the source of the tangerines but the "tangerines per gallon." In an academic article titled "Over the Long Haul," the rural sociologist Matt Mariola succinctly clarifies the most common misunderstanding about food-mile measurements. "Imagine," he writes, "a trailer carrying 2000 tomatoes, traveling 2000 miles from California to Iowa, and using 2000 gallons of fuel...each tomato would be said to have traveled 2000 miles, which is technically true...however, one can more accurately parse the energy use by item and state that a single tomato only accounted for the equivalent of 1 gallon of fuel."[12]

When produce comes with a food-mile measure, as it increasingly does, the figure is essentially meaningless if the number of items with which it traveled goes unmentioned. Similar studies undertaken by the National Sustainable Agriculture Information Service revealed that "when the transportation method was taken into account, the local food system required more energy and emitted more CO_2 than the regional system." Again, if we're going to focus on transportation—as the locavores insist we do—it is critical that we use the right formulas.[13]

Furthermore, insofar as we do focus on transportation, we must realize that it's about more than just the distance food travels from producer to consumer. It also involves the distance the consumer travels to the producer—a figure that rarely, if ever, factors into locavore assessments. Again, Matt Mariola's quantitative work has been especially insightful on this issue. Through an analysis of food-buying habits in Ohio, Mariola notes that local consumption required three shopping trips (farmers' market, orchard, and grocery store), whereas nonlocal shopping demanded just one visit to the grocery store. The differences proved to be significant: 10 versus 38 miles driven, 1.08 versus 2.42 hours consumed, and .56 instead of 2.11 gallons of gas guzzled.[14]

According to Lee Barter, a transportation analyst at Deloitte, an international consulting firm, "any environmental benefits obtained by purchasing local produce from the farmers' market across town were quite likely nullified the moment you drove past the supermarket." He concludes, "It might be better to shop local than buy local." While this conclusion is based on a relatively small number of studies, it still reveals how important it is to consider the full cycle of energy expenditure.[15]

Not to be ignored as we evaluate the hidden links in the life-cycle chain is the energy sucked up by our own behavior in the kitchen. This is a significant factor of consumption that's also generally avoided by the food-milers. As Pirog found, one quarter of the total energy used in the production and consumption of a food product transpires in the kitchen. The typical household wastes more than 1.28 pounds of food a day, 27 percent of which is vegetables. This amounts to about 14 percent of overall food purchases being tossed in the trash. "This issue of waste in the food chain," writes Ronald Bonney, "leaves consumers looking pretty irresponsible."[16]

In addition, in the only comprehensive study done on the relative efficiencies of ovens and stoves, the authors conclude that "environmental impacts depend considerably on the efficiency of the stove used and on the energy consumed due to the consumer's behavior."[17]

Indeed, these findings leave one wondering how much energy could be saved if we threw out less food, cooked smaller amounts, ate less in general, used energy-efficient ovens and refrigerators, composted all organic matter not eaten, and developed more energy-efficient menus (say, by eating more meals that did not require extensive and prolonged applications of heat). In short, if we were really paying attention to the numbers yielded by life-cycle assessments, we'd be better off focusing on what happens to our food after we buy it than on its place of origin. But of course it's hard to turn a variety of small, energy-saving domestic tactics into a token symbol of an eco-correct food philosophy. "Cook efficiently" just doesn't have the same rousing ring as "eat local." Plus it's more work and involves that word too many environmentalists are afraid to mention: sacrifice.

LCAs effectively direct attention to these kinds of activities, but as mentioned, LCAs are currently off the public radar screen. This is about to change. A small coterie of scholars and writers are now starting to integrate these findings into more pragmatic perspectives and, based on the collective evidence, make more reasonable statements about the place of food miles in the general debate over achieving a just food supply. A prominent group of academics from Iowa and Wisconsin—men and women who have spent careers dedicated to sustainable food production—issued a surprising working statement declaring the need to move "beyond 'global' and 'local.'"

One opens the report anticipating yet another sermon on the untarnished virtue of eating local food. Instead the analytical skies open onto a range of insightful criticism. "Too often," the authors observe, "these paeans to the local are founded on axioms and assumptions rather than on good evidence." They continue: "We suspect that those of us with an interest in farming and food are particularly susceptible to the strain of Jeffersonian idealism that has long been an integral feature of agricultural thought in the United States and that gives 'localization' a special appeal." By seizing as we have on the local, they conclude, we make "commitments to pasts that never were or futures that never can be."[18]

Given that these scholars primarily work from a staunch agroecological perspective, one hopes that their skepticism of an exclusive emphasis on localism will convince others to start thinking about food and energy in terms of LCAs rather than dangerously simplistic "farm to fork" paradigms. Such a broadened perspective would create a world of opportunity to do a world of good.

Local Agriculture as a Means of Political Opposition

If LCAs seem like a more complete approach to thinking about food and energy than food miles, resistance to such a transition remains deeply, even ideologically entrenched. Digging up the roots of the buy-local backlash demands that we appreciate the depth of those roots. When we survey the expansive literature supporting the food-miles approach, one thing becomes evident: the prevailing argument for stressing food miles is driven less by concrete evidence of improved sustainability than by a vague quest to condemn globalization. In this respect, buying local is a political act with ideological implications. The ulterior motive of political empowerment makes the LCA perspective, which lacks this power, a difficult one for many consumers to adopt. "Most food is sold with a story," the geographer Susanne Friedberg has observed, and this time around the story comes with an oddly populist twist: food from afar feeds the fat cats. The food anthropologist Heather Paxson captured this sentiment well when she interviewed two Vermont cheesemakers who saw cheesemaking, in Paxson's words, "as [their] personal response to globalization."[19]

Locally sourced food has surely brought considerable benefits to many individuals and communities, and for the consumer, at least, it allows for an easy gesture. In this sense, buying local has evolved into a "lite green" act of conspicuous consumption that offers environmentalists otherwise deeply involved in a commercialized life an easy way to register their discontent with the excesses of modernity. It's going to be hard for environmentally conscious consumers to begin thinking in terms of LCAs when food miles are being used primarily as a cudgel to attack global market expansion, corporate growth and development, the disappearance of the countryside, the supposed decline in community cohesion, and innumerable other pitfalls of modernization. LCAs face an uphill battle because today the local emphasis is as much on identity politics and anticorporate angst as on the realistic achievement of a more sensible system of food production.

The ulterior motives driving the cultural process of localization have academic roots, and are most evident in the way leading scholars of food systems frame agricultural debates. Larry Lev, an agricultural economist at Oregon State University, deems buying local "an alternative to a mainstream food distribution system dominated by large-scale firms...within the global marketplace." Marcia Ostrum, a rural sociologist at Washington State, situates the localist movement in an "increased recognition of the negative impacts of global-level economic restructuring." A group of established academics presents "civic agriculture" as an antidote to "commodifying, concentrating, and globalizing forces" that drive "the corporate trajectory of the current agrifood system." Over and over again it's the same setup: *local is a way to counter the global.*[20]

All of this may seem sensible enough. But such rhetoric doesn't get us any closer to improving our flawed system as it currently operates. It also assumes the impossibility of sustainable agriculture on a global level. Furthermore, the message is overly simplistic in its political connotation: buy local, attack global, feel the inner satisfaction of resistance, change the world.

To be fair, many of these writers are well-intentioned activists hoping that their critique of global capitalism will inspire a just, equitable, and environmentally sound food system. Their intentions are noble: they want to improve our lives. But their prescriptions, which typically involve taking a steamroller to capitalism, tend to alienate the wavering while preaching to the convinced. The person who works hard, tries to be a good citizen, and is concerned with food production is hardly going to be swayed by an argument insisting that he abandon faith in the free market economy. This sort of over-the-top critique of global capitalism might have resonance in academic circles, but it ultimately does little for the cause of sustainable agriculture.

What are we to make, for instance, of the comments of Stan Cox, a senior scientist at the Land Institute, in Salina, Kansas, who writes that "as America mobilizes to protect industrial agriculture against terrorists[,] agriculture itself is doing the very kind of damage that terrorists are said to be planning"? Cox continues with a pie-in-the sky approach to agricultural change when he writes, "If we find no alternative to capitalism, the Earth cannot be saved." Or what about James Gustave Speth, the very thoughtful dean of Yale's School of Forestry and Environmental Studies, when he argues that the only way to achieve genuine environmental change is to find "a nonsocialist alternative to today's capitalism"?[21]

I'm not saying that these radical ideas do not have theoretical merit. (I think Speth's ideas in particular are fascinating.) It's just that when I descend from the ivory tower and say hello to the greeter at Wal-Mart, I cannot imagine such a transition actually happening in the commercial universe I inhabit. Most people I know who work outside of elite professions such as academia and journalism would roll their eyes at such antiestablishment prescriptions. More to the point, they'd also be inclined to respond by doing nothing at all.

More disturbing to me than the anticapitalism argument itself is that it has generally gone unquestioned within the movement. Its advocates, who are not being asked to explore the gray area between the extremes, tend to assume that "local" is environmentally superior and enhances community relations, as if the local setting were somehow immune from the disruptive aspects of normal market forces. This ubiquitously repeated benefit of buying local has led otherwise sober-minded social scientists to don rose-tinted glasses when they assess the nature of basic human interaction.

Indeed, one senses that healthy skepticism has been thrown to the wind when a research associate from the Department of Applied Economics and Management at Cornell can write that small-scale sustainable agriculture will "begin the movement to a more sustainable society in general, where materialism and heedlessness are replaced by community-based values and responsibility." Speaking for the international slow-food movement, Carlo Petrini whips himself into a similar froth of righteousness, remarking that the local economy "is in perfect harmony with nature... The people of a certain place and their local economy are extraordinarily compatible with a philosophy of sustainable development."[22]

When it comes to local food and a sense of community, writes Marcia Ruth Ostrum (in a piece that ultimately challenges the virtues of local food), consumers are bound to be as one because they "can run their hands through the soil that produces their food... even as they make their stand for social and environmental improvements." Vandana Shiva, an outspoken activist for the virtues of local production and slow food, takes the communitarian rhetoric to a new level when, describing the scene at the 2004 Terra Madre gathering in Italy, she recalls, "Despite the diversity and differences, everyone was connected: connected through the earth, our Mother, Terra Madre; connected through food, the very web of life; connected through our common humanity, which makes the peasant the equal of a prince."[23]

Even if it does call for a deep breath, the ring of political empowerment here is appealing. However, given the sanguine extremes to which these opinions stretch, we have an obligation to ask if these earnest communitarian assumptions are in fact grounded in the reality of everyday social relations. Does a local food system enhance the integrity of a community? Some critics are starting to wonder if this is necessarily the case. Writing in the *Journal of Rural Studies*, the sociologist Clare Hinrichs warns that "making 'local' a proxy for the good and 'global' a proxy for the bad may overstate the value in proximity." Building on this suspicion, she acknowledges that many small farms are indeed more sustainable than larger ones, but then adds the critical caveat that "small scale, 'local' farmers are not inherently better environmental stewards."[24]

Often, of course, we have strong evidence that a small agricultural operation is very deserving of a sustainable gold star. Many small farmers maintain an impressive level of transparence, which helps alleviate any lurking concerns about their practices. In turn, their communities ostensibly become more cohesive because of shared pride in their genuine environmental progress. But this process is not democratic or broadly shared. It is generally only the elite few who have the time and money to buy produce from a transparently sustainable farm. Therefore, instead of fostering a community free of competition and greed, local food could just as easily highlight and perpetuate a community's stark, sometimes bitter differences.

Indeed, it very often does. As Patricia Allen, of the Center for Agroecology and Sustainable Food Systems at the University of California at Santa Cruz, argues, when efforts to attain community food security for the poor are joined with efforts to have local systems supply the food, the results are not the strengthening of community bonds but their destruction. Allen questions the premise that communities "will make better decisions about food systems," noting how it depends on "fluid cooperation among groups with quite different interests." Such an expectation is unlikely in *any* social context, but when the social context we're talking about is framed by food, the knives drawn are inevitably sharpened.[25]

One example of the tension that may arise when food becomes a local concern was recently played out in a noted Santa Monica farmers' market. As in any market with limited supplies of a product, consumers compete to acquire the limited goods available. In larger markets the competition is not face-to-face, and thus buying and selling normally proceed with minimal tension. But when consumers carry out transactions in the small but very public arena of the farmers' market, the disputes are face-to-face and as a result can quickly become personal. So when chefs of local high-end restaurants began to send in buyers at the crack of dawn to gobble up local ingredients at the famous Wednesday Santa Monica Farmers' Market, the household consumers who thought the market was theirs alone erupted in protest. As one longtime market denizen explained, "It's not just this little mom-and-pop thing anymore, the way it was back twenty years ago."[26]

The anger between individuals and local restaurants subsided only when it was replaced by another conflict. Corporate buyers from *outside* the community began to arrive with trucks and cart away half the market within a half-hour of its opening. "This is my last day here," fumed one chagrined chef who thought the market was there to serve his restaurant, adding snidely that with so much going to large produce companies, the market has "become some kind of boutique wholesale operation." The farmers, for their part, were the ones in control. They were the decision-makers, and they sold to the first bidder, seemingly unconcerned with assuaging the so-called communal harmony of the venue.[27]

I don't mean to suggest that such disputes characterize the farmers' market. We must, though, remain aware that localizing the food supply automatically means that a small group of people will have enormous influence over what the rest of the community eats (or doesn't). This power imbalance can alienate and anger just as easily as it can assuage and pacify. "The presumption that everyone can participate," writes Allen, "is a magician's illusion." The result is a local food system in which a self-elected cohort of decision-makers deliver to the masses their own subjective vision of what a healthy, virtuous, and environmentally sound diet should look like. The rest just get what they're given, leave, or resist in ways that undermine the process of community development. In this sense, culinary localism can backfire on the community it's supposed to improve.[28]

There's a related element to this argument. When the infra-structure of food production and distribution shrinks to accommodate the local population alone, when middlemen are axed from the supply chain, certain kinds of jobs disappear. Perhaps it goes without saying that these jobs are not employment opportunities that the privileged clientele of the farmers' markets are going to miss. Instead, the burden exclusively hits the "traditionally marginalized," people whose primary concerns in life do not involve securing heirloom tomatoes and baby squash cultivated within a 100-mile radius of their domains. "I participated in a conference session," recalls Patricia Allen, "in which the leaders of a food security project were proud of its success in reducing imports of food from outside the locality. They were uninterested, however, in the negative effect this localization might have on those who had depended on the previous arrangements."[29]

The essence of this section can be reduced to a single, if controversial, observation: culinary localism inevitably boils down to some form of arbitrary cultural (or agricultural) power. Theoretically, this exclusivity could change, and it would be great if it did, but for now it's impossible to avoid the conclusion that the locavore movement leaves many American consumers alienated rather than inspired to think about, much less work toward, agrarian sustainability.

And thus the locavore's dilemma comes full circle. Whereas the push to develop alternative local food systems began as a way of democratizing fresh food, the quest to keep matters local has thus far ended up empowering the self-styled tastemakers while excluding the masses. Melanie DuPuis, an often strong booster of localizing the food supply, asks, "Who gets to define 'the local'? What exactly is 'quality' and who do you trust to provide you with this quality? What kind of society is the local embedded in?" Pondering these questions, she ends up confronting a scenario in which "a small, unrepresentative group decides what is 'best' for everyone and then attempts to change the world by converting everyone to accept their utopian ideal."[30]

Regrettably, this sounds very close to the critique that locavores have been making about agribusiness for decades. When one of the movement's most thoughtful and well-informed advocates admits that localism can be "a way for local elites to create protective territories for themselves," we can be hopeful that meaningful change is on the horizon.[31]

Buy Local

Not only does the "eat local" argument have its inherent problems, but it sets up locavores for the very turn of events that agrarian resistance movements have fallen prey to for over forty years: a corporate takeover of their ideas once they become popular enough to be marketable. In fashioning itself as an alternative to the conventional food system, the locavore proposition has reduced itself to a brand. Like any good brand, it presents an image of purity while concealing a range of flaws.

As the French reliance on *terroir* proves, a nation, a region, and a locality can play the brand game just as well as any corporation. France's emotional investment in its agricultural traditions certainly has deep roots in a genuine and collective national sentiment. Nevertheless, one cannot overlook the fact that local producers benefit substantially when state-sponsored designations keep legitimate competition at bay. When France booted Mondavi out of the country in 2001 for not fully grasping the essence of *terroir*, local producers celebrated the decision for reasons beyond the fact that French culture had somehow been preserved. Profits, too, had been protected. Under the guise of a cultural quest to honor tradition, vintners successfully guarded precious market share.[32]

Thus, when Britain's *Farmers Weekly* magazine promotes the slogan that "local food is miles better," as it currently does, one suspects that a similarly economically inspired strategy is couching itself in the more benign guise of environmental sustainability. This trend is going mainstream, and in so doing it exposes the brand to being used in ways that true locavores would abhor.

The surest indication that "eat local" is being coopted and reduced to the equivalent of an advertising slogan is the phrase's current popularity with agribusiness marketers and conventional food retailers. Just as "organic" was quickly exploited and transformed by corporate interests once its market share became worthy of corporate notice, so it goes with "eat local." Writing in *Business News*, Dominique Patton calls food miles "one of the most effective marketing tools for UK-produced food." The major supermarkets Tesco and Marks & Spencer, without paying a whit of attention to the LCAs of the products they sell, are planning to place little airplane labels on food flown into the country. The justification is supposedly environmental—"it would be disingenuous of us to not put aeroplane stickers on these products," says an earnest Tesco representative—but it's hard to overlook the fact that, as another executive notes, local food "is the fastest-growing part of our business." Tesco, in short, wants to corner an emerging market.[33]

These efforts are eagerly encouraged by domestic agribusinesses in the UK, who also see prospects of gold in the promotion of green. As Patton explains, "Food miles have gained more traction than other miles because they fit particularly well with concerns about the waning domestic farming sector." Surveying agribusiness's sudden sympathy with the "eat local" philosophy, Bill Vorley of the International Institute of Environment and Development observes that "it's quite ironic that mainstream agriculture, which has been on a free trade wagon for years, is now using the food-miles debate to promote their goods." But what matters when it comes to exploiting the "eat local" brand is not consistency but marketability. As Ryan Smith, a researcher at SRI International, notes, "Businesses are taking the opportunity to differentiate themselves from their competition, especially in the supermarket sector, where branding is very important." Adds Emma Howard Boyd, another SRI researcher, "It is no longer about principles but also profit." Such a comment has an eerie ring to anyone who watched the organic movement go into crisis mode over a similar transmutation of its founding values.[34]

The branding of "eat local," as well as the subsequent corporate exploitation of that brand, has taken place in the United States with equally paradoxical outcomes. In 2008 the Chipotle Mexican Grill, a Denver-based fast-food chain, vowed to purchase 25 percent of one item at each store from local farmers as part of its "Food with Integrity" initiative. This decision, which included buying local pork in Virginia from Polyface Farms, was widely heralded by locavores as a harbinger of change for fast food in general. It came, moreover, on the heels of a Wal-Mart promise to spend $400 million a year on local produce as part of its "Commitment to You" program. In a similar vein, Bon Appétit Management, which operates more than 400 dining halls throughout the country and serves more than 80 million meals a year, has determined, as one newspaper report put it, to make "local sourcing a centerpiece of its brand." It's all part of their "Farm to Fork" program.[35]

The corporate commentaries that accompany these well-packaged transitions provide a hit list of environmentally inspired quotables. A high-profile green gesture, however small, evidently allows otherwise conventional food producers to take high moral ground—a point the media, smitten with tales of corporate responsibility, rarely mention. The Bon Appétit press release, for example, praises the company's "radical approach to the business of food service by bringing sustainably grown foods to the American public." A regional operations manager from Chipotle explained his company's dedication to the "eat local" philosophy by pointing out that "for so many people, it's about price...For us, it's about building relationships and knowing we'll have a better product over the long run." One could be forgiven for thinking there's a rat in the rhetoric. After all, most of the laudatory coverage failed to note that Chipotle purchases millions of pounds of animal flesh every year, making the Polyface pork purchase a well-publicized drop in the bucket of the company's overall meat expenditures.[36]

Corporations are not the only ones that have capitalized on the "eat local" mantra in order to greenwash their images and boost profits at the expense of a brand originally designed to criticize commercialism. As Clare Hinrichs has argued, there's a "politics of food system localization" that's evident in state-sponsored efforts to promote goods produced *in the state*. Putting aside the question of how "local" has been allowed to substitute for "the state" (works best in Rhode Island, not so well in Texas), media productions such as Iowa's "banquet meals," vast smorgasbords of Iowa food initiated by the Leopold Center for Sustainable Agriculture, highlight how a "defensive localism" can easily morph into "food patriotism." As Hinrichs observes, the definition of "'local foods' has subtly shifted from food raised 'in this county or one nearby' to food raised 'in Iowa.'"[37]

It all seems fairly innocuous, until you consider the implications of this shift. A movement once dedicated to the proposition that local food was environmentally sound food is now serving the purpose of state boosterism. Praising the success of the first banquet, which took place in 1997, the food policy expert Neil Hamilton tellingly remarked, "These efforts will do more to create opportunities for Iowa farmers and add more 'value' to our food system than any TV commercial." It was with such marketing-driven logic that "eat local" became a brand signifying virtue, something that Iowa, setting the model for other states to follow, used chauvinistically to promote products made by Iowa businesses, regardless of what they were making, how they were making it, or the resources being exploited in the process. And thus another original intention of the locavore movement went up in the smoke of factory-farmed pork and monoculturally grown corn.[38]

Scaling Up/Down

Branding "eat local" leads to another problem, one that goes beyond the threat of being coopted to serve the ulterior purposes of an opportunistic corporation or an innovative chamber of commerce. By their very nature, small agricultural operations fit poorly into the established infrastructure of food production and distribution. If forced—that is, if small operations integrate into larger food systems—this mismatch could prove fatal for the locavore project as a whole. Joel Salatin, the evangelical-libertarian-radical ecologist who heads Polyface Farms in Swope, Virginia (and who was introduced to fame by Michael Pollan's *The Omnivore's Dilemma*), certainly appreciates the opportunity to provide sustainable pork to Chipotle. At the same time, he admits with characteristic candor that "the average local foodie has no idea why farmers like us can't access a larger portion of the market...We've been a square peg in a round hole for Chipotle."[39]

As Salatin's comments suggest, the economics of scaling up local operations and successfully weaving them into preexisting global food systems face serious obstacles. This isn't to condemn the small guy for being small. It's only to say that these obstacles demand that the small guy fundamentally change his ways in order to compete in the big guy's system. If the Chipotle idea of sourcing pork locally catches on, a place such as Polyface Farms will confront two choices: either allow market share to go to another small producer or scale up to capture that market. One doesn't need to be an economist to grasp these options, but one would have to be an idealist to think that small producers as a rule are happily going to forgo more business. This looming paradox underscores the importance of finding ways for systems such as Polyface and Chipotle to coexist independently rather than undertaking a form of "cooperation" that's bound to ultimately undermine the small farming ethic at the expense of the larger endeavor.

As I've repeatedly argued, we have an obligation to foster more sustainable larger systems to feed the world. At the same time, we must encourage small sustainable efforts to serve niche markets. As it now stands, however, "eat local" is a brand that's scaling up to match the patterns of larger systems, a move that will automatically dilute the values that inspired the effort to keep food local in the first place. Because those founding values are quite sound—because the locavore ethic has a viable place in a larger portfolio of solutions—we should honor the role they play by supporting them where they currently work rather than expecting them to scale up into bloated versions of their former selves.

As Salatin notes, the logistical consequences of pushing the square peg into the round hole are rarely appreciated by consumers. It's good to seek local produce, but to insist that such behavior should be universal has unexplored negative outcomes. For one, producers of sustainable food on a small scale cannot supply their products on a year-round basis. Not only is a constant supply a modern luxury that most consumers will always demand from retailers, but how could any storage and distribution service stay in business if it depended on seasonal produce from small growers spread over a vast region? Adding to the distribution conundrum is the problem of scale. Mundane as it seems, the small guy cannot provide food in quantities that even midsized wholesalers and retailers demand in order to justify a contract economically. In essence, to relocalize the food supply nationally would be like replacing cars with skateboards and telling everyone to use the highway.

In regions of the country that enjoy high levels of local production, distribution systems are indeed becoming flexible to accommodate the needs of small and midsized growers. In those exceptional areas where geography supports small-scale farming, this is as it should be. But there are built-in limits to how far such a transition can go in most places. At the very least, in order to justify and support a locally crafted distribution system, a region requires not only comparative geographical advantage but also a reliable cadre of relatively well-off and highly educated consumers willing to pay a lot more for microgreens and baby squash. These regional systems are truly wonderful when they emerge organically, but as natural manifestations of a grassroots movement, they're the exceptions that prove the rule.

The larger infrastructure of food distribution is intricate. Realistically, it's not going crumble because a bunch of locavores come along, get great press, and insist that everything scale down. While there's much room for making our current distribution networks more efficient, the prospect of undertaking a wholesale restructuring of global, national, and even regional transportation in order to accommodate the niche interests of small farmers and their locavore loyalists is little more than a pipe dream for the vast majority of regions in the developed world. More realistically, if the small guy wants to reach a big market, he'll have no choice but to scale up—something that "big organic" did, while in the process selling its sustainable soul to the diabolical designs of big agriculture.[40]

The argument that we must relocalize the nation's distribution networks to accommodate small growers ultimately runs into an inconvenient question: *should every region even have a local food system?* Regions with climate and soil conditions poorly suited for diversified agricultural production must dedicate substantial inputs to fossil fuel and water. This is true whether the operations are big or small, mom-and-pop or franchised.

Should regions that are seeking self-sufficiency in environmentally stressed locations be accommodated with a custom-designed distribution and processing system—not to mention a community willing to engage in the contradiction of sacrificing precious local resources to support a supposedly environmentally friendly ideology? If, for example, the only way a region that's highly populated but perpetually dry can grow local is through costly and environmentally damaging irrigation projects, should residents eat local? Should cities like Tuscon, Las Vegas, and Phoenix—three of the cities in the country that have the most limited water supplies—import water to nurture a local foodshed? As Jennifer Wilkins, a scholar at Cornell's Division of Nutritional Sciences, writes, "In the long run, of course, and increasingly in the short run as well, significant food production may not be possible in these regions." At the least, we need to start systematically mapping where localism is viable and where it is not.[41]

Locavores will often respond to this line of attack by arguing that people should not be moving to these areas in the first place. But again, that kind of logic sends us back to never-never land. Unless one can envision the government in a country like the United States seriously telling citizens and corporations that they cannot settle in a particular region because the resources do not conform to a locavore vision, we're back to the thorny reality that some places simply cannot, on environmental grounds, justify a localized food system.

Even in locales that have great potential to provide a region with considerable food, there are reasons to be skeptical that it's an achievable idea. Consider fruit and vegetable production in New York. The Empire State is naturally equipped to grow a wide variety of fruits, including pears, cherries, strawberries, and some peaches. But none of these compare to its ability to grow apples and grapes, which dominate production, accounting for 94 percent of all fruit grown. At current levels of fruit production, apples are the only crop that could currently feed New Yorkers at a level meeting the U.S. Recommended Dietary Allowances. Every other fruit that the state produces is not being harvested at a level that would provide all New Yorkers with an adequate supply. Other fruits, such as bananas and oranges, are not produced at all because conditions are unfavorable for growing them. What does this situation mean in terms of feeding the state with the state's own produce? In a nutshell, it means citizens would have to give up tropical fruits altogether; rarely indulge in a pear, a peach, or a bowl of strawberries; and gorge on grapes and apples—most of them in processed form, as juice, canned, or as concentrate.[42]

Eating state vegetables poses its own problems. Of all vegetables produced in New York, only nine of the eighty most consumed cannot be produced within the state. This statistic is encouraging for the prospect of local consumption. Not only is the region naturally conducive to growing a diversity of vegetables, but it's already doing so to such an extent that it could provide enough beets, cabbage, onions, pumpkins, snap peas, and sweet corn to feed the state populace an adequate diet of vegetables. So what's the trouble?

The devil, as usual, is in the details. As with fruit production, to move vegetables from New York fields to New York forks would demand, in Wilkins's terms, "a rebuilding of the processing industry." Whereas the global economy's infrastructure allows the importation of fresh produce all year round, consumers of New York–only produce would have to accept processed fruit and vegetables in the off-season. Since the stuff would not be exported, it would be frozen, canned, juiced, or pickled. Whereas the conventional system of production and distribution has in place a series of large-scale processing centers capable of handling these tasks in a handful of isolated locations, localities do not.[43]

Do you really want a local cannery? Herein lies the rub. As three scholars writing in the *British Food Journal* explain, "In recent decades large-scale food processing and production has been undertaken in factories on industrial estates, but a return to small units within communities may well bring environmental problems such as smell, pollution, waste disposal, visual intrusion, and nuisance for those communities." Localities might be thrilled with the prospect of a sprawling farmers' market in their neighborhood, but what about a small fish processing plant designed especially to meet local needs? One imagines it wouldn't be long before a "defensive politics of localism" became "not in my backyard," perhaps punctuated with "Eat local, process elsewhere" bumper stickers. Moreover, given that the New York case study is one that covers a relatively large area of production (it's 400 miles from New York City to Buffalo), these problems would be exponentially compounded for locavores who wanted to keep diets within a 100-mile radius.[44]

Hub and Spoke

So how do we start rethinking matters of scale, scope, and distribution? First we must back off the food-miles gauge. As we've seen, more and more studies are making this case. For example, in May 2007 a group of scientists gathered in London for the Carbon Footprint Supply Chain Summit. Judging from the esoteric nature of the topics slated for discussion, conversations veered from the nerdish to the wonkish. Fortunately, the organizers saw fit to distill the conference's main findings down to a few easily digestible abstracts and graphs. One chart highlighting the scientists' conclusion on food miles, called "Assessment," captures in as succinct form as I've seen the arguments I've been developing throughout this chapter. It reads: "1) Comprehension by public of food miles: HIGH; 2) Measurement and calculation of food miles: EASY; 3) Planet saving ability: POOR."[45]

And that, in a nutshell, is it. Food miles are readily popular primarily because they're easy to grasp and calculate. None of this is to suggest that we should ignore the distance our food travels. However, it does urge the open-minded consumer to reassess the relative importance of eating local, given the broader dynamics of energy expenditure during food production. The facile assumption that local is better must go.

It makes much more sense, once this clarification has taken place, for concerned consumers to focus attention on factors of production and consumption that *really* matter—that is, those that most actively undermine the goal of providing food in a sustainable fashion. Buying local is smart when natural conditions justify the production of local goods. Given the stubborn realities of geography, however, chances are slim that one local environment can sustainably accommodate the diverse range of goods that make up a healthy modern diet.

Globally, freshwater resources are by no means equally distributed. In fact, 2.3 billion people in twenty-one countries live in geographies that are designated "water-stressed basins," which means that there are only 1000 to 1700 cubic meters of water per person per year. Another 1.7 billion, according to the UN's Food and Agriculture Organization, "live in basins under scarcity conditions (with less than a 1000 m^3 per person per year)." What these figures mean is that "much of the world's human population growth and agricultural expansion is taking place in water-stressed regions." It's fine and good for naturally lush regions of the developed world to pursue the noble goals of local production and consumption, but the last thing we want to do as stewards of the environment is universalize such an ethic. After all, the imperative of sustainability demands that more than half the world should get its food from elsewhere.[46]

The locavore approach might do a very good job of explaining how regions naturally predisposed to produce a diverse local food supply can do so. It says very little, however, about how we might export from these areas to water-stressed regions that cannot provide their own food without extensive importations of water. It says very little, in other words, about trade.

Throughout modern history, humans, always desirous of something new, crisscrossed oceans and mountains to pursue a basic human endeavor: exchanging food. There's little chance that we're going to cease this historically inbred itinerant behavior because a small cohort of locavores erroneously argues that everyone must go local to save the planet. The new locavore challenge should thus be incorporating models of environmentally sound trade into their broader efforts to improve our food supply.

The refusal to do so will leave the locavore movement stuck on several questions. Where will the land come from for a localist transition to happen en masse? What about labor? The farmers? The knowledge? The discipline? The sacrifice? How many college graduates are realistically going to go into farming, not as a temporary hobby but for life? Right now less than 2 percent of the U.S. population provides our food. Even if that number expanded by a factor of five—an occupational shift without precedent—we'd have nowhere near enough growers for a relocalized food supply.

When 60,000 people gathered in San Francisco in the summer of 2008 to celebrate the essence of local food, slow food, and small farming, the press went gaga. But nobody at this culinary Woodstock asked the basic logistical questions. Nobody pondered the reality of *how* this change would take place. Again, universalize the "eat local" movement and think through the consequences. I've spent more hours than I care to admit doing just that, and all I can come up with, over and over again, is *I don't see how it could work*.

Fortunately, there are more achievable goals for us to reach, and many of them are elaborated in the pages ahead. But for now we can work to develop renewable energy sources to power the energy-hogging phases of large-scale food production (for instance, using solar energy rather than natural gas to make fertilizer), food storage systems that are energy-efficient, and sustainable home kitchens and cooking habits. We should also support agricultural practices that reduce land dedicated to food production (while increasing yield and fostering wilderness preservation), recycle safe agricultural waste back into the land, and reduce the number of farm animals clogging agricultural systems.

I know, I know: dull stuff. It's so much sexier to reiterate the mantra of eating local, growing rooftop gardens, foraging for wild dandelion balls, and keeping backyard hens. And all this is wonderful. We *can* keep things local—we *should* keep things local—but we must also stop insisting that our behavior is, if universalized, a viable answer to the world's present and future food problems. One of the most critical steps we can take toward a genuinely feasible, sustainable system of global food production is not necessarily to eat local but to think global. We should also probably come to terms with the fact that there's nothing sexy or fashionable about feeding the world an environmentally sustainable diet. It requires work, thought, compromise, and sacrifice.

Ultimately, we need to go beyond "local" and "global" and all the moral judgments these terms convey in order to establish a complex food system that's intelligently integrated into worldwide environmental conditions. Imagine a number of regional food systems bound together with a series of hub-and-spoke arrangements designed to accommodate the basic environmental reality that certain foods grow especially well in certain places and at certain times of the year. In this scenario, the hubs would be the tender sweet spots of food production, areas where the climatic and geological conditions justify the midscale production of goods for local and distant markets. The spokes would be the clean, energy-efficient lines of travel and transport. Trade—often long-distance trade—would be assumed, but everything at the hubs would be open to regimes of improved efficiency.

To a large extent the global economy has naturally developed such a model of production and distribution, albeit with glaring imperfections. We don't buy coffee beans grown in New Jersey, bananas from South Dakota, or wine from northern Canada for good reason: the laws of comparative advantage (when untarnished by subsidies; see Chapter 6) wouldn't allow for such absurdities. A more consciously designed and internationally sanctioned program of trade would systematically underscore the power of the hub-and-spoke logic, rewarding producers who locate their operations in areas where the environmental conditions are most appropriate and economically punishing those who try to coax abundance from a desert in order to take advantage of cheap labor, affordable land, subsidies, or preexisting irrigation systems.

As consumers, moreover, we can foster the hub-and-spoke system just as readily as we can foster the "eat local" philosophy. When an English consumer purchases fresh, in-season green beans locally and then, when the beans are out of season, buys them from Kenya rather than from a local hothouse, he supports the hub-and-spoke logic. When a Bostonian chooses sustainably raised farmed fish sent from Alabama instead of endangered cod caught with a beam trawl and processed a few miles away, she adheres to the hub-and-spoke logic. When a flour mill buys foreign wheat from minimally irrigated land and harvested with fuel-efficient harvesters rather than from a local producer who uses dull blades and grows in water-stressed land, it adheres to the hub-and-spoke logic. Granted, much more information must become available for us to make proper decisions within an LCA framework. But if we can measure the distance food can travel, we can certainly measure the carbon footprint created by the major inputs of production.

But all those miles! you protest. Yes, indeed, all those miles. Even granting the importance of LCAs—that is, even in light of the fact that transportation is a relatively small factor when it comes to the energy expended before food gets to our fork—those miles still matter. It is thus fitting that in 2007, transportation wonks from the UK met in order to deliver a challenge and offer extensive advice on how to achieve transportation efficiency. Promising to follow the lead of "fact, not emotion," the group called on the food industry to "reduce the social and environmental costs of domestic food transport by 20 percent by 2012."

Eating local, interestingly enough, never came up. Their argument, in the awkwardly titled "Report of the Food Industry Sustainability Strategy Champions' Group on Food Transport," aimed for "friendlier miles" rather than fewer miles. And rather than calling for a lifestyle change among millions of consumers in order to possibly reduce one small factor of production, the scientists, who declared the importance of "working with the grain," explored the feasibility of dozens of energy-reducing tactics in the transport sector. In the end, though, they settled on "six big initiatives" to achieve the 20 percent reduction. They are greater-capacity vehicles, out-of-hours deliveries, engine specifications, vehicle telematics (better route planning), transport collaboration (industrial carpooling), and logistics systems redesign.[47]

And you're thinking to yourself, *Yawn.* Sure, things like vehicle telematics and transport collaboration are not the stuff to inspire movements or drive media reports. But they are, as it turns out, the stuff of real environmental change. And so, as conscientious consumers, we might have to forgo the trendy green slogans and take on a more challenging task, one that asks us to think more critically, creatively, and comprehensively about how food is produced and consumed. Naturally, it'd be easier just to "eat local" and call it a day. But that short bike ride to the farmers' market would only obscure the fact that we have many miles to go.

2

Organic Panic:
Discovering Agriculture's Golden Mean

Clearly more strategies are needed for both organic and conventional growers. —PAMELA RONALD

My interest in food and agriculture owes a great deal to a farmer named Eliot Coleman. I was originally seduced by Coleman's vision of small-scale organic farming through the allure of his 1989 book, *The New Organic Grower.* To this day I remain a dedicated fan. As an organic grower with enough of a cultish following to have earned himself a heroic Wikipedia page, Coleman has, during forty years of farming, led by example. His Four Season Farm in Maine produces organic vegetables and meats throughout the year in fist-shaking defiance of those who say you can't grow healthy vegetables in the dead of a New England winter.

In every way imaginable, Coleman embodies the purest organic commandments—they're evident in his farming methods free of synthetic chemicals, in his reverence for soil fertility, in his steadfast belief that nature is "impeccably designed," and in the venom that drips from his pen over "the crushing onslaught of petrochemical agribusiness." It's with legitimate pride that Coleman wrote to me,

"We use no pest control products, whether chemical or organic. We refer to our approach as 'plant positive' (strengthening the plant) rather than 'pest negative' (killing the pest)." Good for Eliot Coleman, good for the insects, good for the plants, and, of course, good for you and me.[1]

And good for organic agriculture, right? The answer to this question would seem to be obvious. Coleman's choices strike me as indistinguishably cultural, agricultural, and ecological. But the environmental benefits of the system he promotes outweigh all other impressions. Traditional organic agriculture forbids the use of synthetic fertilizers and synthetic pesticides. It avoids feed additives for livestock and rejects all plant growth regulators and hormones. Its practitioners rely as much as possible on biological pest control methods, composting, crop rotation, and green manuring techniques.

"Deep organic" in particular generally vows to stay small, place process ahead of profit, avoid the middleman, market goods directly, and work from the premise that nature is the best farmer. Because the Colemans of the organic world offer such a sharp contrast to industrial-organic and conventional operations, many influential food writers have swooned over them and told us that *the* main task is to protect the founding ideals of organic agriculture from the ever-hovering talons of agribusiness and its taste for chemically driven growth.

And one can see why. The organic option offers a powerful critique of the established norm. It's a critique, moreover, that's been well developed, everywhere from the ivory tower to the popular press to the everyday concerned consumer. However, despite my genuine respect for the agroecological ideals promoted by Coleman and others, I do not think that organic is the answer to our broken food system. It's certainly one answer among many others, but it is by no means the only strategy that, along with reducing food miles, we should spend our time trying to achieve.

To explain why not, I'll provide a systematic analysis of organic agriculture. There are, as I have noted, organic principles that deserve high praise, but at the same time organic remains a model of food production burdened by many misconceptions and unacknowledged limitations. My argument goes beyond criticizing "big organic"—a red herring more than anything else—to highlight deeper problems affecting organic resources, ideology, practices, and yields. In the end I hope to show that when thinking about organic and conventional, it makes more sense to conceptualize "a continuum of farming systems" than to become mired in a rigid organic/conventional or big/small dichotomy.

With all due respect to Coleman and organic farming, I hope to show that an overemphasis on the organic option has kept us from building more inclusive and achievable models of sustainable food production capable of feeding billions of people.

Doing the Math

Because organic farming bans synthetic chemicals—namely nitrogen fertilizers and synthetic pesticides—it generally yields less per acre than conventional farming. This claim is hotly contested among scientists, but on the whole organic farming seems to demand more land to produce less food.[2] It's commonplace to note how the lower inputs that define organic practices improve biodiversity in the plots under cultivation. Usually left unmentioned, however, is the impact that even slightly lower yields have on agricultural expansion and biodiversity in the wild.

Agricultural sprawl is an insidious form of development that threatens the world's remaining natural resources. "If organic farming were to be widely adopted," write two scientists in the 2004 *Proceedings* of the International Crop Science Congress, "lower yields would require more land (25–82%) to sustain production." The Tuskegee University plant microbiologist C. S. Prakash puts it this way: "Converting from modern, technology-based agriculture to organic would mean either reducing global food output significantly or sacrificing undeveloped land to agriculture." Or, as Norman Borlaug, the famous agronomist who started the Green Revolution in the 1940s, explains, "Growing more crops and trees per acre leaves more land for nature." It goes without saying that humans are far less competent at nurturing biodiversity than nature is. We must keep this point in mind when we hear the argument that organic farming leads to improved biodiversity.[3]

To be sure, there are many cases where the two forms of agriculture, organic and conventional, break even on yield counts. There are even a few documented cases where organic production exceeds conventional output. Every organic advocate I've ever asked about yields has responded that *theoretically*, organic yields could be consistently higher than conventional ones. Faced with the question of organic farming's yield potential as a whole, Raoul Adamchak, Market Garden Coordinator of the University of California–Davis Student Farm, hedges the issue: "It depends on the crop, the place, the farmer, the variety, the type of crop rotation used, and whether cover crops take the place of crops."[4]

But as statistics that Adamchak himself quotes in the excellent book *Tomorrow's Table* confirm, conventional methods tend to do a better job at wringing more food from less land. This well-documented disparity is in no way a justification for continuing with the status quo of conventional production. To the contrary, it's an opportunity to envision alternatives that combine a judicious and conservative system of chemical application—something that organic farming promotes—with high agricultural yields—something that organic sometimes achieves, but not consistently enough to make it the basis for global food production capable of producing 60 percent more food on the same land by 2050. Once again, the goal is a compromise that takes us beyond the established categories.[5]

Thinking beyond the conventional/organic dichotomy requires

placing organic production, which is popularly understood to be inherently more environmentally beneficial than conventionally produced food, in a much more critical perspective. Organic food is currently garlanded with so many laurels that a comprehensive evaluation of its drawbacks often strikes readers as an effort to promote conventional production. But to criticize organic is not necessarily to endorse conventional. It's mostly (but not always) true that organic soil is healthier than conventionally formed soil, that it leaches fewer antibiotics and growth hormones into surrounding habitats, and that it's responsible for less surface-to-air ammonia emission. At least from the perspective of soil inputs, organic can be considered more energy-efficient, because it rejects forms of synthetic fertilization that demand 30 gallons of gas for one acre of corn.

But granting these benefits (which, we will see, are not always as evident in practice as they are on paper) should not preclude a fair assessment of what organic too often fails to accomplish. After all, what organic production is unable to do with enough reliability is something that a viable system of global food production *must* always do: produce increasing quantities of food on the same, or even a smaller, amount of land than is currently under cultivation. For all their faults, this is something that conventional systems do very well and, with the application of judicious technologies, can be made to do better. The problem, in many ways, is as much a mathematical conundrum as an environmental matter.[6]

For better or worse, the reality of worldwide demography and population expansion demands that we think in such terms. Norman Borlaug explains, "If all agriculture were organic, you would have to increase cropland area dramatically, spreading out into marginal areas and cutting down millions of acres of forest." Results of research conducted by British scientists support Borlaug's claim, demonstrating that "more land is always required for organic production (65% to 200% extra)." Due in part to organic farming's use of cover crops to replenish the soil's nutrients, land requirements in this study were at least 65 percent higher than for conventional milk and meat production, 160 percent higher for potatoes, and 200 percent higher for bread wheat production.[7]

Studies of rice have found that organic production in California yields 50 to 70 percent of conventional production, while organic corn yields are two thirds of conventional. Organic tomatoes demand six to ten times the land required for conventional tomatoes and use twice the energy to produce. When the Rodale Institute, an organization explicitly dedicated to organic agriculture, conducted an eight-year test comparing crop yields, the best results they could achieve were 20 percent lower yields, with 50 percent reductions being common.[8]

The extensive land requirements of organic production are further inflated by the demand for animal manure that is produced and collected off-site. It is true that a small, tightly integrated organic farm can effectively balance livestock and crop ratios and thus efficiently capture manure on location to fertilize a modest range of organic crops. Such a balance, in fact, is critical to creating a sustainable food system, and there must be inducements for farmers to pursue this sort of integration when it's feasible to do so (although the markets they reach will be quite small).

But larger organic operations capable of producing for broader markets require substantial external supplies of manure to compensate for the soil's lack of nitrogen fertilizer. Should organic agriculture ever undertake the project of feeding the world, these larger operations would be the ones running the show, so we must not overlook the fact that organic manure production requires either considerable amounts of pastureland or feed to fatten cattle. Not only that, but the manure that organic farmers import contains nowhere near the level of nitrogen contained in synthetic fertilizer. Literally tons of manure would be needed per acre. Advocates of an exclusive transition to organic production are quick to condemn conventional agriculture for the energy required to make nitrogen fertilizer. They do so, however, without calculating the energy needed to keep a major source of organic fertilizer—cows—up and running.

It's this limitation that has led the UCLA molecular biologist and National Academy of Sciences member Bob Goldberg to assert, "At most, organic farming practices can feed 4 billion people." As we have seen, the world's population is scheduled to reach 9 to 10 billion by midcentury. So either way we're left with lots of people, lots of poop, and potentially not enough food.[9]

In light of these deficiencies, the Green Revolution is commonly held up as the successful counterpoint to organic agriculture's relatively low yields. This profoundly important agricultural transition, which started in the mid-1940s and continued through the 1980s, centered on the technological effort to boost the world's crop yields in order to feed an impending "population bomb." From the narrow measure of sheer grain output, it was a wild success.

Through a productive combination of plant breeding (creating dwarf varieties of wheat and rice that could hold up more grain per stem), chemical inputs (synthetic fertilizers, herbicides, and pesticides), and mechanization (tractors, plows, irrigation systems), agronomists, farmers, and policymakers were able to win what the population geneticist Paul Ehrlich famously called "the battle to feed all of humanity." They were able to do so with dramatic increases in output per acre, thereby preserving rainforests and marginal lands from agricultural expansion and in turn enhancing wilderness biodiversity. "Without the development of high-yielding crop varieties over recent decades," writes Pamela Ronald, "two to four times more land would have been needed to produce the same amount of food in the United States, China, and India." That's a frightening prospect—thankfully, one we've avoided.[10]

The raw numbers alone cut to the core of the Green Revolution's qualified accomplishments. Over the past half-century, the principles of high-yield farming fed a world population that doubled. It did so with food that was 75 percent cheaper. Between 1965 and 1970, India and Pakistan watched wheat yields increase twofold, bringing both countries to the brink of self-sufficiency. In Asia, cereal production also doubled between 1970 and 1975, while land under cultivation grew by only 4 percent. For the world as a whole, between 1960 and the present, grain production has increased 250 percent, while the average person in the developing world now eats 25 percent more calories as a direct result of increased yield per acre. According to the International Food Policy Research Institute, "Most industrial countries achieved sustained food surpluses by the second half of the 20th century, and eliminated the threat of starvation." Grain production, as I will later argue, has unfortunately gone to feed far too many domesticated animals. Nevertheless, the Green Revolution can take legitimate credit for the accomplishment of feeding the world's humans—something that organic agriculture, at least as it currently operates, would probably never have done.[11]

But the story of the Green Revolution has a dark underside. The movement came with severe environmental costs. Borlaug, who designed a dwarf wheat variety in 1943, won the Nobel Peace Prize, and is often credited with having saved more lives than any other human being in history, bristles when these costs are enumerated. Castigating environmentalists who condemn the Green Revolution for its environmental excesses, he explains, "They do their lobbying from comfortable office suites in Washington or Brussels. If they lived just one month amid the misery of the developing world, as I have for fifty years, they'd be crying out for tractors and fertilizer and irrigation canals and be outraged that fashionable elitists back home were trying to deny them these things."[12]

Borlaug might have a point, but to be fair to fashionable elitists, those pushing policy papers in D.C. aren't as clueless or hardhearted as he makes them out to be. For all its accomplishments with explosive yield increases, the Green Revolution relied on extensive and unrestrained chemical and industrial inputs. In so doing, it drew the blueprint for an environmentally damaging model of agribusiness that currently plagues food production throughout the developed world. When Michael Pollan talks about the food system's addiction to fossil fuel, he's talking about the legacy of the Green Revolution. The popular moral driven home by the Green Revolution was that the means, however wasteful or forceful, justifies the end. Because the means—industrial irrigation; synthetic fertilizers, herbicides, and pesticides; and aggressive forms of mechanization—accounted for much of the Green Revolution's bumper yields, environmentalists have rightfully raised objections to them.

They've noted, for example, that the fossil fuels driving these inputs went a long way toward offsetting gains in crop yield, thus shortchanging the future for the moment. They further note that the Green Revolution diminished crop biodiversity by favoring monoculture over polyculture, and laid the basis for intense corporate consolidation of food production. Through such a heavy reliance on a few staple crops and a steady stream of fossil fuels, today's industrial agricultural systems, which took their cues from the architects of the Green Revolution, have set conventional agriculture on a course of chemical dependence, genetic homogenization, and unsustainable production. Critics have pointed to all these problems, and they're correct to do so.

Hence the current state of our agricultural alternatives. The two dominant ideals of food production now before us, low-yielding organic and high-yielding agribusiness, urge us to take a side. Taking sides in this debate, however, is a bit of a disingenuous act, if only because it assumes that there's a clear distinction between organic and conventional production. The promotional mantras for each form of agriculture—organic will save the earth!/conventional will feed the world!—certainly suggest that the differences are like night and day.

But are they? Socially conscious consumers know that the conventional norm of agribusiness-driven food production is environmentally, if not morally, bankrupt. There's no need to make that case here, as it's made in many other places. However, partly because of its yield issues, organic does not fully deserve the golden halo it gets to wear. As a careful elaboration of the underlying facts of organic agriculture will suggest, the distinctions that the idealized version of organic promotes are in reality more blurred than crystalized. This is especially true when it comes to the contentious and frequently misunderstood issue of chemical applications.

Chemicals

Organic agriculture is often praised as a "clean" or "pure" alternative to the chemically intensive practices of industrialized agriculture. Indeed, acre for acre, organic agriculture employs far fewer chemicals than conventional operations. One obvious point of distinction centers on the fact that organic agriculture forbids the use of synthetic fertilizers. Nitrogen fertilizer, which adds nitrogen to the soil (and, unfortunately, to the air and water), requires substantial inputs of natural gas to produce. In fact, 5 percent of all natural gas goes toward manufacturing fertilizer.

Excessive applications of synthetic fertilizers not only consume large quantities of fossil fuels and contribute to global warming (through the production of nitrous oxide), but they also compromise the soil's ability to hold nutrients, cause extensive riverine and oceanic "dead zones," and might even lessen the ability of naturally occurring bacteria to hold nitrogen (a plant's most critical nutrient) in the soil. Writing in *The End of Food*, the journalist Paul Roberts, hardly an alarmist on environmental matters, describes the impact of nitrogen used in agriculture as "pervasive and devastating."[13]

Organic agriculture also disallows the use of synthetic pesticides. These chemicals today are much safer than their pre-1970 counterparts. Nevertheless, chemicals such as malathion, atrazine, and

Sevin—not to mention a range of other organophosphates—leach into drinking water, can cause reproductive problems in lab animals, may cause endocrine and respiratory problems in humans, and persist in the food supply as residues on fruits and vegetables. Many of these pesticides and insecticides kill more than their intended host, ridding the environment of a range of beneficial insects and soil microbes that foster a more dynamic ecological system. Although advocates of organic agriculture rarely note that these chemicals also directly result in more productive agricultural operations, they routinely tout organic's superiority because of its "chemical-free" approach to growing food, thereby reinforcing the misleading impression that a solid line separates organic and conventional systems. As we will see, however, organic practices rely heavily on a range of natural chemicals, many of them quite dangerous.

Research conducted by scientists without industry connections are beginning to challenge the line of demarcation between organic and conventional growing methods. Foremost among these scientists is Bruce Ames, a biochemist, molecular biologist, member of the National Academy of Sciences, winner of the Tyler Prize for Environmental Achievement, and director of the National Institute of Environmental Health Sciences Center at the University of California at Berkeley. Ames places the issue of pesticides in an interesting perspective, one that ultimately asks us to rethink the supposed benefits of the "organic" designation. By no means does he believe that synthetic chemicals used in conventional agriculture and eschewed by organic growers are innocuous. But he does argue that our obsession with their dangers overlooks the fact that, as he writes, "99.9 percent of the toxic chemicals we're exposed to are completely natural."[14]

The implications are significant for organic agriculture. When we eat an average plant, organic or not, we "consume about 50 toxic chemicals," most of them natural pesticides occurring both in the food and as residue on it. Tests done on rats—which, granted, may have little predictive value for humans—show that there are virtually no differences with respect to health consequences between natural and synthetic chemicals. They were equally carcinogenic when delivered at high doses. Reinforcing this point, Ames notes that "the natural chemicals that are known rodent carcinogens in a single cup of coffee are about equal in weight to a year's worth of ingested synthetic pesticide residues that are rodent carcinogens." He has even gone so far as to say that because synthetic pesticides better increase the supply of cancer-fighting fruits and vegetables, "pesticides lower the cancer rate." As he sees it, the benefits that accrue from eating a steady diet of fruits and vegetables far outweigh the detriments of consuming trace amounts of mildly toxic pesticides sprayed upon them.[15]

This line of argument, of course, must be approached delicately. But as counterintuitive as it may seem, it has a strong following. Writing in the prestigious journal *Science*, other researchers joined Ames in showing that a sleeping pill, a glass of wine, a cup of coffee, and a glass of orange juice each have, according to toxicity studies done on rodents, a higher "potency index" than the synthetic pesticides lindane and captan. So does a glass of chlorinated tap water. When the Oxford University scientist Dr. Robert Peto determined that the primary cancer-causing risks in the United States were smoking, genetics, and a low-fiber diet, scientists at the Environmental Protection Agency (EPA) followed up with a report that noted, "The occurrence of pesticides as dietary pollutants seems unimportant."[16]

Writing in a 2006 issue of the journal *Critical Reviews in Food Science and Nutrition*, scientists concluded, according to one summary of the piece, that "there was no evidence that eating organic food was healthier" than eating conventional food. "The bottom line," according to Dr. Elizabeth Finkel, a microbiologist, "is that there is tremendous variation in the nutritional make-up of fruit and vegetables regardless of whether they were grown by organic or conventional means."[17]

None of these findings discredit the historic muckraking mission of Rachel Carson. Nor do they undermine the need for strict and enforced chemical regulations. To the contrary, as I have argued in my book *American Pests*, they suggest that the extensive pesticide reforms enacted in the wake of *Silent Spring* have left us with pesticides that are far safer than the organophosphates and hydrochlorides, not to mention the arsenic- and lead-based insecticides that became commonplace in conventional agriculture before Carson exposed their dangers.

Unfortunately, reexamining the place of chemicals in conventional and organic agriculture can provide an opportunity for distortions. Ideologically driven critics of organic agriculture, most notably archconservative ideologues affiliated with the Hudson Institute, have cynically deployed Ames's findings as ammunition to defend the status quo of commercial agriculture, using the research as a green light for agribusiness to dump synthetic chemicals indiscriminately. This is, however, a distortion of what Ames is doing. One can accept Ames's argument that natural chemicals, like synthetic ones, are an integral risk of food production and consumption and still pursue the overlapping goals of agricultural sustainability, high-yield farming, and intense, well-funded government regulation.

Just as unfortunately, though, the Hudson Institute is not the only guilty party in obscuring a rational reassessment of agricultural chemicals. Rhetoric from the organic lobby leveled against synthetic chemicals has also resulted in less than forthright portrayals. "Along with chemical weapons," writes the Soil Association, "chemicals used in farming are the only substances that are deliberately released into the environment to kill living things." Equating chemical warfare and chemical farming is just another case of polemics and propaganda. A more productive tack would be to perpetuate a healthy skepticism of chemicals based on accurate scientific information, rather than rejecting them outright based on ideological presuppositions, scientific ignorance, or fear of the unknown.[18]

However, the damaging rhetoric continues. Staunch proponents of organic systems often misleadingly characterize the relationship between organic agriculture and chemical applications. "Organic food excludes pesticides," declares Craig Sams, the president of Whole Earth Foods in London. But this very common declaration is simply not true. As the plant pathologist Laura Pickett Pottorff writes, "If we think organic gardening means vegetables free of any chemical pesticides, we don't have the story quite right." Indeed, if the risk of synthetic pesticides has been overstated by organic advocates, organic's own reliance on chemicals has been vastly understated to perpetuate a marketable image that what's going on in organic agriculture is "all natural," in the sense that nature, rather than the farmer, is running the operation.[19]

The difficulty of framing a productive discussion about agricultural chemicals brings us face-to-face with an all-too-familiar hurdle: popular misconceptions about nature and farming. Rob Lyons, a journalist in the United Kingdom, sums up this problem well when he writes that "the underlying temper of our times is that anything processed or industrialised can be seen as adulterated and harmful, while anything that appears to be natural or close to nature can be regarded as pure and uncorrupted." The reality of contemporary food production, whether organic or conventional, whether large-scale or small, stubbornly fails to follow this purified/corrupted script.[20]

Agriculture by its nature demands human interference with nature's rhythms, and these interferences, synthetic or not, are necessarily contrary to what "nature" intends. No matter how sustainable the process, agriculture is designed to transform nature and yield outputs. Clearing a field with scythes, plowing a field with a tractor and a metal plow, planting hybrid seeds that have been bred over decades for resistance, applying chemicals—organic or not—with mechanized sprayers, employing irrigation systems, weeding fields with hoes mass-produced on the other side of the world, just looking at a vast forest and envisioning fields—these are only a few examples of how agriculture at its core remains an industrial process centered on the efficient production of commodities.

No matter how "primitive" or "pure" the operation may seem, every farm on some level is a factory. This point is critical, for it is only when we start to question the organic rhetoric about "natural farming" that we can make room for the judicious use of agricultural chemicals—something that, as we will see, is integral to any form of production that is sustainable, high-yielding, profitable, and amenable to midsize, diversified farms.

Eliot Coleman notwithstanding, organic farmers grow crops that are no less plagued by pests than those of conventional farmers; insects generally do not discriminate between organic and conventional as well as we do. While organic farmers are far more likely than conventional farmers to practice environmentally benign forms of biological control, and while they're also more likely to sensibly diversify their crops to reduce infestation, most farmers have no choice but to rely on chemicals as necessary supplements to their operations. With pests often consuming up to 40 percent of the crops grown in the United States, most organic growers do so as a matter of course. They might refer to these substances as "botanical extracts" or "biorationals," but according to Ned Groth, a senior scientist at Consumers Union, these toxins "are not necessarily less worrisome because they are natural."[21]

Consumers, swayed by the "chemical-free" reputation of organic foods, tend to take false comfort in the impression that organic products lack potentially harmful external inputs. However, organic agriculture struggles with its own demons of chemical dependency. The fact that farmers have been applying natural chemicals to agricultural systems for thousands of years does not mean that these applications are innocuous, especially when they're used to promote the interests of commercialized organic agriculture. As with the synthetic pesticides and fertilizers used by conventional growers, the chemicals applied by organic farmers are relatively safe when responsibly applied but could easily precipitate environmental and health problems if delivered in excessive doses.

Take sodium nitrate. This active compound, which is mined exclusively in South America, is employed primarily by organic farmers growing winter vegetables in dry soil. They use it as a soluble fertilizer to enhance the soil with nitrogen. In addition to the environmental costs of mining and shipping the compound, sodium nitrate contributes to groundwater pollution by furthering freshwater eutrophication (intensification of phosphorous and nitrogen) and salinization. Once applied, sodium nitrate fertilizer, which contains perchloride from the caliche mud from which it's mined, leaches that perchloride into surrounding lakes and rivers.

Recent work on perchloride demonstrates that it interferes with iodine uptake by the human thyroid gland, a discovery that has led scientists to start investigating its impact on drinking water. This concern has been serious enough for the EPA to add perchloride to the Contaminant Candidate List, encouraging more research into this potentially widespread environmental problem. In addition, critics of synthetic nitrogen fertilizer point out how much energy is required to produce that product, but they've yet to undertake an analysis of the energy that goes into acquiring sodium nitrate destined for organic farms, a measurement that would allow a more accurate comparison of organic and conventional energy costs.[22]

Organic growers are also allowed to use copper, sulfur, and copper sulfate as natural fungicides. According to Julie Guthman, a geographer who writes extensively about California's organic agriculture, "Sulfur is said to cause more worker injuries in California that any other agricultural input." Miners who harvest sulfur dust to be sprayed on organic grapes tend to suffer chronic respiratory problems. According to the Pesticide Information Project, "pulmonary function may be reduced" with heavy exposure to sulfur dust. The dust is generally harmless to land animals, but the Department of Health and Human Services has found that it is toxic to fish. A study of a Canadian forest with high levels of sustained sulfur contamination discovered extensive topsoil acidification of pine trees, which had also developed a diminished ability to take nitrogen from the soil. For all these reasons, one study opines that sulfur could be "a greater environmental risk than many synthetic fungicides."[23]

Regarding copper sulfate, the English politician Lord Taverne calls it "the most poisonous fungicide there is." The EPA backs him up with several studies classifying copper sulfate as a class I toxin: "highly toxic." The compound is dangerous enough to warrant a permit if used in regions close to endangered aquatic animals and is also "highly toxic" to the tissue of fish, where it bioaccumulates. The impact of copper sulfate on organic soil is powerful enough to counteract many of the organic compounds' soil-enhancing qualities. It persists indefinitely and can kill organisms in the soil, including earthworms.[24]

One study of female vineyard employees working near copper sulfate (and other pesticides) found 6.2 times more copper in their breast milk than in the milk of women who worked on the vineyard away from the pesticides. Studies of mice exposed to copper sulfate showed their DNA to be damaged. Many plants that absorb copper sulfate experience enough stress to significantly reduce their ability to undergo photosynthesis.[25]

Copper is obtained through the energy-intensive processes of smelting, leaching, and electrolysis and thus demands considerable energy expenditure before winding up in a plastic bag for sale. A study of the impact of copper fungicide on coffee trees found that "root growth decreased with increasing copper fungicide spray increasing." Of greater concern, scientists have documented through a study of avocado orchards the fact that earthworms are repelled by copper fungicides, a discovery that led the researchers to conclude: "Our results highlight the importance of limiting future application of Cu-based fungicides." Copper heavily accumulates in the soil after spraying, and it does not biodegrade. Assessing this development through a study of apple production, scientists writing in a prominent environmental pollution journal argued that unless measures were taken "to control copper accumulation," the future of sustainable apple farming could be in jeopardy.[26]

Another mineral commonly used by organic farmers is zinc phosphide. More often than not, it's used to kill rodents in grain crops. The World Health Organization (WHO) notes that zinc phosphide is "of high mammalian toxicity" and kills not only mice and rats but prairie dogs and squirrels. Cows, pigs, goats, chickens, and rabbits have been severely poisoned by zinc phosphide. When it's been used as a household product, cats have died as a result of "secondary poisoning"—eating a dead rodent. The mineral is toxic to fish and highly toxic to birds—again, all according to the WHO. In Australia, the Queensland government has warned farmers against zinc phosphide, noting the "poisoning risk to children and pets." It does not allow the mineral to be placed in "agricultural storage" because "it is an acute, fast acting poison."[27]

Toxic plant extracts used by organic farmers for insect control, including rotenone and pyrethrins, are also natural inputs often considered to be harmless to the environment. However, these pose health and environmental risks of their own. Rotenone is moderately toxic to birds, highly toxic to fish (it was used by Native Americans as a piscicide), kills bees when used in combination with pyrethrum, has been shown to kill turtles and other amphibians, exterminates a range of beneficial mites, and, according to the Occupational Safety and Health Administration, "can cause damage to liver and kidney." Fish farmers use it to eliminate "trash" fish before restocking. One study that investigated the impact of rotenone on animals concluded, "Overall, the effects of rotenone toxicity are widespread."

In 2000 scientists performed tests that established a possible connection between rotenone and Parkinson's disease. Four years later they concluded a study on the environmental impact of rotenone by warning that "it is extremely important to raise the awareness of potential dangers of rotenone poisoning."[28]

Pyrethrin has problems as well. According to the Pesticide Information Project, it is "extremely toxic to life, such as bluegill and lake trout, while being slightly toxic to bird species, such as mallards." It's been shown to kill lizards. The EPA classifies it as a "likely human carcinogen." When manufacturers mix pyrethrin with a synergist such as piperonyl butoxide, they make pyrethrum, which is the most readily used natural insecticide on the market today.[29]

Other botanical chemicals that organic regulations allow include ryania (made from a South American shrub), nicotine, sabadilla (made from tropical lilies), and neem extract (taken from the Indonesian neem tree). Some of these products, especially nicotine, are quite dangerous to mammals, while others, like sabadilla, remain fairly harmless. Although botanical chemicals generally biodegrade rapidly and thus do not run off into watersheds, they all must be imported, packaged, and distributed by chemical companies such as Dow Chemical, many of them anathema to the organic movement. Plus the fact that these botanicals do break down so rapidly means that they have to be applied in heavier doses and more often than many synthetic compounds.[30]

Much of this information lies buried in scientific journals. However, there's encouraging evidence that a more balanced message about organic chemicals, as well as information fairly comparing synthetic and natural chemicals, are beginning to seep into the public sphere. In Sunman, Indiana, for example, a popular gardening magazine recently ran an article on natural insecticides. Rather than assume, as almost always happens, that "natural" is necessarily better for our health and the environment than synthetic, the editors of *Gardens Alive Catalog* declare with refreshing candor that "there is a misconception among many gardeners that organophos-phates and other synthetic 'chemical' insecticides are dangerous, while botanical and mineral insecticides are not. This is not neces-sarily true." They then go on to note that "some botanicals, such as insecticidal soaps, are nearly harmless to mammals, but, in fact, nicotine sulfate and rotenone are more toxic than, say, the chemi-cals malathion or carbaryl (sevin)."[31]

The point here is not to use these comparisons to criticize organic production per se, or to imply that conventional produc-tion holds all the answers. It is just to recognize, as Dr. Elizabeth Finkel observes, that "purism gets in the way of practices that are better for the environment and more sustainable for farmers." Nei-ther system of production can by itself sustainably provide food for billions of people. The purpose of dismantling the myth of organic purity is to start blurring the misleading line between organic and conventional. Working from the premise that a responsible food system capable of producing food for the world must tolerate some chemical inputs, we must start thinking about alternatives to get us beyond our current impasse.[32]

Soil and Cycles

The founders and most prominent leaders of organic agriculture were religiously dedicated to the proposition of healthy soil. Their passion for rich humus was at its core reactionary in nature, tilting as it did into the heavy winds of artificial fertilization and agricul-tural industrialization that followed World War I. Albert Howard, the author of *An Agricultural Testament* and an early pioneer of organic methods, explained in 1947, "Agricultural research with inorganic fertilizers is misleading [because] the great nature law of return, birth-growth-reproduction-death-decay, is ignored."[33]

His predecessor as organic agriculture's leading spokesman was Rudolf Steiner, a Croatian-born scholar of German literature who became deeply engaged in the connections between nutrition and agricultural methods. "If there is to be nothing but the mineral fertilizer that has now become so popular," he complained in 1927, "well, gentlemen, your children, more particularly your grandchildren, will have very pale faces." Steiner, who delivered over six thousand speeches in his lifetime, had a tendency to stray into some quirky agricultural territory, but ultimately his kaleidoscopic vision of soil fertility came down to one thing: "proper manuring."[34]

Lady Eve Balfour and J. I. Rodale carried Steiner's and Howard's message of soil health into the 1970s and beyond. Rodale's popular magazine *Organic Gardening* joined Balfour's Soil Association to advance the notion that the conscientious farmer treated his or her soil with "all organic residues which originated on the farm." More than any other belief, an unwavering faith that synthetic fertilizers ruined the soil while on-site organic material vitalized it has united the organic movement from its earliest incarnations to the present day.[35]

The idea of fertilizing soil with organic matter derived from on-site sources is an appealing one. But as we have discussed, it can be achieved only on a very small scale by the most talented of farmers. I'm skeptical that it's realistically achievable in larger systems of commercial agriculture. Recent scientific studies have started to explain why.

The most radical organic farmers, very much wedded to the timeless guidelines set by their spiritual founders, pursue methods that enrich soil with natural minerals, green manure, animal manure, and ley crops. It is through these on-site enrichment techniques that they aim to reduce environmental stress and achieve a more sustainable form of agricultural production. These benefits, however, depend heavily on efficiently distributed nitrogen inputs for plants. (Plants must have a steady and well-regulated supply of nitrogen to grow, and though nitrogen is in the air, most crops cannot "fix" and absorb it.) And it is on this point—this very important point—that the assumption that natural is better crashes into the complex realities of fertilizer application and nutrient distribution on larger farms.

Nitrogen is a tough element to control. According to Holger Kirchmann, a soil scientist at the Swedish University of Agricultural Sciences, and Megan H. Ryan, a plant biologist at the University of Western Australia, "the N [nitrogen] input in organic farming tends to be quite imprecise, being unevenly distributed in the crop rotation and not necessarily well-adapted to the needs of the following crop." In addition to the difficulty of carefully directing nitrogen applications, organic methods of soil enrichment often fail to maintain required levels of phosphorous (P) and potassium (K). "More of these nutrients," write Kirchmann and Ryan in reference to P and K, "are removed through harvested products than applied to the soil." Robert Mullen, a soil fertility expert at Ohio State University, recognizes the many benefits of manure as a source of fertilizer but adds that manure "has a problem. It is an unbalanced nutrient source."[36]

Other difficulties abound. In a speech delivered to the OECD Workshop on Organic Agriculture in 2002, Tom Bruulsema explained, "To meet all the crop's needs, [organic fertilizers] have to be applied at high rates, which may lead to increased risk of loss and negative environmental impact." Many organic farmers compensate for this imbalance by importing organic manures. This importation, however, is a violation of the Steiner-Howard premise, insofar as it's just another case of organic farmers, in Bruulsema's words, "gain[ing] nutrients that originated from conventional farms."[37]

Other organic farmers—perhaps a majority—buy conventional manure and compost it. Composting is a process that does not occur naturally in nature. It is done in part to break down contaminants in the manure. But many agrochemicals cannot be broken down through composting. Cattle farmers feed over 25 million pounds of antibiotics a year to their animals. These antibiotics appear in the manure and in turn can show up in the vegetables they fertilize. Health experts warn that the consumption of fruits and vegetables containing antibiotics can create resistant strains of bacteria. The European Union banned the use of antibiotics as a feed additive in 2006, but in the United States antibiotics are still given to promote animal growth. Even midsized organic farms, however, cannot reliably track the history of their manure.[38]

Conditions will vary for every individual farm, but in the end, as Kirchmann and Ryan concluded, "there is a substantial risk of nutrient depletion in organic systems with a directly associated reduction in yield." Add to these nutrient problems the rarely acknowledged fact that organic manure often contains more heavy metals than conventional manure. It turns out that the process of composting concentrates heavy metals at a higher level than if the manure had not been composted. This process can in some cases lead to higher levels of heavy metal content in organic soils. Considering these inherent vagaries of organic fertilizing, it's not hard to see how the reality of a self-sustaining system, or even an organic system reliant on external additions, rarely conforms to its articulated ideal.[39]

One might counter that at least the nutrients from organic sources do not leach into the surrounding water and air. But even this long-held assumption is debatable. Based on extensive field studies conducted in Sweden starting in the 1990s, scientists found that nutrient leaching could in some cases be higher for organic agriculture than for conventional systems. Nitrogen was used more efficiently by plants in conventional systems than in organic ones. To be exact, under controlled conditions, 65 percent of the nitrogen in organic plots went into the crops and 35 percent leached, whereas 81 percent of the nitrogen in conventional plots went into the crops and 19 percent leached. Green manures in particular caused especially high rates of leaching losses and, as the authors put it, "much higher leaching of P [phosphorous] than inorganic synthetic fertilizers."[40]

Naturally, any effort to grow food necessarily involves the removal of plant nutrients during harvest. However, organic advocates like to promote their organic systems as "closed," meaning that the nutrients taken from the soil are systematically recycled back into it. In reality, however, examples of successful closed systems are rare. Even if they were commonly attained, the land requirements to make enough manure to fertilize enough plants would be unsustainable. There seems to be no escaping the persistent specter of external inputs, whether in organic or conventional systems, large operations or small, synthetic or natural, in order to meet the needs of an expanding population with the use of limited land.

Fortunately, the closed-loop model is not the only way to think about responsible soil health. We can also conceptualize farming in terms of an efficient transfer of resources. This idea has just as long a legacy as organic's recycling ideals, if not longer. In 1911, Franklin Hiram King, the author of *Farmers of Forty Centuries*, undertook an intensive study of farming systems throughout Asia. Paying particular attention to how farmers redistributed waste, he persuasively argued that the most efficient agricultural systems he encountered effectively incorporated external sources of nutrients, including wood ash, household trash, and even human waste. The farmers' objective was not to create a perfectly closed and self-perpetuating ecological system, but rather to replace the soil's nutrient loss with the most efficient and effective external soil additives available at that time.[41]

This approach soberly accepted the fact that "nutrient depletion of natural resources was necessary to maintain high yields," acknowledging that "any agricultural system will become depleted in nutrients... unless there is a regular addition from an external source." The implications of this quotation should not be overlooked: between the generally unachievable ideal of a closed loop and the wasteful outsourcing of externalities that characterizes agribusiness, there are endlessly viable combinations of soil inputs—many of them yet unexplored—that farmers might use to dramatically improve the sustainability of their agricultural operations. Thinking of the matter in rigid terms, with conventional being wasteful and organic being clean, prevents a creative exploration of alternative combinations. We have to feed the soil to enhance yields, most of the nutrients will inevitably have to come from afar, and so the goal should be to undertake the task as responsibly and pragmatically as we can.[42]

Fertilizer Efficiency

Surveying the world's current use of synthetic fertilizers, there's little good news to highlight. The status quo, as we're repeatedly told, cannot hold. With grain production anticipated to increase by almost 40 percent by 2025, the environment will be devastated if today's rates of nitrogen application and leaching are not radically curtailed. As I will later argue, the quickest way to diminish wasteful fertilizer applications significantly would be to stop producing grain to feed livestock. Sixty percent of all nitrogen fertilizer use is for cereals. If one could wave a magic wand and radically reduce meat consumption, all discussions of fertilizer abuse would come to an abrupt halt.

Here in the real world, however, we will for some time be staring into the face of yet another frustrating paradox, one that's only going to intensify as the world's population expands: synthetic fertilizer is essential for achieving high yields, but when it fails to enter the plant, it destroys the environment.[43]

So how do we proceed without categorically rejecting synthetic nitrogen fertilizer? Yet again we have to seek reasonable compromise. In a 2008 *New York Times* piece, Dr. Robert J. Diaz, a scientist at the Virginia Institute of Marine Science, made a remark that happened to cut sharply through the fat of the fertilizer debate. He said, "Nitrogen is nitrogen; if it's on land it produces corn. If it gets in the water, it produces algae [which suck up all the oxygen]." This observation is brilliant in its simplicity, highlighting the critical point that nitrogen becomes a problem only when it escapes the plant. So before we declare with earnest environmental conviction that farmers should abandon synthetic fertilizers, we must consider a more realistic middle ground. What if farmers could use less fertilizer as well as ensure that the fertilizer is almost completely absorbed by their crops, rather than being taken up by the air, soil, and water that sustains us? Such a scenario is becoming increasingly possible.[44]

In the underworld of soil science research, scientists are exploring ways to enhance what they call NUE, "nitrogen uptake efficiency." In a 2006 essay, Achim Dobermann, of the University of Nebraska's Department of Agronomy and Horticulture, writes that "interventions to increase NUE and reduce N losses to the environment must be accomplished at the farm level." After reminding us that on average, only half of nitrogen soil inputs are taken up by plants, he goes on to describe the ways in which soil scientists, plant biologists, and farmers are working to improve this figure.[45]

Without going too deeply into the details, we are coming to learn that NUE is in many respects a matter of improved management and openness to new technology. Farmers who apply fertilizer in the spring, who employ "controlled release" fertilizers, who make pinpointed applications immediately before or after flowering, and who plant seeds that have been bred for more efficient uptake have seen substantial improvements in overall NUE. "It has been demonstrated in many studies," writes Dobermann, "that 30 to 50% increases in NUE can be achieved through fine-tuning of N management practices."[46]

Even without a concerted effort among environmentalists to promote these strategies, NUE in corn in the United States increased by 36 percent between 1980 and 2000 and by 32 percent in Japan between 1985 and the present. What makes these uptake figures even more encouraging is the fact that they're beneficial both for the environment and for the farmers' profit margins. Moreover, the limits to this progress do not seem insurmountable, and with the help of improved plant breeding, many scientists envision reaching 90 to 100 percent NUE.[47]

Organic advocates unwilling to look at the matter of soil productivity through a broader lens are apt to remain unswayed by these figures, or by the potential of NUE to substantially decrease the damage caused by synthetic fertilizer. So in a last-ditch effort to encourage an open mind, I offer a final point to consider on the matter of nitrogen fertilizer: 50 percent of all nitrogen leached into the world's soil comes from Chinese farmers. This statistic matters a lot, because there is no cohort currently less predisposed to go organic—lacking as they do the infrastructure, incentive, and institutional motivation—than the millions of Chinese farmers currently dumping massive quantities of synthetic fertilizer into the soil.

This is not to say that one day the ideals of the eco-agrarian philosophy might not migrate from the enclaves of Berkeley, Cambridge, Madison, and Austin to the impoverished fields of northern China, where, as King taught us in *Farmers of Forty Centuries*, organic methods once flourished. Anything is possible. But until this remarkably unlikely shift happens, doesn't it make sense to try to substantially reduce the environmental consequences of our current practices? In other words, looking at this matter in global perspective, doesn't reform seem a lot more likely than revolution?

The Golden Mean

My goal here is not to give my organic-loving friends a sour stomach. I admire the underlying objectives of organic agriculture very much, I often choose to buy organic, and I think that organic farming has a bright future as an invaluable form of niche production. Eliot Coleman and thousands of other organic farmers and small-farming advocates have made significant contributions to our food and agricultural knowledge over the past thirty years. We should be grateful.

The problems I have with organic agriculture have less to do with how it is currently practiced than with the inflated claim that it's the only alternative to today's wasteful conventional production. The insistence on such a narrow and exclusive option is especially shortsighted given that it is a highly specialized approach to farming that now feeds less than 2 percent of the world's population.

To reject the ideals underscoring the organic ethos outright, of course, would be folly. In the proper context they work exceptionally well, and more important, they promote agricultural standards that can effectively inform larger, better-capitalized, and farther-reaching operations. But the problem with pushing the small sustainable model too far is that, as Pollan and others have already shown, it breaks down when asked to scale up. We cannot afford to put all our eggs in such a modest and unstable basket.

My intention, both in this chapter and in the book as a whole, is to reframe the debate about sustainable food production in a way that opens it up and encourages us to seek less ideologically crafted alternatives—ones that reform the environmental abuses of industrial agriculture, lend themselves to pragmatic regulation and enforcement, preserve the profit motive, and adapt to local, regional, national, and global economies and infrastructures.

Working from the premise that the small/sustainable/organic models are just one general answer among many others to the failures of the world's food systems, the following chapters develop in greater detail what some of those options might look like.

Klaus Amman, of the University of Bern, offers guiding words of wisdom: "Looking for sustainable and equitable farming methods means...to refrain from any kind of ideological debate and concentrate on pragmatic decisions to find the best solution for a given region." Rejecting a one-size-fits-all approach to a sustainable global food supply, he adds, "Roads to success are many, and we must pursue them all."[48]

3

Frankenfood?: A Case for Genetically Modified Crops

Sometimes the lack of full certainty, in an environment of manageable risk, should not be used as the reason to postpone measures where genetic modification can legitimately be used to address environmental or public health issues. —AUSTRALIAN ACADEMY OF SCIENCE

With food as with people, first impressions matter most. It's worthwhile to keep this point in mind when considering that the general public's introduction to the concept of genetically modified (GM) foods came through monarch butterflies. In May 1999, just three years after the United States approved the use of GM crops, an assistant professor of entomology at Cornell University published a short report in the scientific journal *Nature* documenting his discovery that under controlled circumstances, pollen from genetically modified corn killed the larvae of the monarchs.

The media pounced, with the *New York Times* running the story on its front page under a caption calling the butterfly the "Bambi of the insect world." Antibiotech interests, led by the organic industry, spread the news far and wide. Friends of the Earth asked members in a mass mailing, *"If deadly toxins that kill butterflies are being introduced into our food supply, what effect are these toxins having on you and your family?"* For all intents and purposes, popular opinion (including my own at the time) effectively made up its mind. Fatefully, it would be through this emotional lens that concerned consumers would see the supposed health dangers of eating genetically modified crops, as well as the broad environmental threats they evidently posed.[1]

Speculation about what would happen with the introduction of GM crops evolved into one of the more overblown litanies of future destruction ever attached to a specific form of technology. Mae-Wan Ho, a scientist who works in England, announced that genetic engineering "will spell the end of humanity as we know it and the end of the world at large." The director of Greenpeace UK argued that "genetically modified crops pose a greater threat to the environment than nuclear waste or chemical pollution." Needless to say, a 2005 Pew survey found that more than half of the people it questioned opposed allowing GM crops into the food supply (with respondents evidently unaware that 61 percent of all corn and 89 percent of all soybeans grown in the United States *already did* come from GM seeds). From the perspective of public opinion, at least, this case was closed.[2]

But from the perspective of sound science, it was anything but. Within days of the story's publication, scientists began to sniff around the research. Within months, they were denouncing it. Their critiques were systematic and withering: in nature, monarch larvae and butterflies do not even eat corn pollen, only milkweed; the Cornell entomologists had purposely used a specific Cry protein (1 out of 170 available) already known to kill caterpillars (Cry proteins attack an insect's gut); they had kept no records of the amount of pollen dusted on each leaf; they had force-fed the larvae corn pollen for four days straight; and they had never considered the timing of larva hatching and pollen shedding as it occurs in nature. They assumed what proved to be a highly unlikely correlation between butterfly births and the release of pollen. These methodological problems were only the most obvious ones with the study.[3]

A handful of loyal defenders backed the research, but scientists around the world proceeded to dismiss it as more fear-mongering and publicity-hounding than sound science. One entomologist (a Cornell colleague of the authors) noted that the experiment was analogous to a person's going to a movie, eating 100 pounds of popcorn, and dying from salt poisoning. As the embarrassing condemnations piled up, six studies published together in the *Proceedings of the National Academy of Sciences* confirmed the safety of GM corn, finding no immediate risk to the monarch butterfly. In fact, Jeffrey Glassberg, the president of the North American Butterfly Association, concluded that more monarch butterflies died from common insecticides than from genetically modified corn pollen—an ironic observation, given that GM corn has the potential to lower insecticide use. Less diplomatically, another opponent of the study within the Cornell department wondered aloud, "How many monarchs get killed on the windshield of a car?"[4]

These assessments, tactful or otherwise, were eventually reported in the mainstream media, but they appeared on the back pages and, most notably, they all ran during the dark days immediately after September 11, 2001. "The world might have a different attitude to the safety of genetically modified crops if it had not been for the terrorist attacks on New York and Washington," explained the editors of SciDev.net, an on-line publication sponsored by the journals *Nature* and *Science*. In the end, then, this case was reopened and even overturned, but only among the scientific community. Popular opinion, the ultimate arbiter, did not budge. GM crops thus continue to face an uphill battle, and the debates about them only grow more polemical as a result.[5]

The butterfly anecdote is an apt one for understanding our troubled relationship with the technology of genetic modification. On the surface, there's an abundance of passionate condemnation;

beneath it, there's another, much more complex story. What I will try to do in this chapter is encourage skeptics of genetic engineering to forget about the butterflies and the (unfulfilled) doomsday predictions and take another look at this technology, which, if used wisely, can potentially serve the interests of sustainable global agriculture.

Keeping Biotechnology in Perspective

Let it be said from the outset that biotechnology is not going to save the world. It will not end hunger or single-handedly resolve our many agricultural problems. There are certainly legitimate concerns to monitor when it comes to biotechnology. Its impact on agriculture and the environment might ultimately prove to be modest. All of which is to say that I approach the matter of genetic modification and the environment with hedged optimism, guided by an assumption best stated by the eminent Harvard scientist Richard Lewontin: "No unequivocal conclusions can be drawn about the overall effect of genetic engineering technologies." At best, genetic engineering can play a niche role in the multifaceted approach to sustainable agriculture. It can be an important piece in the larger puzzle, but still just a piece.[6]

A second caveat: my cautious advocacy of GM crops does not mean I'm shilling for agribusiness. I'm not interested in the status quo of food production and have no tolerance for corporate malfeasance within our food system. As critics rightly point out, the companies that now monopolize the relevant technology, notably Monsanto, have generally used their discoveries to further the interests of agribusiness. They've done so with little concern for the environment or public interest. My support of biotechnology is thus decidedly not blind support for the corporations that currently employ it. Nor is it advocacy for the way it's now being used. In fact, I think that the only place for this technology ultimately to be located is in the public domain.

Resistance to biogenetic modification, which I will fully detail, is more often than not a way of disingenuously registering resistance to corporate abuse and globalization in general. The fact is, most Americans who object to GM crops lack the scientific grounding to back their objections with concrete information. More often than not, their problem is not with genetic engineering per se, but with what "Frankenfoods" vaguely represent—corporate greed and global exploitation. This opposition prevents the technology from moving into the hands of nongovernmental organizations (NGOs) and other public-interest institutions, not to mention ethically incentivized corporations, which could use it to further the ideals of regional agriculture, broader productivity, agricultural diversity, and global food security. There's a baby going out with the bathwater here, and I think it should be saved, valued for its potential worth, and placed in more nurturing hands.

Bt

Detractors of this technology argue that there are too many unknowns. They've justifiably raised concerns about what *could* happen: GM crops could cause allergic reactions or antibiotic resistance in humans; they could create superweeds that choke the planet; they could lead to unpredictable diseases as a result of their tinkered internal architecture. Many, but not all, of the worries have some merit, and thus they highlight the need for the strict regulation and testing of genetic modification technology. For all the concerns, though, genetic modification should not be strangled by a paralyzing use of the precautionary principle—the idea that we should test for *all possible drawbacks* before adopting a new product or technology. Genetic engineering, like any technology we currently employ, might very well prove to have defects that we've never anticipated. We must keep in mind, however, that farmers have planted over 2 billion acres of land with GM crops and none of the predicted health consequences have resulted. To become mired in endless testing—something we do not do for conventional crops—would be to overlook one of the most exciting environmental aspects of GM varieties: their ability to reduce the extensive agricultural use of synthetic pesticides. The risk, in short, is there, but given the already proven benefits, it's worth taking.

The practice of spraying synthetic toxic chemicals, as Rachel Carson made clear with the publication of *Silent Spring* in 1962, has been a devastating agricultural habit for over a century. It's arguably one of the most persistently damaging things humans have inflicted on the environment. Despite many improvements in the United States and other developed nations, such as the phasing out of organophosphates, the problem continues today. As John Wargo, the author of *Our Children's Toxic Legacy*, writes, "As we [enter] the twenty-first century, an additional 5 to 6 billion pounds of insecticides, herbicides, fungicides, rodenticides, and biocides are added to the world's environment each year." The stuff is still all around us.[7]

We have doused the earth with billions of pounds of arsenic, lead, and DDT, among hundreds of other organophosphates and chlorinated hydrocarbons. We have spiked our rivers and larded our landscapes with carcinogens and other slowly deteriorating toxic substances. It therefore seems logical that the environmentally concerned citizen would quickly embrace any pragmatic opportunity to wean agriculture off these extensive chemical inputs. It seems that any self-respecting environmentalist should entertain every viable option of reducing the application of dangerous pesticides.

Not so. The sinister political game being played over a soil bacterium endowed with insecticidal properties reveals the gutter into which the biotech debate has fallen. In 1987 scientists successfully transferred to tobacco and cotton crops the insecticidal protein from *Bacillus thuringiensis*, thereby genetically modifying these crops to protect themselves better without increasing external applications of insecticides. The bacterium is called Bt-toxin. Antibiotech activists erupted in protest. They immediately demonized "Bt crops" as the essence of Frankenfoods and put loads of money where their mouth was with well-placed advertisements and savvy marketing campaigns—all without hard evidence of Bt's alleged harmful qualities. In the United States the Green Party bullied popular opinion with an advertisement calling Bt technology "the gravest moral, social, and ecological crisis in history."[8]

Whatever the underlying motivation to distort the Bt case, anyone following this rhetorical slugfest would be hard-pressed to believe that the Bt-toxin is a naturally occurring soil bacterium that nature has endowed with enzymes that target damaging insects. Indeed, Bt-based insecticides have been used for decades by *organic farmers*, who praise the plant extract as an environmentally safe form of insect control that fits seamlessly into the organic approach. Not only does the bacterium repel many invasive insects, but it biodegrades rapidly and has shown no known dangerous side effects since it was first used as a commercial pesticide back in 1958.

What makes it so effective? Bt insecticides are safe to humans and the environment because the Cry proteins in the spores of *Bacillus thuringiensis* are innocuous until they're triggered by the digestive juices of vulnerable insects. Then, and only then, do they turn toxic. Precisely what happens with the Bt-toxin is, in its own way, a masterpiece of natural adaptation. Certain insects that ingest the bacterium cease processing potassium. As a result, they become paralyzed and die as their cells drown in a cascade of water. As so often happens with life down in the dirt, one organism's demise is another's meal ticket. Indeed, the besotted gut mucosa of the dead insect becomes a fertile breeding ground for millions of Bt spores, which proceed to grow exponentially, catch a gust of wind, and dust the topsoil with a layer of the natural repellent.

If anything can be called natural, this would seem to be it. But "natural," of course, is a hotly contested term in the debates raging over GM foods. This point bears careful consideration. To many observers, capitalizing on Bt comes off as high-tech wizardry—artificial and excessive human intervention in "nature" that turns real food into Frankenfood. To be fair, it's not hard to see why opponents of biotechnology have deemed firing the Bt-producing gene into the cells of corn, potatoes, and cotton plants an aberration from the normal course of events. There certainly is a basic difference between spraying or dusting Bt insecticides on select plants and arranging in a lab for those plants to produce the toxin internally. The human intervention in the latter case is far more intense and, for many consumers, the source of understandable skepticism.[9]

But to get hung up on the laboratory distinction is to miss a critical point. Placed in perspective, Bt technology is entirely consistent with the long and dynamic history of agricultural innovation. In a fundamental sense, the decision to embrace biotech solutions reflects what farmers have been doing for millennia: observing the natural world at work, drawing on available technological methods, and harnessing nature and technology to our productive advantage.

Within the past one hundred years this innovation has taken the form of systematic plant breeding. When plant biologists crossed disease-resistant wild crops with a commercial variety of the same crop, they began the now established agricultural habit of introducing resistance into crops through the transfer of genes. Today, according to Pamela Ronald, a plant pathologist at the University of California at Davis, "most of the crops we eat contain such disease resistance genes." Thus the genetic transfer has been going on for decades, with nary a complaint registered about the human intervention in plant breeding.[10]

But now, somewhat arbitrarily, many of us are deeply bothered over biotechnology. We shouldn't be. Genetic engineering (GE) is often portrayed as a radical break from "natural" agricultural practice, but as Ronald points out, this is not the case. "In the same way that the introduction of genes from wild species through breeding revolutionized farmers' management of pests," she writes, "so can the introduction of GE revolutionize control of diseases, insects, and nematodes for which there is presently no solution." As the renowned plant physiologist Lloyd Evans confirms, genetic engineering "brings greater speed and specificity to plant breeding" rather than altering the process in any fundamental way. Looked at from another angle, the introduction of GM crops is part of the natural evolution of the human-driven process of making plants serve our needs—a big step, but one that pales next to the agricultural transformation once initiated by, say, the harvester or the tractor. (Plus GM crops have almost certainly harmed fewer people than these machines.)[11]

In the public arena, this argument from the perspective of agricultural history has fallen flat. This is unfortunate. After all, when contemporary critics recoil at the supposed artificiality of biotechnological intervention—as Prince Charles does when he opposes biotechnology because it "does not proceed in harmony with nature"—it's clear that we need a more informed and thoughtful perspective on this widely misunderstood issue. We might begin with an agricultural ethic that was popular back in the nineteenth century, at a time when most Americans still ended the day with dirt under their nails. Then another Charles—Charles Darwin—famously remarked, "What a book a devil's chaplain might write on the clumsy, wasteful, blundering, low and horridly cruel works of nature." This is a refreshing antidote to the popular Thoreauvian notion that nature can do no wrong. And it came from a man who knew a thing or two about the natural world. Even if nature could farm for us, as one founder of the organic movement, Albert Howard, said it could, why on earth would we trust it to do so efficiently?[12]

The idea that nature is not perfect—that it is humanity's task to responsibly improve it to our advantage—has deep roots in a noble tradition. It led a nineteenth-century plant breeder and Darwin advocate named Luther Burbank to systematize what farmers had been doing since the dawn of agriculture: making plant life more accessible, abundant, and edible through human ingenuity. As breeders crossed oranges and lemons, wheat and rye, dozens of different plums, apples, and pears, and anything else that would stand to be hybridized, agriculture became more efficient and responsive to the vagaries of human desire. Ultimately it churned out food—good, healthy, diverse food—for millions of people. Luther Burbank was heralded as an American hero for innovations that would prove to be revolutionary for future farmers.[13]

Why we've so drastically changed our opinion on the topic of manipulating nature is an important question. I can only suggest that more people were literally closer to the earth in Burbank's day, and as a result they better understood the complexity of the human relationship with it. "Nature," Burbank wrote, "has time without limit, but man has immediate need for better and still better food…and our present state of civilization depends largely upon the improvements of plants and animals *which have consciously and half-consciously been made by man.*" People intuitively got this idea. Echoing Burbank was the famous zoologist of the early twentieth century David Starr Jordan, who wrote, "By grasping the ways of nature man…*creates species* by using nature's methods." Critics of industrial agriculture today lament the decline of traditional agricultural beliefs. Rarely, though, do they note that this one has survived.[14]

Today we've sequestered ourselves in urban and suburban enclaves. Generally speaking, even the hobby farmers among us are disconnected from the earth as our forebears knew it and are thus prone to bouts of agricultural romance. Still, we have insightful agricultural thinkers such as Richard Manning, who echoes this older realization about man and nature by explaining, "Domestication is human-driven evolution, a fundamental shift in which human selection exerts enough pressure on the wild plant that it is visibly and irreversibly changed, *its genes altered.*" Richard Lewontin, in a similar vein, writes that "the history of domestication is precisely the history of the genetic modification of organisms." Only in the past half-century has our perception of "nature" been so miscon-strued as to make even remotely plausible the well-publicized head-line posed by the Turning Point Project: "Globalization vs. Nature." As if this were a legitimate description of a dichotomy we humans now face.[15]

Biotechnology is just one step on a long historic path of grad-ual agricultural innovation. This point is, of course, hardly at the forefront of our minds as we negotiate our way through the grocery aisles. It's not as if we all have the time (or inclination) to study the intricacies of agricultural history, plant breeding, or the finer points of gene transfer. But the emergence of a new link in the agri-cultural chain—in this case Bt technology—provides us with a rare opportunity to educate ourselves and achieve responsible progress. This moment is critical to developing a pragmatic and environmen-tally conscious ethic of eating that transcends ideology and politics. We should seize it with all the information at hand and regulate it accordingly.

Reducing Pesticides

Rarely mentioned in our public debates over biotechnology is the fact that Bt technology not only has the potential to significantly reduce pesticide applications, but that it is, according to many stud-ies, already doing so. Evidence of this reduction has been most evi-dent with cotton. Cotton is an unusually resource-intensive crop, requiring enormous insecticide inputs. In India, Bt cotton, which is primarily protected from the American bollworm, has enabled farmers to reduce the use of harmful pesticides by 80 percent. Non-Bt cotton crops in India suffered almost three times as many bollworm infestations as Bt crops did, according to a 2003 study. Chinese farmers report similarly beneficial environmental (and economic) outcomes with Bt cotton. One study found another 80 percent drop in pesticide use.[16]

Not only have studies confirmed lower rates of spraying, but because Chinese farmers typically spray from leaky backpacks and use especially toxic chemical cocktails that often include DDT, there have been lower rates of farmer poisonings as well (to the tune of four times lower). South African farmers who typically sprayed eight times a season now, by growing Bt cotton, spray only twice a season, lowering their insecticide costs by a third. Enhancing optimism over Bt crops is the fact that in killing only the offending insects, Bt has increased insect biodiversity to such an extent that natural predators of cotton weevils have thrived, increasing at a rate 25 percent higher than they would have if crops had been sprayed conventionally. One can rightly argue that monocultural production is a bad thing and should be ended. But the immediate implication is that Bt cotton lessens the harmful environmental impact of monoculture by reducing the use of pesticides.[17]

All these benefits have been evident enough for many scientists to highlight the potential for a productive partnership between biotech and organic models of food production. It's no coincidence that when environmentally conscious growers in the 1990s began to search for less chemically intensive approaches to farming, they turned to biotechnology for possible answers. Nor is it a coincidence that the USDA, when drafting standards for organic production in 1997, included GM crops in its list of acceptable commodities (although it received 275,000 letters vehemently disagreeing with this inclusion).[18]

Farmers in Kern County, California, passed a resolution expressing their opinion that "biotechnology is a promising component of progressive agricultural production." The organization California Clean, which formed in partial response to a prevailing belief that federal organic standards had become too lax, drew up a list of regulations that, tellingly, allowed the use of Roundup, an herbicide sprayed on resistant GM crops, for spot treatment of weeds. It thus takes little imagination to see how biotechnology could be compatible with the larger goals of sustainable agriculture.[19]

The most common Bt food crops on the market—rice, corn, and soon possibly potatoes and wheat—have recently started to join cotton in diminishing dangerous reliance on conventional chemicals. Comparative analyses of conventional and genetically modified rice varieties in China have shown that conventional crops were sprayed seven times more often, required over ten times as many pesticides, and called for nine times as much labor. Farmers who used GM varieties reported no pesticide-related health problems, while non-adopters had an 8.3 percent annual rate of injury. GM rice, moreover, consistently led to higher yields. At UC Davis, Pamela Ronald has recently created a GM variety of rice that's resistant to bacterial blight disease, an innovation that will soon result in substantial increases for farmers throughout Asia. She interprets her discovery not as a boon to agribusiness but as a way to show how "applications of GE to reduce the adverse environmental effects of farming [can] enable farmers to produce and sell more food locally."[20]

Bt potatoes have followed a similar, if less realized, trajectory of environmental progress. Varieties engineered to contain the CryIIIA protein have proven resistant to the Colorado potato beetle, one of the most devastating pests ever to attack cash crops. Regrettably, McDonald's decision not to buy new potato varieties (GM and non-GM alike) has led producers to withdraw Bt varieties from their inventories. There is, however, a strong possibility that eastern European and Russian potato growers will provide a large enough outlet for this Bt crop as the Colorado potato beetle takes hold there. There may also be demand from Central American farmers, whose potato crops are currently being decimated by the Guatemalan tuber moth. If these markets do open, there will be an increase in the potential to diminish reliance on dangerous chemicals to control potato pests.[21]

There have been modest insecticide reductions with corn as well. A lot of corn farmers never spray at all because their corn is grown to become corn syrup, ethanol, or cow feed—a horrific environmental scenario altogether, but one in which blemishes are tolerated. In these cases, of course, Bt corn does not result in measurable reductions in insecticide usage but is used only to increase yield. However, corn destined for human consumption or for other markets that demand blemish and worm-free corn requires considerable spraying. In these cases there have been substantial reductions with Bt corn, as farmers have been able to spray on average once or twice rather than seven or eight times a season. Insofar as farmers do have to spray GM crops, the Bt protein allows corn farmers to pinpoint the timing of their applications better, spraying poison only when the borers are in larval phase and as a result protecting the biodiversity of nontarget insects. If Bt corn were not available, according to a study done by the National Center for Food and Agricultural Policy, farmers would end up annually dousing their crops with an additional 2.6 million pounds of insecticides to battle the ceaselessly invasive corn borer.[22]

Another point to consider is that Bt corn has a much lower chance of suffering an outbreak of fungal toxins, aka mycotoxins, than conventional corn. Fungal toxins harbor carcinogens that proliferate rapidly when corn is stored for even a short amount of time in tropical and subtropical climates. Studies have confirmed a strong connection between mycotoxins and neural tube pregnancy defects. GM corn substantially reduces this danger.[23]

A few more figures should round out my point about Bt crops and pesticide reduction. A 2002 study conducted by the National Center for Food and Agricultural Policy found that in 2001 the most common biotech cultivars being planted—corn, cotton, soybeans, and virus-resistant papaya and squash—were solely responsible for a national pesticide reduction of 46 million pounds. The study praised this figure but also noted that if planters consistently planted the thirty other available GM cultivars, they could cut pesticide use by another 117 million pounds per year. Add in the reduced spraying that could come from developing virus- and fungus-resistant crops—predicted to be about 91 million pounds—and the study ends up confirming what amounts to a significant drop in pesticide, insecticide, and fungicide application. One would think that these figures, which would at least have made Rachel Carson optimistic, would also pique the interest of her antichemical advocates. This has not been the case, in what has thus far been a missed opportunity to grow commercial crops with fewer environmentally dangerous pesticides.[24]

To be sure, there are many studies that show the exact opposite—that is, that GM crops have done nothing to reduce pesticide use. As with the question of organic versus conventional yields, the issue is one of the most controversial in agriculture. The discrepancy in these studies reflects that fact that findings are often crop- and site-specific rather than reflective of a categorical truth. There is much room to disagree on this issue, and to disagree based on solid scientific evidence. It is for this reason that I pay attention to what fair-minded scientists have said about genetic engineering. The molecular biologist Don Deoring explained to the *Atlantic Monthly* that the judicious use of Bt technology could result in "a virtually chemical-free agriculture." Patrick Moore, a founding member of Greenpeace, has said point-blank, "I have come to believe in the promise of agricultural biotechnology." He continues: "The environmental movement's campaign against biotechnology in general, and genetic engineering in particular, has clearly exposed its moral and intellectual bankruptcy."[25]

David Sandalow, the executive vice president of the World Wildlife Fund, has said of biotechnology that "the huge potential benefits include increased productivity of arable land" and "decreased pesticide usage." Per Pinstrup-Andersen, the former director general of the International Food Policy Research Institute, believes that "the shift to Bt from standard chemicals is packed with potential."

Even Jason Clay, the vice president of the Center for Conservation Innovation and a tough opponent of genetic engineering, concedes that GM crops have led to pesticide reduction and notes that Bt technology "is particularly important for producers in arid environments."[26]

It is hard to see why Bt crops could not be taken out of their current big corporate context and considered as an integral part of small or medium-scale, sustainable, and even organic farming practices. Whatever the reason for ignoring these exciting possibilities, whatever the underlying rationale for the seditious war on GM crops, we must, as environmentally concerned eaters, cut through the rhetoric, consider the science, and—without false expectations—cautiously support the role of this technology in creating a viable model of sustainable food production.

Reduced Tillage

In this and the previous chapter we've seen how heavy applications of synthetic fertilizers and pesticides do serious environmental damage. Two other inescapable agricultural practices that are just as destructive to the environment are tilling fields and applying conventional herbicides. The first loosens the topsoil and creates the conditions for erosion and runoff. The second leads to an accumulation in the soil of dangerous chemicals that can harm wildlife and, if carried away with the topsoil, damage aquatic ecosystems. It is therefore significant that GM crops have the power to reduce these deleterious practices as well.

Scientists have genetically engineered crops in addition to Bt crops to be herbicide-resistant. The most conspicuous example of this technology is something you may have heard of, Roundup Ready crops. Roundup is a relatively safe, highly effective, broad-spectrum herbicide made by Monsanto (whose patent expired in 2000) that kills weeds but does not kill the GM crops the weeds threaten. In most public discussions about sustainable farming, the benefits of genetically engineered herbicide resistance and the tillage that this technology prevents have been either overlooked or drowned out in anticorporate venom. Nevertheless, the environmental implications are potentially significant. At the least, they deserve careful consideration as an important element of sustainable agricultural systems.

The plow might be a sacred symbol of agricultural productivity, but it wrecks the soil and, as we've known for a long time, compromises basic agricultural health. In her 1943 book, *The Living Soil*, Lady Eve Balfour declared that "the criteria for a sustainable agriculture can be summed up in one word—permanence, which means adopting techniques that maintain soil fertility indefinitely." Tilling soil to manage weeds, however, does precisely the opposite; it dries soil out, causes chronic erosion, and in so doing renders soil impermanent. It is for this reason that, also writing in 1943, Edward Faulkner noted in *Plowman's Folly* that "there is nothing wrong with our soil except interference." For Faulkner, as his book's title suggests, interference meant the plow.[27]

These ideas persist to this day. In his fascinating recent volume, *Dirt*, David Montgomery explores the impact of tillage on agricultural societies dating back thousands of years, spanning every geographical region, and stretching across vast expanses of time and place. Indeed, if there is a single common downfall in the history of agriculture, it would be, in Montgomery's words, the fact that "soil erosion began to exceed soil production only after introduction of the plow."[28]

Healthy soil has a densely interwoven but porous structure. It's often described as a stack of frozen peas pocked with pores and bound with fungal tendrils and plant roots. The two primary purposes of this structure are to hold water in place and keep the soil and its microbial nutrients from blowing or washing away, or, in Lady Balfour's view, to keep it "permanent." Sometimes no-till farming is called high-residue farming, because the previous season's crop stubble settles upon the soil and offers organic cover. This structure allows the soil to hold more of its carbon content (about 25 percent more), thereby reducing greenhouse gas emissions while ensuring soil health.[29]

Soil that is spared the blades of a tiller has other merits. It reduces labor input, improves the quality of surface water, decreases soil compaction (enhancing water retention), lessens fertilizer usage, reduces nitrogen runoff, lowers a farm's fuel demands, and promotes microbial diversity (and biodiversity in general). According to the Conservation Technology Information Center at Purdue University, "Land left in continuous no-till can eventually create a soil, water, and biological system that more closely resembles characteristics of native soils before the advent of agriculture." To the ears of an environmentalist, this is beautiful music.[30]

But the environmental benefits of reduced tillage extend well beyond the agricultural plot itself. Because no-till and reduced-till farming lessen the need for nitrogen fertilizers while securing and preserving the soil structure, they reduce the sedimentation of rivers, enhance surrounding water quality, increase a "steady-state" level of organic matter, and even foster widespread natural (biological) pest control by supporting a broad diversity of beneficial soil microbes and in turn the insects, spiders, and worms that symbiotically thrive among them.[31]

A more balanced and varied insect population enables local bird populations to flourish, which in turn leads to natural pest control. Scientists discovered, for example, that quail chicks feeding in untilled GM soybean fields needed only four hours to find enough grubs to feed themselves, whereas it took twenty-two hours on tilled soybean plots. Conservation tillage also reduces the plowing of pheasant nests. Small mammals are supported by this improved environment, as is marine life, because lowered nutrient runoff diminishes the frequency of hypoxia, a condition that results when excess phosphate and nitrogen deplete oxygen in the water and endanger fish and crustaceans.[32]

If the benefits of reduced tillage are so obvious, why haven't farmers pursued the technique throughout history as a matter of course? The old answer was of course a maddening one: weeds. Indeed, weeds, the bane of every farmer's existence, would strangle crops unless fields were tilled. Thus when Edward Faulkner declared in *Plowman's Folly* that "the use of the plow has actually destroyed the productiveness of our soils" and insisted that "there is simply no need for plowing," real farmers concerned with growing on a commercial level—and thus unable to weed by hand—could only listen in disbelief. *Don't plow?* All well and good in theory, they thought, but how were they supposed to control acres and acres of wild plants threatening to undermine their livelihoods?[33]

One popular solution, offered in the late 1940s, was to try to substitute synthetic chemicals for the plow. Dow Chemical was eager to peddle the requisite deadly herbicides, including paraquat and atrazine, and farmers, hooked as they were on monocultural practices, were eager for any help they could get to reduce tillage, fight weeds, and increase yields. Agent Orange emerged from this broad effort and went on to achieve infamy in Vietnam. Other companies producing chemical concoctions into the 1960s and 1970s, such as Sherwin-Williams and Monsanto, quickly came to the rescue as well. But these solutions, including metribuzin, imazaquin, and chlorimuron, while popular, were loaded with environmentally damaging baggage.[34]

Nonetheless, willing to place short-term agricultural gain over long-term environmental damage, millions of farmers sprayed with dangerous, carcinogenic weed killers. They had to spray repeatedly, mix a cocktail of (on average) eight herbicides (because conventional herbicides are each specific to a small range of weeds), and conform to an elaborate spraying schedule in order to match the fickle cycles of various weed invasions. As with insecticides, this was an agricultural version of an environmentally damaging chemical dependency in the process of being normalized.[35]

Making matters more difficult, as well as environmentally

dangerous, was the fact that conventional herbicides persisted in the soil long enough to compromise efficient crop rotation. There is a reason that organic farmers are required to allow a field to sit for three years before the crops grown on it can be called organic. The slow rate of decomposition among standard weed killers means that farmers wanting to plant, say, corn in a soy plot have to wait an extra ten months for the persistent herbicides to degrade. Not only does a fallow field collect foreign weeds, but this delay shrinks yields and often inspires further agricultural sprawl into diminished supplies of arable land.

Perhaps the most depressing aspect of the agricultural turn toward herbicides is the fact that this comparatively hit-or-miss, resource-intensive approach to controlling a wide variety of weeds with an equally wide variety of poisons did not substantially obviate the need for tillage. And so farmers continued to till their homesteads, all the while destroying topsoil, fostering further agricultural encroachment on new land, releasing excess carbon dioxide into the atmosphere, and clogging the rivers and oceans with nitrogen and phosphate runoff. Only now they were doing it while adding harmful weed killers, the toxins of which also leached into the surrounding ecosystem.

With the advent of GM technology, however, agricultural options have changed. No-till farming is no longer unrealistic. And the positive "downstream" environmental outcomes of reduced tillage have become notable enough for scientists to start systematically cataloguing their impact. According to 2002 figures, no-till practices, which immediately increased 35 percent after the introduction of biotech crops, diminished water and wind soil erosion by a billion tons a year, a 30 percent reduction from the 1980s. Reduced soil erosion in turn saved Americans $3.5 billion in water treatment and storage and flood management.[36]

Mechanical tillers, which are inefficient gas guzzlers, were frequently parked in the barn permanently. This is a particularly good thing, given that the fuel required for field operations on tilled land is five times that required for nontilled land. Thus conservation tillage has saved over 300 billion gallons of fuel a year, leading to a 1-billion-pound drop in carbon dioxide emissions. David Montgomery suggested to me that the government would be much better off ending fertilizer subsidies and supporting the mass acquisition of seed drills in order to further the admirable goal of lowered tilling. In the end, he claims, the farmer's main job should be to "produce soil wealth." Genetic engineering technology (which Montgomery backs away from endorsing) helps the farmer do precisely that by offering the option of spraying a single, quickly decomposing, nonselective herbicide called glyphosate.[37]

Glyphosate

Glyphosate is the main ingredient in Roundup and similar herbicides. It kills weeds while selectively sparing the crops that have been genetically modified to be herbicide-resistant. Glyphosate, which can be sprayed *after* the weeds have started to grow—and thus can be sprayed in much lower dosages than traditional herbicides—bonds to a critical enzyme found in all plants that enables the plant to produce amino acids. By attaching to this enzyme, glyphosate disables it, undermining the weeds' ability to produce amino acids and, as a result, protein. Within two weeks the weed withers and dies. Because the GM crop has been endowed with a gene that produces bacteria able to resist glyphosate, however, it thrives. The process is by no means perfect. But—and this is the critical point—it's been effective enough to foster a significant transition to no-till or reduced-till methods for those who have embraced it, thereby supporting the broad range of very real environmental benefits that lowered tillage confers.[38]

While the risks are minimal, this does not mean that glyphosate is harmless. Critics of glyphosate, and thus of GM crops in general, have highlighted the product's potentially toxic effect on humans.

It is important to note, though, that their findings of even mild toxicity have been preliminary at best. A widely circulated 1998 article from the *Journal of Pesticide Reform* offered a "glyphosate fact sheet" that listed as proof of glyphosate's dangers such odd evidence as "rubbing of Roundup in an eye caused eye and lid swelling, rapid heartbeat and elevated blood pressure." (One imagines that having an herbicide rubbed in your eye might have such effects!) Another case offered as evidence referred to "a student athlete who suffered abnormally frequent menstruation when she competed at tracks where glyphosate had been used." (Competitive women runners commonly experience menstrual variations, and who's to say it wasn't some other chemical in the track?) The report goes on to list a litany of health problems "associated with" glyphosate and others that glyphosate "may cause," continually using vague language to avoid admitting a general lack of substantial evidence. While it is important that we keep testing glyphosate, and that we actively regulate all chemicals that go into our food, there is simply not enough proof of its detrimental human impact to forgo its benefits. I wouldn't season your tofu with the stuff, but there seems to be little reason to panic over glyphosate's toxic potential.[39]

More standard professional studies have actually deemed the product relatively safe for humans to handle. The World Health Organization and the Environmental Protection Agency classify glyphosate as "an unlikely carcinogen." Spectrum, a highly respected pollution monitoring company, provides an extensive evaluation of glyphosate. Read the fine print and you'll find that the chemical has "a low propensity for leaching," "readily and completely biodegrades in the soil," and "does not bioconcentrate in aquatic organisms or bioaccumulate in species in higher tropic levels." When more than two hundred wells near Ontario were tested for glyphosate runoff (in an area where twenty-eight farms sprayed with it), not a trace showed up in a single well.[40]

Humans, it must be noted, lack the enzyme that glyphosate

bonds to in plants, a point that the scientist Nigel Halford, writing in the *British Medical Journal,* makes clear before concluding that "glyphosate has very little toxicity to insects, birds, fish, or mammals, including man." Nina Fedoroff, the geneticist and plant biologist, takes it one step further and writes, "Roundup does not harm insects, fish, birds, or mammals (including humans) because none of these creatures have the enzyme [to which glyphosate bonds]." So, all things considered, the risks to human health do appear to be low enough to sanction its cautious use.[41]

A more relevant and immediate environmental concern, however, is the prospect of glyphosate resistance. Extensive monoculture, the ongoing and seemingly irredeemable sin of commercial agriculture, creates a situation in which farmers spraying the same glyphosate variety on the same crop enhance the ability of weeds to develop resistance to the poison. Critics often speak of "superweeds." But this is not the concern here. Like "Frankenfoods," the term "superweeds" is something of a red herring. It refers to the possibility that herbicide-tolerant genes will flow to wild species and result in raging monster weeds that could crowd out other wild plants and destroy biodiversity.

Molecular biologists are actually less alarmed by the superweed scenario than activists are. After all, gene flow has been going on for as long as humans have been cultivating crops (especially with "promiscuous" crops such as corn), and over the long course of agricultural history, it has had minimal impact on genetic diversity. Superweeds, in short, seem to be a classic example of the risk expert Peter Sandman's assessment that "the risks that hurt people and the risks that upset people are almost completely unconnected."[42]

The reason this concern is overblown is fairly basic, and it's also the reason we won't dwell on superweeds beyond this paragraph: gene flow happens only when a crop's wild relatives are within striking distance of the cultivated species. The worldwide exchange of seeds has made this proximity less likely. It's impossible, for example, for corn grown in the United States to flow into wild relatives for the very simple reason that there are no wild relatives of corn in the United States. Crops have undergone a worldwide diaspora and as a result are usually grown far away from their place of origin. But even in regions where gene flow to wild relatives is possible, such as with sorghum in Africa, corn in Mexico, and potatoes in Peru, molecular biologists point out that it's unlikely the resistant gene would, upon pollination, successfully transfer to the wild variety. If it did, the chances of its persisting would be even lower. And if it did persist, it would eventually diminish in power. What advantage, after all, would a gene for herbicide resistance have in a weed not being sprayed with herbicide? Or, as the organic farmer Raoul Adamchak reminds us, "a GE crop is still a crop and crops make lousy weeds."[43]

Superweeds, then, are not our problem. However, common resistance to glyphosate is, and with good reason. Farmers in the Midwest report that the weed waterhemp is starting to show resistance to glyphosate. Resistant strains of giant ragweed and Palmer amaranth recently made an appearance in Tennessee. Unfortunately, these reports may be just the tip of an iceberg. Surveys by weed scientists confirm that farmers of GM crops worry incessantly about weeds developing resistance to glyphosate herbicides. As much as a third surveyed think that resistant species may already be securing a purchase in their fields. "The occurrence of herbicide-resistant weeds continues to increase virtually every year," writes Aaron Hager, a weed scientist at the University of Illinois. This is a frightening prospect, but, one must reiterate, the threat is no different from what is already happening with conventional crops.[44]

The real possibility of glyphosate resistance has predictably led the antibiotech lobby to call for a categorical end to herbicide-resistant crops. But this is like saying we should get rid of antibiotics because some individuals are becoming allergic to them. Again, a little historical perspective is needed. We must recall that farmers have been contending with weeds that have become resistant to synthetic herbicides since the 1940s. "Continue to use the same chemical with the same mode of action year after year," writes Mark Moore in *Farm Industry News*, "and the chances of selecting a weed with resistance increases dramatically." It was as true in the 1950s as it is now, and it's as true for conventional plants as it is for GM plants.[45]

In essence, the basic agricultural problem of resistance, despite its specific GM-crop manifestations, should not be cited, as it often is, as a detrimental feature of GM crops alone. It is a problem that arises from *monoculture*—an old problem, a real problem, and one that calls for reform. But, alas, it's not a crime that can be added to the rap sheet of GM crops. A more diversified approach to commercial agriculture, something that must eventually happen if food production is to be even remotely sustainable, would substantially help alleviate herbicide resistance. Eliminating GM crops, however, would not.

There's also emerging technology to consider. One would be foolish to fall into the common trap of thinking technology is the solution to every agricultural dilemma. Nevertheless, it would be equally foolish to discount its potential in helping agriculture stay one step ahead of the resistance menace. New, equally safe herbicides already in the works will soon join glyphosate to expand and enhance weed-control options in the face of growing resistance. Admittedly, what's starting to look like a corporate-driven cat-and-mouse approach is not ideal. But in combination with advanced "weed scouting" efforts, more precise application schemes, and pre-emergence control tactics, farmers can effectively (and selectively) use new products to pursue a responsible scientific answer to weed control.

To cite one example, farmers in favor of GM crops but troubled by resistant pigweed are having success combining a "preplant" herbicide with an "over-the-top" dose of metolachlor (commercially known as Dual), an herbicide with negligible environmental impact, according to a Cornell University profile. Of course, it's not a solution that asks farmers to diversify. But let's not forget that agricultural scientists have been asking farmers to diversify for centuries and farmers have, regrettably, pretty much ignored them. So this solution equips us with weapons that will subdue nature without destroying it. And once again, it's a solution that accepts the lesser of evils in hope of fostering more sustainable outcomes—in this case, lowered pesticide applications and reduced tillage—while we wait for farmers worldwide to undertake the unlikely collective step of diversifying their farms.[46]

Yields

A third environmental benefit of genetic engineering is its potential to increase yields. The figures that researchers have calculated thus far are, on balance, encouraging. The National Center for Food and Agricultural Policy reported in 2001 that commercial GM crops accounted for 1.8 tons of extra food being produced on the same amount of land. Figures from South Africa, where commercial GM crops have been enthusiastically embraced, show yield increases in maize from 20 to 34 percent. One study, which found similar results, concluded, "In all plots it was found that GM maize gave higher yields and had less stalk borer damage than the comparable non-GM variety." According to a global overview of the environmental impact of GM crops from 1996 to 2004, maize yields increased 9 percent in Argentina, 25 percent in the Philippines, 6 percent in Spain, and 5 percent in Canada.[47]

Other crops seem to have kept pace. A report on GM canola production, undertaken by the Canadian scientists Stuart Smith and Linda Hall, stresses "the direct benefits to growers of increased yield." A summary of independent research put together by the Australian government highlighted several studies showing a 10 percent yield increase for canola and a 3 percent to 10 percent increase for wheat (in trial tests, as GM wheat is not in commercial production).

Many soybean studies have reported yield increases as well. Independent studies reported by CropLife Canada in 2008 showed a 66 percent yield increase between 1997 and 2007 due to the planting of GM crops. Romania reports a 30 percent increase. The Australian study found soybean increase to be "limited." Cotton was the clearest success across the board, with an AgBioForum study finding increases of up to 63 percent in India, 30 percent in Argentina, and 37 percent in Mexico.[48]

It should be noted that another spate of reports presents a very different picture. One organization, Seed to Plate, explains that "hundreds of university yield trials have shown that herbicide tolerant soybeans suffer from a moderate to modest yield drag." (However, reports of GM yield depletion almost always focus on soybeans, the crop that even GM proponents acknowledge performs least well when it comes to yield increase.) No citation is offered, and it is not at all clear what "moderate to modest" means, nor is it noted whether "drag" means that production actually fell below that of conventional soybeans.[49]

Still, other reports have supported the charge. Charles Benbrook, of the Northwest Science and Environmental Policy Center in Idaho, explained that yield on Roundup Ready soybeans "can be up to 10% less than the yield of conventional soybeans." Yet another 2001 analysis of the literature, by London's Institute of Science in Society, concluded, based on "8200 trials of soya varieties," that conventional soybeans outperformed GM soybeans by 10 percent on average. Downplayed by anti-GM activists is the finding that, as both these reports noted, overall herbicide use was less for GM soy. But the fact remains: the claim of higher yields for GM varieties is by no means universal.[50]

Pinning down the underlying causes of these disparities is an important task, but on balance the evidence points toward an increase in yields for many commercial crops. This may prove to be critical in preserving biodiversity as we seek to feed the world.

Biodiversity

Perhaps the best way to appreciate the connection between genetic engineering and biodiversity is to think for a moment about what's happening on undeveloped land—land that remains for all intents and purposes wild. A lot of the action is, of course, visible. A walk in the woods shows some of the complex, competing, and interdependent relationships among insects, worms, birds, reptiles, amphibians, and small and large mammals as well as plants, grasses, mosses, trees, and weeds.

Most of the action, however, eludes the naked eye. The soil, as the wildlife biologist John Storer once wrote, holds "the hidden history of the earth." It's a story with countless characters, including fungi, bacteria, elaborate root systems, lichens, and molds. On this level the interactions are even more complicated, with lichens secreting acids to leach minerals from rocks, bacteria fixing nitrogen and feeding it to plant roots, and mold decomposing dead plants to recycle into the soil, among millions of other symbiotic processes. Through photosynthesis, the visible and the invisible enrich each other and in so doing sustain an ever-changing ecosystem. This "hive of living things, the eaters and the eaten," as Storer wrote, "adds up to incredible numbers." Even to the experts, the biodiversity of undisturbed land is a mind-boggling and endlessly fascinating phenomenon.[51]

Imagine that this description, which only scratches the surface of the underlying ecological processes at work, was of a forest. Then imagine what would happen if a farmer cleared that forest to plant crops, something that's happening today at an alarming rate. While it might not be like "pouring concrete on the land," as Nina Fedoroff puts it, everything would change. Everything would undergo an overwhelming ecological simplification. The diversity of plant and animal life would yield to a handful of man-made crops totally dependent on human intervention for their existence and survival. The composition of the soil would adjust to support the particular needs of these privileged plants. The delicate balance of insects, "the eaters and the eaten," would give way to the pestiferous dominance of a predaceous few. The mammalian world would be distilled to a species or two. Only the strongest weeds would survive the onslaught, and they would, with their subterranean weapons, fight to choke out the man-made plants in a ruthless attempt to monopolize the soil's nutrients. No matter what form of agriculture followed, nature would be transformed to follow the rules of domestication.[52]

It was for good reason that James Lovelock, the famed originator of the earth-friendly Gaia theory, advocated intensive farming on limited land in order to allow more land "to evolve entirely free of human interference." Indeed, wouldn't it be better if the land was never cleared in the first place? Can humans possibly do any better than nature in promoting biodiversity?[53]

Of course they can't. And this is where GM crops enter as a major player in the larger discussion. Because, as we have seen, GM crops have the potential to increase agricultural yields, they also have the potential to reduce expansion into undeveloped regions, such as rainforests, where natural biodiversity is most intense. When forests are cleared, plowed, and transformed into agricultural acreage, the level of diversity falls drastically. Ultimately, the best way to foster biodiversity is to leave the land alone.

Critics of biotechnology assert that it fosters monocropping and undermines crop biodiversity. They have a strong point. However, despite the fact that agribusiness has unfortunately reified this assumption, there is no inherent connection between GM crops and monoculture. If used judiciously and for responsible purposes, genetic modification technology could just as easily foster crop diversification.

With the world's population growing rapidly and with hundreds of millions of citizens from China and India experiencing better standards of living, the task of agriculture in this global century is to produce more food on less land, or at least to produce more food on the same amount of land, and to do so in an ecologically friendly manner. In truth, if agriculture and biodiversity are to be complementary endeavors, having lengthy debates about crop diversification is like arguing over the eco-efficiency of a firehose while the house burns. Instead, we must figure out how to increase crop yields and protect marginal lands from further agricultural exploitation.

This argument is bolstered by the current status of agricultural land use. Much of the land that the world's farmers now cultivate is the most productive on earth while being endowed with the least natural biodiversity. This is as it should be. We've "plucked the low-hanging resource fruit," and that fruit has served us well. However, the lands that are currently being eyed for agricultural expansion, such as rainforests, are marginal for farming but are the richest on earth in terms of natural biodiversity.

This is exactly where we must tread lightly, if at all. This is where plucking the resource fruit becomes more costly, even deadly, to the environment. Look at it this way: centuries of converting the Great Plains of the United States from native grasslands into cultivated monocrops is rightly considered a historic case of enormous environmental devastation. If the same level of transformation ever occurred in a Peruvian forest, however, the biodiversity lost would be immensely larger. As the ecologist Michael Huston notes, a small patch of tropical rainforest (several square miles) might very well sustain a greater number of "aboveground species" than all of North America. Not only are we on the verge of expanding food production into vast amounts of land, but we're planning to do so on land that is the most biodiverse on earth. This is an impending disaster, and yet another reason that the focus, perhaps more than anything else, must be on environmentally responsible crop yields of food grown for people to eat, which the judicious use of GM crops can help us achieve.[54]

The Case of Africa

Most yield-enhancing GM crops are commercial crops produced by agribusiness for markets in developed countries already flush with supply. While for the purposes of biodiversity we need to pay more attention to yield figures for commercial crops in a place like Brazil, with its rainforests, than in the United States (no rainforests), there is another aspect of sustainability and yield figures that we must always keep front and center.

Where we really need high-yielding crops is in the places where agricultural conditions are especially dire, where agribusiness is not producing for processing plants and fast-food joints. We need high yields not necessarily for commercial crops like soy and corn, which are rarely directly eaten by people, but for subsistence-oriented foods like sweet potatoes, papayas, cassava, millet, beans, and sorghum, which are central to so many poor nations' diets. It is essential to the future of responsible biotechnology that research focus on genetic modifications that will enable crops to flourish in arid and saline-heavy soils. Such yield increases would not only improve biodiversity but help ameliorate worldwide access to food. It is for all these reasons that I'll conclude by focusing on the place where the stakes for agricultural biotechnology could not be higher: Africa.

I recently visited North Africa. Everywhere I looked I saw people who spend the vast majority of their lives in the fields, farming, hauling hay and water, following sheep, tending donkeys, and working to keep food on the table in an environment racked by aridity and sky-rocketing food prices. And there I was, earnestly reading a book about the history of *terroir,* a beautifully packaged volume arguing that foodies in the United States have a moral duty to nurture *terroir*—the taste of place—as an integral aspect of our cuisine. *And why not?* I would have thought if I had been reading my book back in Austin. But I was in Africa (and not even sub-Saharan Africa, where the problems are worse), and it suddenly seemed very wrong for me—a person from a country where 2 percent of the citizens farm and 66 percent are overweight—to be getting worked up over such a precious matter while cavorting across a continent where 70 percent of the population farms and people starve in the streets.

Terroir is a nice idea, but I would imagine it's a low priority when 80 percent of your land is sapped of moisture and half your budget goes for food, as is the case throughout Africa. As Robert Paarlberg shows in his excellent book *Starved for Science: How Biotechnology Is Being Kept Out of Africa,* agriculture on the continent is currently affected by a perfect storm of rapid population growth, drought exacerbated by climate change, and the persistence of damaging agricultural practices. Not only is hunger widespread in the face of this mounting crisis, but environmental problems are especially severe as a result of postcolonial African farming habits.

"The continued expansion of conventional cultivation systems," writes Paarlberg, "has depleted soil nutrients, forcing farmers to cultivate new lands, which causes deforestation." This expansion in turn "has caused massive soil erosion, watershed destruction, siltation of surface water, and death of aquatic life." If any place were a prime candidate for a technology that would foster increased yields on less land, it would be the technology-poor continent of Africa, especially the sub-Saharan region.[55]

Antibiotech activists have not proceeded with the best interests of African agriculture in mind. Working through a range of influential NGOs staffed with green-collared "experts" from developed countries, these powerful interest groups have placed first-world ideology ahead of third-world reality. Organizations including Greenpeace International, the International Federation of Organic Agricultural Movements, and Networking for Ecofarming in Africa have lobbied African governments to eschew yield-enhancing technologies such as GM crops in favor of organic and other alternative methods.

In essence, given that most of African agriculture is already de facto organic (because farmers cannot afford chemicals), these NGOs gush forth free money and expertise to help Africans continue business as usual. With organic agriculture as currently practiced requiring more land for lower yields, this approach is fuel to a fire that's already engulfing the region's remaining arable lands.

This irresponsible effort to keep GM crops out of Africa has inspired some incomparably thoughtless remarks. President Levy Mwanawasa of Zambia, after rejecting a shipment of GM food aid desperately needed by the starving citizens of his country, explained, "Simply because my people are hungry, this is no justification...to give them food that is intrinsically dangerous to their health." What would such men say about the Philippines, another poor part of the world, where small farmers who adopted GM varieties saw yields increase by 37 percent, insecticide costs drop by 60 percent, and profitability per hectare almost double? Or what about South Africa, the exception on the African continent, where Bt maize has successfully battled the corn borer, improved yields, and made farmers more money per hectare?[56]

The fact that both supporters and opponents of GM crops frequently resort to the Green Revolution to frame contemporary debates about food technologies indicates how polarized the debates are. The pro camp says, "See, look what happens when you use technology to grow food—people thrive," and the anti camp says, "See, look what happens when you use technology to grow food—the environment takes a beating." But as often as the Green Revolution is brought up as a way to think about the situation in Africa, the reference misses the point completely. It's yet another distraction in a debate that cannot afford to be anything but totally focused on achieving pragmatic and applicable solutions.

The Green Revolution was about cash crops and chemical

inputs, but what could happen with genetic engineering in Africa and other poor regions of the world involves subsistence crops and chemical reduction. And while NGOs and African governments have been resisting the integration of biotechnology into African agriculture for over a decade, scientists have been pioneering GM varieties that could play a critical role in helping Africans feed themselves while significantly protecting biodiversity in the process. Environmental and human justice could potentially converge on a range of improved African crops—beans, cassava, millet, sweet potatoes, and white maize—that are genetically altered to be drought-tolerant, able to grow in saline soil, and capable of assimilating added nitrogen, among other beneficial qualities.

What would a heat-tolerant cowpea or a water-efficient wheat variety or virus-resistant cassava and papaya or sweet potatoes engineered to grow in African soil do for Africans, African agriculture, and the continent's environment? We honestly don't know. They've been strong-armed out by the advocates of organic food and by pressure from European markets not to touch GM crops exported from Africa. Africans have every right to reject these technologies, of course, but shouldn't they at least be given a chance to make that decision on their own, with all the facts before them? As an angry French farmer quoted in my *terroir* book explained, "My struggle remains the same...the right for the people to feed themselves as they choose."[57]

A skeptic of biotechnology could grant these points and still argue that as long as this technology is controlled by a handful of corporations intent on monopolizing patents in the interest of profit, any humanitarian or environmental benefits will be unachievable. This is a valid point. Monsanto is in this game not to save the world but to make money, a fact that Roger Beachy and Ernie Jaworski, two of the pioneers of GM foods for Monsanto, bluntly acknowledged in a joint interview with me. There's a reason that, say, drought-tolerant cassava is not on the market: the demand is simply too small for a company with the scope and research expenditures of Monsanto to pursue. The handful of corporations manufacturing GM crops has, not surprisingly, stuck to the money-making lines of soy and corn.[58]

But this situation is not the dead end it appears to be. When I asked Beachy how we were supposed to get niche GM crops to poor farmers in Africa, Jaworski, now in his eighties, answered for him "Bill Gates! Bill Gates! The Gates Foundation!!"[59]

The process of producing GM crops specific to the environmental needs of Africa begins with two necessary components. First, financial resources are required. In 2006 the Bill and Melinda Gates Foundation donated $100 million to establish the Alliance for a Green Revolution in Africa (AGRA), with Kofi Annan as its inaugural chair. Its mandate is to fund the research and production of drought-tolerant crops using "the best and most appropriate science and technology, including biotechnology," as Robert Horsch, another founder of genetic engineering technology at Monsanto, who was asked to be a senior advisor for AGRA, explained in an interview.[60]

Second, there has to be easy and open access to proprietary technologies. Whereas critics of biotechnology frequently portray the main players as hoarding access to knowledge, this is largely a misconception. As Robert Paarlberg has discovered, "It is actually in the poorest countries, where commercial markets for seeds are so small, that the big companies are most often willing to license their proprietary technologies on a royalty-free basis for local use, since they have no significant sales to lose."[61]

Remarkably, this has been done with the disease-resistant sweet potato, beta-carotene-enriched Golden Rice, and nutritionally enhanced sorghum. With technologies available, with international pressure on big corporations to make green gestures, and with the Gates Foundation lavishing research dollars, the pieces are falling into place for a future generation of smaller, locally tuned African corporations able to make GM niche crops available to African farmers. And not just African farmers. Consider just a sampling of the options and the potential benefits that might follow for countries such as India and China and throughout South America and Southeast Asia: rice enhanced with vitamin A, slow-ripening mangoes that enable poor farmers to reach wider markets, virus-resistant papayas, allergen-reduced peanuts, and soybeans that produce healthier oil.[62]

Every technology takes time to go from the purview of the few to the realm of the many. As biotechnology approaches its twenty-fifth birthday, the time is right for it to find a larger audience. It can, I believe, legitimately do this in the name of human justice, sustainable agriculture, and environmental biodiversity.

Coda

And thus I rest my case for this controversial piece of the larger puzzle. I wish I could do so with a final home run of an argument, a parting shot that is airtight and undeniable, ending the discussion once and for all. But that's not to be. As I have gone to great pains to show, the issue of genetic modification is, and probably always will be, fraught with confusion, passion, and ambiguity. Every defense I make in this chapter has a counterargument, every point a counterpoint, many of them persuasive. Our job as ethical eaters in the twenty-first century is, however, not to seek timeless environmental commandments, nor to settle on a single food ideology. Instead, it is to continue our debates on grounds that are swept free of agricultural romance, ideological localism, scientific ignorance, and elitist solipsism.

If the terms of our food fights can be opened a bit, the largest barrier to a judicious use of GM crops—public opinion—could come around to viewing it as a viable, though by no means perfect, step toward sustainable global food production. And not just for our own community, but for the world around us, a world full of places we've never been to or, for that matter, thought much about.

4

Meat—The New Caviar: Saying "No," or at Least "Not as Much," to Eating Land-Based Animals

To be an environmentalist who happens to eat meat is like being a philanthropist who doesn't happen to give to charity.—HOWARD F. LYMAN

I promised at the outset of this book not to preach. A patronizing list of eating dos and don'ts is the last thing anyone needs. Not only are bookstore shelves already sagging under the weight of dietary self-help manuals, but these earnest volumes are typically rigid, often insulting to our intelligence, and, within a year or two of publication, outdated. Instead, my main goal (which I hope is clear by now) is to provide insight into how we might *think* about food and agriculture in ways that are both pragmatic and environmentally relevant.

As twenty-first-century environmentalists, we have a personal responsibility to lay the foundation for culinary and agricultural literacy, a mind-set that accepts complexity, challenges assumptions, and enriches itself over a lifetime of thoughtful eating. My idea of culinary literacy enables the concerned eater to parse the myths and promotional tactics that have infused discussions about food today and develop a personal and well-grounded approach to achieving a responsible diet. Ideally, at least, this is the goal—not to lecture, not to reduce what we must do to a catchy mantra, but to help establish the basis for an ethical diet.

But alas, if only for a chapter, I must (more or less) preach. In the upcoming pages, I argue that a necessary precondition for eating a sustainable diet is to radically reduce meat made from animals that dwell on land. I insist on this change because conventional meat production is unavoidably degrading to the environment. No matter how hard we strain to find rays of hope in this grim picture, no matter how much we'd like to find a magic loophole of sustainability, it does not exist. Even the supposedly more sustainable alternatives—grass-fed beef, free-range chickens and happy pigs that frolic in mud and grow fat on grubs—have environmental consequences that are severe enough for us to conclude that these products should be nothing more than a rare treat, indulged in maybe a few times a month, and in quantities that would frustrate an ascetic (say, twelve pounds a year!). As the opening quotation by Howard Lyman suggests, being a meat-eating environmentalist is a tough contradiction to uphold.

I've looked far and wide for an exception to this dour assessment. Indeed, I've tried to find a rationalization that would allow the serious environmentalist to enjoy his meat and wear his green stripes too. Regrettably, I could find none, and thus I'm left to argue that if you want to start changing the environment with your diet, one of the most productive things you can do is quit eating meat. Unlike most other dietary decisions, this one can be completely controlled by the individual consumer. It just takes will—a great deal of will—and that willpower is, I believe, best strengthened with objective information about the global production and consumption of meat.

General Perspectives

As I undertook the research for this book, I never expected to reach such a radical conclusion—a conclusion that may very well be the book's most important. Nevertheless, every environmental problem related to contemporary agriculture that I've investigated ends up having its deepest roots in meat production. Every rock my research discovered and upturned revealed meat. Monocropping, excessive applications of nitrogen fertilizer, addiction to insecticides, rain-forest depletion, land degradation, topsoil runoff, declining water supplies, even global warming—all these problems would be considerably less severe if global consumers treated meat like they treat caviar, that is, as something to be eaten rarely, if ever.

Yeah, right, you're thinking. Of course, maybe you'd think differently if you toured a feedlot, as I did in April 2008, and saw (and smelled) thousands of cows penned in chutes, knee-deep in their own feces, with troughs of corn and soy feed under their noses, all under one roof, chained, marked, and thoroughly demoralized. But the reality is that most of us will never visit a confined animal feed operation (CAFO), and most of us will never stop eating meat. Eating meat is one of the most natural and historically entrenched human habits. "Our eating habits," writes the ethicist Peter Singer, "are dear to us and not easily altered." Lester Brown, the president of the Earth Policy Institute, has—mistakenly, I believe—called eating meat an "innate appetite." The vice president of the Humane Society has said that "it's probably harder to change your diet than it is to change your religion." Realistically, then, substantial, if gradual, reduction remains the only achievable option. How to work a modest diet of meat into the golden mean of agriculture is the challenge.[1]

This chapter encourages a serious reduction in meat consumption by laying an evidentiary basis so thick that any serious environmentalist must at least come to terms with the paradox of being a meat-eating environmentalist. I undertake my quest knowing first-hand what a serious sacrifice it is to cease eating meat. Indeed, after finishing the research for this chapter, I did it myself. Much as I'd like to claim otherwise, it's been hard, *very* hard. But I've persisted with my decision, eaten well, and stayed healthy and energetic. Sure, I cannot pass a BBQ shack (seemingly on every corner in Austin) without having a Pavlovian meltdown. But the fact is that I've grown fiercely dedicated to my choice, because I know that a diet that's almost exclusively plant-based has direct environmental consequences for the better.

Understanding the place of meat in global food production is critical to understanding virtually every other argument I make in this book. The proposals I've made thus far for establishing agricultural models that are midsized, commercially viable, sustainable, and linked into a global economy cannot be achieved without a sharp drop in worldwide meat consumption. To be perfectly blunt, if the world continues to eat meat at current rates, there's simply no way to achieve truly sustainable food production. For all the rhetoric and gesturing and good intentions, the effort would be a complete wash. The broad environmental consequence of such a failure is frightening to contemplate. It would assuredly involve irreparable degradation severe enough to seriously compromise the health of future generations.

A few examples should highlight the intimate connection between meat production and other important agricultural reform proposals. First, consider agricultural biotechnology. While it's true that genetic modification currently supports the wasteful monocultural production of selected cash crops, this emphasis would change dramatically if demand for grain and soy grown to feed livestock dropped. A diminished market for grain and soy in turn would give researchers more incentive to explore markets for niche crops in developing countries—crops with broader humanitarian and environmental applications. In essence, if you accept the premise that the major problem with genetic engineering is how the technology is currently monopolized and applied, then the best way we can, as individuals, address this concern is by reducing our intake of meat and meat-related products.

A second example involves nitrogen fertilizer. As we've seen, nitrogen fertilizer, when used to produce corn and soybeans to feed livestock, leads to all manner of environmental wreckage, most notably the growing dead zones that plague oceans throughout the world. Remove the enormous feed demand, however, and the very real prospect of using nitrogen fertilizers more responsibly, especially as progress is made on improving nitrogen uptake, grows considerably. The main benefit here is that farmers could cultivate a wider range of crops on commercial farms while maximizing yields (with the assistance of modest nitrogen use) and minimizing sprawl (owing to reduced land needs as a result of higher yields). Conserved land would preserve biodiversity, prevent runoff, and improve aquatic ecosystems.

Again, though, the balance that's so necessary for reducing nitrogen applications and enhancing nitrogen uptake hinges directly on a major drop in meat production. Otherwise, grain demand remains high, and with it the careless and extended application of nitrogen fertilizers and the environmental problems resulting from it.

A third example relates to food miles. As discussed in the first chapter, the distance food travels has become a conventional and convenient (if inaccurate) barometer of environmental correctness. Nevertheless, as study after study has shown, "livestock rearing generates more greenhouse gasses than transport does." A 50 percent reduction in meat consumption would compensate for 2937.5 miles driven every year by every family. These are just a few of the ways in which reducing meat production would alter the nature of global agriculture.[2]

Closely related to the broad environmental issues are the specific health problems explicitly linked to meat production, conventional meat production in particular. The most common food-borne bacteria that cause illnesses, including *E. coli*, *Campylobacter*, and *Salmonella*, come primarily from meat. In fact, most feedlot cattle today have *E. coli* lining their intestines. Then there are the frightening prospects of mad cow disease, the rendering of downer cows to produce livestock feed, and anemic regulatory apparatuses that are, especially in the United States, geared primarily toward profit rather than consumer safety.[3]

Manure poses an especially messy problem for public health. Its excessive production on factory farms requires the construction of manure lagoons, among other poorly regulated storage facilities. Rain and melting snow can easily pull heavy metals, nitrates, bacteria, and viruses from these sprawling poop ponds into local water supplies. In 2001, according to the Sierra Club, the EPA forced several hog farms in the United States to supply bottled water to residents living around the farms because lagoons had seeped manure and contaminated drinking water.[4]

An especially insidious health problem involves the emission of hydrogen sulfide from the manure lagoons. This broad-spectrum poison has been linked to severe headaches, nausea, diarrhea, and death. And the stench emitted from factory farms is dangerous too. It can cause widespread respiratory problems, gastrointestinal disorders, and even fatigue and depression. Of course, what's bad for the environment is always bad for individual health, but the by-products of meat production make this connection more immediate, personal, and directly toxic.[5]

In the end, the environmental and health-related consequences of meat production are one and the same. To make the strongest possible argument for reducing global meat consumption, this chapter will therefore attack the issue head-on, using as a framework the Aristotelian basics: land, air, and water (the fire, shall we say, is in the opposition). This approach demonstrates how the devastation of meat production resonates widely, thoroughly infecting the global environment—an environment that encompasses our health, the health of our ecosystems, and even, I might venture, our moral health.

The urgency and complexity of these problems with respect to land, air, and water is, I believe, best understood when meat consumption is examined through two lenses: the energy it takes to produce meat, and global trends in meat consumption with respect to population.

First, the energy used to produce meat is astronomical. To appreciate its extent, begin with the environmentally friendly baseline of grains. Grains produce between 1.5 and 2.5 food calories for every calorie of fossil fuel burned. This is a net gain underwritten by the sun, which is providing most of the energy and thus doing the work for free.

Compare that scenario to meat production, in which much of the energy derives from fossil fuels mined and burned by humans to power the process "from semen to cellophane." Land-based animals happen to be terribly inefficient converters of plant protein into edible flesh. It takes considerable energy even to stand up and maintain body temperature, after all, and this is what land-based animals use much of their energy to do. As a result of these inescapable inefficiencies, the production of range-fed beef requires 3 calories of fossil fuel for every 1 calorie of meat produced. Rendering beef from animals confined in feedlots, however, takes this expenditure to a new level, requiring 33 calories of fossil fuel for every calorie of meat produced. Pigs, chicken, lamb, and dairy products fall in between, but beyond the precise numbers, what matters most is that all these meat products operate at a net energy loss. We eat these foods, and no matter how "sustainable" the production, on some level we waste energy. Even if a cow is eating grass that's fed by the sun, the cow does not turn all the energy from the grass into meat, and thus energy is lost.[6]

In fact, we're only starting to appreciate the nature and consequences of this systematic misapplication of resources. The figures noted above do not include the many transportation stages in the supply chain (to the slaughterhouse, to the processor, to the whole-saler, to the retailer, to the home). Nor do they take into account the fact that meat must be cooked at high temperatures, and often for a long time, to be made safe for consumption. The implications of this capacious energy sink are hard to quantify, but according to one estimate, the energy used annually to produce meat for one person living in the United States is the same amount of *total* energy expended by a person living in a third-world country over the course of a year. Looked at another way, the energy needed to produce meat is so high that if the average meat eater in Australia reduced his or her meat consumption by half, the saved energy would be enough to run that household for an entire month.[7]

The second major perspective to keep in mind when evaluating the environmental impact of meat production on air, land, and water is how population pressure affects consumption trends. Between 1961 and 2002 the worldwide consumption of meat rose from 71 million metric tons a year to 247 metric tons a year—almost a fourfold leap. During this time the world's population roughly doubled. People have been begetting more people, and these people in turn have been wolfing down more meat per capita than their ancestors did.[8]

In 1958 the average amount of meat eaten per year by a European was 123 pounds; today it's 196 pounds. In the United States, the 1958 amount was 196 pounds; today it's 273 pounds. Between 1961 and 2002, per capita yearly meat consumption in Sweden rose from 110 pounds to 167 pounds, in New Zealand it went from 248 pounds to 312 pounds, in Ireland from 121 pounds to 233 pounds, and in Cyprus from 62 pounds to 288 pounds. The numbers astound. All in all, we're witnessing exactly the opposite of what needs to happen in order for sustainable global agriculture to become a reality. Indeed, according to current figures, meat consumption across the developed world has taken off like a rocket.[9]

The most challenging numbers, however, come from developing nations—places with large populations of poor people on the verge of being able to afford diets higher in meat protein. In Brazil, for example, per capita meat consumption has spiked from 61 pounds a year to 174 pounds. In China it's gone from 8 pounds to 119 pounds. Cambodia has seen an increase from 10.8 pounds to 30.6 pounds. Angola has gone from 15 pounds to 42 pounds. From 1981 to 2001 the Chinese consumption of grain dropped 45 percent in urban areas, while meat consumption rose 278 percent. "Every society that I've looked at, when incomes go up," writes Lester Brown, "one of the first things people do is add [meat] protein to their diets." These figures are proof positive.[10]

Given that it takes 16 pounds of grain to make 1 pound of beef, ponder for a moment the global transfer of energy from plants to animals required to sustain this behavior if it were universalized. We now have, as a global community, 1.3 billion cattle roaming in our midst. They join 16 billion chickens, a billion pigs, a half billion turkeys, and 800 million goats. The world already raises and slaughters 45 *billion* chickens a year, 23 million a day in the United States alone. Slaughterhouses in the United States now kill hundreds of millions of cows, pigs, and sheep a year, as well as billions of chickens. And as staggering as these numbers are, they're growing exponentially. The world's land supply is being overwhelmed. And it's being overwhelmed by animals that by design waste energy, harm the environment, and, when eaten excessively, ruin our health.[11]

The resources needed to maintain this endlessly growing cycle of breeding, exploitation, and slaughter are running out. Given the nature of this trend, it's a frightening prospect to consider the environmental consequences of a predicted doubling of the world's population between now and 2060. Adding to the impending squeeze of this disaster is the frustrating calculus of personal sacrifice: even if the world's meat consumption stagnated, population increase alone would take an already serious environmental problem and transform it into a devastating one. Vaclav Smil has thought through this scenario and noted that if the world's growing population decided to eat the same amount of meat that the world's affluent now consume, we would need 67 percent more land than the earth has. In this sense, there will be no choice: the world will simply *have* to start eating less meat.[12]

Of course, it would be much better if we could make this decision of our own volition instead of waiting for an environmental catastrophe to make it for us. It is with this goal in mind that we can now turn to the environmental evidence and start to digest what I hope amounts to a compelling reason to reconsider eating meat.

Air

Looking at cows roaming around a verdant pasture, you'd probably never guess that what you're witnessing is global warming at work. Indeed, whether confined or pastured, grass-fed or grain-fed, cows—and livestock in general—contribute significantly to rising concentrations of greenhouse gases in the atmosphere. The UN's Food and Agriculture Organization (FAO) estimates that livestock are the cause of 18 percent of all global warming. Every stage of livestock production emits carbon dioxide, methane, or nitrous oxide, all climate-changing gases that scientists believe are altering the global environmental in ways that will fundamentally change how humans live—and procure food—for the rest of our existence.[13]

The impact of livestock on climate change and air quality has been historically overlooked in large part because the causes are so dispersed, and in most cases hard to visualize. Some global warming contributions are direct, such as the methane released from decomposing manure, the carbon dioxide and methane generated from "respiratory processes," land degradation through extensive grazing, and the deforestation required to graze cattle and grow their food. Other contributions are indirect, such as the fuel burned to produce fertilizer in order to grow grain for livestock, the energy expended to render an animal into meat, and the nitrous oxide emissions created by the aquatic runoff of chemical fertilizers. In addition to generating these greenhouse gases, livestock production, as we have seen, adds enormous quantities of toxic and noxious chemicals to the air, contributing to air pollution, degrading the quality of life for surrounding residents, and instigating several acute public health problems.

Because these processes are largely invisible, however, we rarely pay them the same heed we might to, say, the kind of car we drive. However, what's happening out in the pasture and on the feedlot is arguably of greater environmental concern than the amount of fuel being burned in our SUVs (or our Priuses). As the FAO notes, transportation of all forms worldwide accounts for 13.5 percent of global warming gas emissions. This compares to 18 percent for livestock. Food milers, if they really want to help the environment, would be much better off giving up meat than buying local.[14]

Of the many contributions to global warming attributable to livestock production, the heavy application of nitrogen fertilizer may be the most universal. The use of nitrogen fertilizer in and of itself is not, as I've argued, necessarily problematic. In fact, as proponents of the Green Revolution have long claimed, it has probably saved millions from starvation throughout the past century. When nitrogen fertilizer is applied to foster the unrestrained growth of monocultured crops intended to feed livestock, however, the equation, and thus the environmental consequences, fundamentally shift.

According to the FAO, nations with intensive livestock production dump a majority of their nitrogen fertilizer onto crops destined for the guts of their farm animals. The most notable of these crops is maize, but soybeans, sunflower, rapeseed, barley, and sorghum are also cultivated in increasing amounts for the sole purpose of fattening animals to feed people. In 2006, more than a third of all grain produced in the world entered the mouths of animals destined for the abattoir. In the United States, an astounding 80 percent of all grain produced went toward animal feed.[15]

The UK leads the world in the gross misapplication of nitrogen, dedicating 70 percent of its nitrogen fertilizer to produce feed *and* pasture forage. Corresponding figures for the United States and Canada are, respectively, 51 percent and 55 percent. Germany uses 62 percent of its nitrogen fertilizer for such a purpose, and France 52 percent. The emission of carbon dioxide, the most abundant greenhouse gas, as a result of manufacturing these fertilizers amounts to about 41 million metric tons a year. Without demand for meat, these inputs would be significantly reduced.[16]

The production of nitrogen fertilizer is the most common energy sink, and thus the most common cause of global warming gas output, associated with growing crops for livestock feed. However, "on-farm energy use"—energy dedicated specifically to growing crops that go toward feeding livestock—is the most intensive. The manufacturing of seed, herbicides, and pesticides, as well as the fossil fuels burned to run the machinery that distributes these inputs, are included in this category of farm expenditure. All these demands lead to the extensive consumption of energy, and once again, it's all done in the name of feeding the world meat.

According to a study of agricultural production in the state of Minnesota, the "on-farm energy use" required for cultivating maize and soybean for cattle and pig consumption made up "by far the largest source of agricultural CO_2 emissions." Extrapolating from the Minnesota figures, the FAO suggests that greenhouse gas emissions generated by "on-farm fossil fuel use" could be 50 percent higher than those generated by the manufacturing and application of nitrogen fertilizer. These inputs, which are largely beyond the consumer's purview, must be taken into consideration when we choose to buy meat.[17]

Grazing animals in pastures—something even CAFOs do for a few months of an animal's life—also contributes to significant increases in global warming gases. Cows, pigs, lambs, and chickens currently trample about 66 percent of the earth's dry land area.

When pastureland vegetation is gradually degraded by manure, fertilizers, pesticides, and repetitive pounding underfoot, desertification is the common result. The 1992 Rio Earth Summit defined desertification as "land degradation in arid, semi-arid, and dry sub-humid areas resulting from various factors...including human activities." The Millennium Ecosystem Project says that desertification "poses one of the greatest environmental challenges today."[18]

Indeed, the implications of this process for global warming are quite serious, with some estimations attributing about 20 percent of all global warming gases to "land use change," of which desertification is a major component (deforestation being another). Desertification systematically ruins and removes topsoil and vegetation, which releases carbon dioxide into the atmosphere instead of sequestering it in healthy plants that would otherwise use it for photosynthesis. Making matters worse, the inability of destroyed vegetation to capture carbon dioxide ultimately leads to what scientists call a "desertification–global warming feedback loop." In this scenario, carbon that's released from desertification causes global warming, and then in turn global warming exacerbates desertification. According to Yvo de Boer, the top climate official at the UN, desertification and global warming are "two halves of the same coin." Livestock are the main engine of this vicious cycle.[19]

The animals themselves are a factor as well. According to the FAO's groundbreaking report *Livestock's Long Shadow,* cattle alone account for over 50 percent of the world's total output of carbon dioxide generated from respiration. For cows grazing a lush pasture, carbon dioxide emissions do not escape into the atmosphere but instead are recycled through plants, which are consumed by the cows and stored in cattle tissue. This is good, because in a balanced scenario, cows actually sequester carbon. (Herein lies one justification for choosing grass-fed beef over feedlot beef.) But the reality of overgrazing is such that land degradation is the norm, and as long as the world keeps increasing its consumption of meat, it always will be. When the vegetation in the pasture is compromised, it is incapable of properly recycling the atmospheric carbon dioxide emitted by grazing cows. The unabsorbed carbon goes into the atmosphere as a global warming gas.[20]

Even if cattle and vegetation coexisted in harmonious ecological balance, though, the respiratory impact of livestock would continue to be an issue. Livestock give off 86 million metric tons of *methane* a year. Methane is twenty-one to twenty-four times more efficient at trapping heat than carbon dioxide. Moreover, it can linger in the atmosphere for as long as fifteen years. The FAO report puts the matter in formal terms: "In the rumen, or large fore-stomach, of [ruminant animals], microbial fermentation converts fibrous feed into products that can be digested and utilized by the animal. This microbial fermentation process, referred to as enteric fermentation, produces methane as a byproduct, which is exhaled by the animal."[21]

The sanitized language is really just a polite way of describing burps and farts, which ruminants produce with environmentally detrimental regularity. A 2008 study showed that livestock gas emitted from Argentine cows—up to 1000 liters of flatulence a day—threatened coral reefs in the Caribbean. When it comes to methane emissions from cows, buying grass-fed hardly lets the consumer off the hook: grass-fed cattle actually produce four times more methane than feedlot cattle, when measured on a per-cow basis. Grass contains lignin, which is hard to digest, and cows rely on microflora in their gut to do this job, the result of which is, alas, more belches, more flatulence, and thus more methane.[22]

Ruminant gas foretells ruminant waste, and this much more conspicuous by-product of beef production hits the ground with its own set of heat-trapping troubles. Whether domesticated farm animals are digesting grain or grass, the manure they dump releases substantial amounts of methane and carbon, especially when it is liquefied and collected in lagoons. This problem has become especially acute in recent years as animal feed producers stuff their products with increasingly dense concentrations of nutrients. These overpacked nutrients, once evacuated, produce greater amounts of methane than older feeds ever did.

Pigs are the guiltiest culprits when it comes to manure-produced methane. A hog farm with 50,000 pigs (which is big but by no means out of the ordinary) accounts for a half million pounds of urine and manure *every day*. Over 90 percent of pigs mature in "megapiggeries," and these environmentally devastating operations rely as a matter of course on "lagoon waste management" (these lagoons can be 25 feet deep and 18 acres long), thus making a huge contribution to methane output, decreased air quality, and global warming. Pigs might top the methane-output charts, but cattle are hardly immune to the manure-methane scenario. Feedlot cows need poop lagoons just as feedlot pigs do, and as mentioned, grass-fed cows are actually worse methane emitters than grain-fed cows.[23]

The final greenhouse gas that meat production creates is the most potent: nitrous oxide. Very little nitrous oxide exists in the atmosphere, but what's there as a result of human activity is environmentally costly: nitrous oxide traps heat 296 times more effectively than carbon and sticks around for 110 to 150 years. Unlike carbon and methane, nitrous oxide also contributes to ozone depletion. The sources of nitrous oxide exist throughout livestock's extensive supply chain, but the central polluting component once again involves feed. The fertilizers used to grow feed and prepare pastures for grazing are to blame for the volatization of 3.1 million metric tons of ammonia a year. This volatization frees up nitrogen to bond with oxygen and go on to form 200,000 metric tons of nitrous oxide annually.[24]

When cheap nitrogen fertilizers are employed instead of anhydrous (dehydrated) ammonia (examples of anhydrous ammonia include fertilizers such as urea and ammonium bicarbonate), the volatization problem is further exacerbated, with the amount of nitrogen lost by ammonia up to seven times higher. Even more nitrous oxide comes from nitrogen runoff into aqueous ecosystems, with 8 to 10 million metric tons of nitrogen pouring into aquatic zones and forming another 200,000 metric tons of nitrous oxide.[25]

A final fact to consider when exploring the connection between meat production and nitrous oxide is livestock's inability to effectively assimilate nitrogen into flesh. When growers apply nitrogen fertilizers, plants can absorb up to 70 percent of the nitrogen. Although there's plenty of room for improvement here, it's better than the 14 to 34 percent rate at which cows, pigs, and chickens absorb nitrogen. The unprocessed excess is, of course, excreted, and in the case of animals fed a steady diet of concentrated feed, the millions of pounds of excretion send yet more nitrous oxide churning into the atmosphere.[26]

These phenomena, with the exception of the poop, are invisible. The noxious impacts of conventional meat production, however, are not. This claim holds especially true for the underprivileged people who live near factory farms, slaughterhouses, and packing plants. In his compelling piece "Power Steer," written for the *New York Times Magazine*, Michael Pollan recalled how he started to smell "a bus-station-men's-room" stink more than a mile away from the feedlot he studied. Stories of manure stench and fly infestations ruining towns and the lives of the people who live in them are becoming legion. Ken Midkiff, in his provocative book *The Meat You Eat*, writes extensively about families existing in a perpetual state of nausea as a result of manure lagoons and, in one case, thousands of dead hens found rotting inside a hot factory shed. It is not at all unusual for families working and living around factory farms to walk outside their homes and gag.[27]

The Sierra Club, publicizing its "Tour de Stench" in western Kentucky, noted in a press release that the odor wafting from the dozens of chicken processing plants in the area routinely caused schoolkids to vomit during recess. These odors, as we've seen, carry toxic airborne chemicals—compounds such as ammonia and hydrogen sulfide—that, while not contributing to global warming, damage human health. Residents living close to hog factories in particular suffer abnormally high rates of respiratory problems, intestinal disorders, and depression.[28]

Environmentalists are well aware of the connection between meat production and air quality. Not surprisingly, several initiatives are under way to mitigate emissions of carbon dioxide, methane, and nitrous oxide. Efforts to improve livestock farming by reducing deforestation, increasing the carbon content of currently cultivated soil, and reclaiming degraded pastures have the potential to lessen the harmful impacts of raising animals for food considerably. The same holds true for strategies to reduce methane emissions by improving animal diets and refining manure management practices. In the same vein, genuine attempts to prevent the release of nitrous oxide by storing manure in an enclosed tank rather than an open lagoon are in the works. All these options, of course, hold great appeal and should be pursued as temporary measures as we work to reduce meat consumption in the long term.

Ultimately, however, these solutions are left for others to design and implement. We can only stand by and encourage these plans (which is, admittedly, all we can do when it comes to many of the thorniest agricultural issues). But this is not the case with meat. The thing with meat production is that we can, as individuals, play a direct role in initiating environmental change. Indeed, we're able to do something direct and concrete by slowing down or stopping eating meat altogether. Unlike other food commodities, the production of meat is driven exclusively by demand. We can thus forcibly shape the future of agriculture by properly answering the question Jim Motavalli, the editor of *E: The Environmental Magazine*, asked at the dawn of this century: "Do real greens eat meat?"[29]

Land

In addition to contributing significantly to global warming, livestock are taking a toll on the world's shrinking supply of arable land. Pasture set aside for livestock composes two thirds of the world's agricultural land. In light of increasing global meat demand, the most obvious problem this causes is direct land degradation. According to the UN Environment Programme, land degradation includes soil erosion (of which cattle cause 85 percent in the United States), chemical and physical deterioration of the soil, and the "long term loss of natural vegetation." The key results of this destruction are declines in both biodiversity and land productivity. Cattle are by far primarily responsible for each problem.[30]

Defenders of the livestock industry frequently argue that cattle graze on land that is unfit for alternative agricultural purposes. When I wrote a piece for my local newspaper on the damage that beef cattle do to the landscape, a rancher wrote to scold me: "Try growing wheat on the same ground that a cow can produce beef on!" This argument, a standard one, is disingenuous. Not only does it ignore the point that land left untouched can become a thriving ecosystem, but it confuses cause and effect. Extensive grazing is exactly what makes land less useful for crops or reforestation in the first place. "Take away the cattle," writes Erik Marcus, the author of *Meat Market: Animals, Ethics, and Money,* "and in a surprisingly short amount of time, most ranching areas become revitalized." Instead, too many ranchers degrade land with intensive grazing and then, as if the problem were there from the start, defend their actions by claiming that there's no other viable use for such worn-out land.[31]

Revitalizing degraded land is, as Marcus argues, often a real option. Instead, business proceeds as usual and depressed yields due to livestock degradation plague developing continents such as Africa, where production has dropped by as much as 40 percent as a result of soil erosion. It is certainly true that livestock manure can be a valuable source of soil fertility when the animals are carefully integrated into cropping systems. But the global demand for meat is preventing the achievement of such a balance. To wit, an alarming 73 percent of African land in dry areas—areas that get minimal rainfall but where the soil is able to hold much of the moisture—is deemed degraded. This figure is surpassed only in North America, where 74 percent of the land in dry regions is degraded, which is to say rendered unfit for growing crops that could normally survive dry-land conditions (such as dryland wheat). The latter figure is not surprising, given that since 1800, land turned over to grazing has expanded by a factor of six. Today in the United States, 44 percent of all land has cattle or sheep on it. Again, the sad part about this wholesale encroachment onto dry land is that it's land that could otherwise be used for something that's becoming increasingly radical: growing plants for people to eat.[32]

The decline in biodiversity on degraded land is another tangible consequence of livestock expansion across the globe. Decreases in microbial biodiversity are virtually incalculable, but the drop in readily observable land species tells a more measurable story. According to the Millennium Ecosystem Assessment, extinction threatens about a third of all amphibians, a fifth of all mammals, and an eighth of all birds. The World Conservation Union adds that almost 13 per cent of the world's plants face extinction.[33]

The most devastating attack on biodiversity comes from deforestation. For most of human history, dense forests, which happen to nurture the world's highest rates of biodiversity, carpeted the landscape of Central and South America. One reason for the proliferation of rich forestland in these regions was the fact that pre-Columbian American Indians lacked livestock. Although they burned forests to clear some areas for planting and hunting, they had no need to clear land systematically for pasture or to cultivate grain to feed cattle. With the post-Columbian proliferation of livestock, however, this situation changed dramatically. Today the rainforest is eroded at the rate of 11 acres a minute in order to grow soybeans for cattle feed. "Pasture development," writes the Oxford University geographer Michael Williams, "may well be the primary cause of deforestation everywhere in Latin America." To a very large extent, the claim holds true for Europe, South and Southeast Asia, and India as well.[34]

A 2004 FAO report on the state of global forests offers a statistically sobering look at the extent of global deforestation. Everyone has heard about forest destruction in Brazil—and indeed, the report justifies this concern, showing a rate of deforestation of .4 percent a year. Of course, this is .4 percent of the world's largest rainforest, which adds up to about 3551 square miles a year, and the sheer extent of the devastation is cause for our attention and outrage. But it should not obscure the fact that, as the report also shows, rates of deforestation are much higher in other countries. To cite just a few examples, Argentina and Costa Rica are losing rainforests at twice the rate of Brazil, Ecuador at three times the rate, and Guatemala at four. In Africa, Côte d'Ivoire has a worrisome annual deforestation rate of 3.1 percent, Burundi 9 percent, and Sierra Leone 2.1 percent. The majority of this deforestation is taking place to grow crops to feed livestock. "The conversion of forest to cropland," states the 2007 FAO report on livestock, "was massive over the last centuries and is still occurring at a fast pace in South America and Central Africa."[35]

Another way in which cattle devastate the land involves their impact on riparian zones. Riparian ecosystems are small strips of wetland located between land and streams. Throughout riparian zones, relatively high water tables and flat land grades support soil that nurtures an unusually rich level of biodiversity. For the same reasons that a majority of a rangeland's floral and faunal species congregate in riparian zones, livestock find these delicate patches of biodiversity an especially attractive region in which to cluster. In these areas they feed, rest, socialize, and trample. Depressingly, about 80 percent of the vegetation that cattle graze exists on the 2 percent of a range that's riparian.[36]

Critics of my argument might counter that it's perfectly natural, even healthy, for animals to graze dense floral patches, consume plant nutrients, and deliver their waste back into the soil. This is true, but, as I have said, only when the animals are seamlessly interwoven into a rich ecosystem. This is something that nature alone manages most effectively. When humans manage the system in order to produce beef for the world's billions, we get what's recently happened in the American West, where 90 percent of the region's riparian zones "have been degraded almost out of existence by livestock grazing." As the former rancher Harold Lyman puts it, "Ranchers allow livestock to trample aquatic vegetation without the slightest regard for the role that vegetation plays in anchoring streambeds, filtering out sediments, and breaking down nutrients and pollutants."[37]

The hit that livestock deliver to grassland is equally hard. In some environments, evidence confirms the potential benefits of selectively grazing grasslands with modest levels of livestock. Nevertheless, the negative impacts on grassland biodiversity should not be overlooked when weighing the environmental costs of beef production and consumption. The vast majority of ranchers do not graze modestly. Thomas L. Fleischner, a former chair of the Public Lands Grazing Committee of the Society for Conservation Biology, places the issue in stark historical relief when he notes how "the most severe vegetation changes of the last 5400 years occurred during the past 200 years." The reason for this degradation will be familiar: "The nature and timing of these changes suggest that they were primarily caused by 19th-century open land sheep and cattle ranching."[38]

Fleischner's condemnation of ranching might well have extended even further back in time, across the Atlantic and into England, where the agrarian reformer Reynell Carew lamented "the employing of ground to so mean a profit as grazing." This was in 1685. In any case, whenever the damage to grasslands began to exact its toll on the landscape, it did not take long for the "ecological abuse of the range [to become] entrenched in tradition." This environmental habit, according to Fleischner, means that "scores of native animal and plant species have been pushed to the margins." Thus, while it is true that when managed with scientific precision, cattle can effectively enhance grassland diversity, the fact remains that the imperatives of profit-oriented agriculture lead to intensive grazing practices that ruin rather than revive range grasslands and the intricate ecosystems that depend on them.[39]

Scientific studies have recently added heft to this argument. Writing in the *New Zealand Journal of Agricultural Research*, three scientists with the Chinese Academy of Sciences investigated the impacts of grazing and concluded that "continuous grazing in the erosion-prone sandy grassland is very detrimental to vegetation and soil." They also noted that it caused a significant drop in carbon sequestration. Another study, this one on the "influence of trampling" on central European grasslands and wildlife, found that grazing was the dominant cause of grassland destruction. In an analysis of the ecological connections between livestock grazing and bird populations on the seminatural grasslands of Europe, scientists recommended that current grazing practices be relaxed in order to restore a healthy predator-to-prey balance.[40]

Another evaluation of cattle and grass, this one from the journal *Conservation Biology*, has even made a convincing case that livestock grazing increases the frequency of forest fires in the American West. By reducing understory grasses and hedges in forests, livestock literally lay the groundwork for greater forest density than would otherwise occur. This happens because untrampled grasses used to beat out conifers for a place on the landscape. Without these grasses, fires climb the conifers, get exposed to winds, and spread rapidly rather than crawling slowly across the forest floor. All these assessments highlight the notable claim made by Michael Jacobson, the executive director of the Center for Science and the Public Interest, who explained, "If people stopped eating meat, Illinois, Indiana, and Iowa would be returned to forest and grassland."[41]

In terms of general biodiversity, it's also worth noting that cattle dictate the destruction of a wide range of indigenous animals, even when they do not trample riparian zones or damage grasslands. Rangeland management, whether informal or formal, automatically threatens and often substantially diminishes surrounding wildlife. Simply by choosing to graze an animal, the farmer upends the preexisting arrangement of species. More often than not, he'll then work to rig the game. Erik Marcus drives home this point well, writing, "Just about any animal with a spine is considered a varmint and is liable to be shot, trapped, or poisoned" when cattle move onto land.[42]

In the United States, to cite a well-documented example, ranchers have legally killed billions of animals, including prairie dogs, wolves, bears, coyotes, rattlesnakes, and, most notably, buffalo. In 2005 alone, the USDA's Wildlife Services killed 86,000 coyotes at the behest of ranchers grazing cattle and sheep. From a less obvious perspective, millions of pounds of insecticides have been deployed to combat cattle ticks, fleas, and flies. Interestingly, however, the attempt has more often than not backfired, with insects proliferating beyond their original numbers as a result of their insidious ability to resist conventional insecticides. Either way, the ultimate result is the same: biodiversity is compromised, the predator-prey balance is upset, and the environment suffers the consequences.[43]

To best appreciate the impact of livestock on landscape, it helps to recall an experiment undertaken in Oregon starting in 1991. The Hart Mountain Refuge is a 278,000-acre tract of land that, in addition to the adjacent Sheldon National Wildlife Refuge, was barred from grazing. This was a radical change. For over a century the land had endured constant grazing by cattle owned by nearby ranchers.

By the late 1980s, according to one report, grazing "had turned the refuge into a danger zone for wildlife...had trampled springs and streambanks, had transformed grasslands to sagebrush, and grazed young aspen and willow shoots to the nub." Even as land quality precipitously declined, ranchers introduced more cattle, eventually creating a habitat "suitable only for mule deer and a few hardy birds." After the Wilderness Society successfully lobbied the U.S. Fish and Wildlife Service to ban grazing until 2009, remarkable changes took place. As the writer Kathie Durbin, who carefully followed the story, explained, "The cows are gone. The desert is blooming. The birds are returning...two wildlife refuges finally have the chance to allow wilderness to work itself out."[44]

Water

It's often assumed that global water supplies are predominantly consumed by industrial operations. However, industry uses only 20 percent of the world's water supply. With household consumption accounting for 10 percent, this leaves the rest—70 percent—going toward agricultural purposes. Livestock's share of this figure varies region by region, but to provide a sense of how predominant it is in general, consider that about 70 percent of the water in the American West goes directly into raising pigs, chickens, and cattle.[45]

This amount is not surprising, given that it takes 2400 liters of water to make a hamburger (as opposed to 13 liters to make a tomato) and fifty times as much water to produce a pound of meat as to grow a pound of grain. Our water supply is shrinking. However, ranchers fail to consider these inefficiencies, and producing meat has led them to tap aquifers, rechannel rivers, and drain wetlands with little regard for the inherent (not to mention market) worth of these resources. At some point the logic will have no choice but to become depressingly obvious. But for those currently willing to take the long view, the journalist Fred Pearce has offered some hand-writing on the wall: "Water shortages equal food shortages."[46]

The claim is worth keeping in mind, given livestock's aggressive attack on the world's water supply and quality. Wetlands and aquifers are especially at risk because of the massive amounts of water meat producers suck from them. Wetland ecosystems, which are seasonally or permanently under water, exceed even rainforests and grasslands in their wealth of species biodiversity. Grazing is, of course, a major part of the problem. The National Institute of Water and Atmospheric Research surveyed the literature on the link between grazing and wetland water quality and concluded unequivocally that the impact is not only detrimental but also dire. Moreover, producing cattle feed is also a factor in the widespread destruction of these once rich ecological centers. Over the past century almost half of the world's wetlands have disappeared. No agricultural factor has been as critical to this decline as the raising of livestock.[47]

Underground aquifers have come under equal fire. Diesel-powered pumps now extract 800 gallons of water a minute from the world's largest aquifer, the Ogalalla, in order to grow feed for cattle from Texas to South Dakota. A single pig farm in Dumas, Texas, Ken Midkiff reports, uses 4 million gallons of water a day to slaughter over 16,000 hogs. David Pimentel, a Cornell ecologist who has studied this problem extensively, notes that aquifer depletion is even worse in other countries. Groundwater reserves throughout China and India are dropping at alarming rates, sometimes up to 4 meters annually, and African countries, which export thousands of tons of beef to the EU, are irrigating rivers dry to keep cattle sufficiently watered.[48]

Adding to the demise of water supplies is the fact that cattle emit contaminants into aquifers. Unless a deep layer of clay separates a manure lagoon from the underlying aquifer, seepage of dangerous bacteria, antibiotics, growth hormones, and chemicals such as fluoride and heavy metals is hard to avoid. Responsible societies should make a concerted effort to preserve and even improve aquifers for those who will inherit our land. In reality, though, we are, as a result of a shortsighted diet addicted to meat, creating an environment that our children will have a harder and harder time using to produce food.[49]

Meat production's heavy reliance on a steady supply of water does more than wastefully consume a precious resource. It also fouls the water and, often with legal protection, pours it back into the ecosystem. Go back to the Dumas pig farm. Not only does the factory remove from the water supply 4 million gallons a day, it also discharges into the environment that same 4 million gallons of water, now polluted. This is a horrific example of recycling. The discharge at Dumas, which is typical of pig farms, returns to the water supply (according to Midkiff) raw sewage, blood, and grease.[50]

At a Tyson's chicken farm in Noel, Missouri, the processing of more than a quarter million chickens creates over 800,000 gallons of wastewater a day, an effluvia of blood, intestinal material, grease, fat, and solvents. It all ends up in the Elk River. In McDonald County, Missouri, factory farms raise and process 13 million chickens and several hundred thousand turkeys. It comes as no surprise that as of 2004, every natural body of water in the county was on an "impaired waterbody" list.[51]

The problem of livestock-induced water pollution is global. In fact, it's a huge, mostly unacknowledged mess. Antimicrobials, endocrine disrupters, hormones, antiparasitics, pesticides, antibiotics, and an array of feed additives designed to foster disease-free, pest-free, and absurdly fat livestock are never fully absorbed by animal tissue. These products join the detergents and disinfectants used excessively in dairy production to foul freshwater supplies wherever livestock are raised, milked, and slaughtered. The problem has become so prominent that the bacterial ecosystem worldwide is becoming resistant to common antibiotics.[52]

Conventional meat consumption thereby encourages an insidious arms race in which half the antibiotics manufactured today are fed to animals who in turn release them into the water supply, where bacteria develop a resistance that only calls for more potent antibiotics. Hormones entering the water supply have caused pronounced neurological and endocrine changes in wildlife dependent on polluted streams, rivers, and wetlands. Estrogen runoff has led to sex changes in fish and genital cancer in mammals. An ecosystem is interconnected, and so humans are hardly immune from these alterations. What happens on the microbial and microscopic levels puts us and the environment at fundamental risk.[53]

It's not just estrogen and growth hormones, either. Much as mineral fertilizers that are used to grow feed crops contribute to air and soil pollution, so they contaminate water. According to research undertaken by several prominent ecologists, "the increased consumption of fertilizer over the past 50 years has made agriculture an ever-increasing source of water pollution." They add that "the livestock sector is a major cause of this increase." In the United States, the UK, Canada, France, and Germany, livestock account for more than half of all nitrogen and phosphorous used in agricultural production. So many of these excess nutrients work their way into the water supply that the 2007 FAO report concluded, "We can reasonably surmise that the livestock sector is the leading contributor to water pollution derived from mineral fertilizers on agricultural lands." A 2004 study found that millions of people in the United States drink from wells with nitrate levels that exceed legal standards. This statistic is just one of many that has led the FAO authors to assert that the impacts of livestock-related nutrient runoff "represent a cost to society which may be ... enormous."[54]

Taking concerns to an even deeper level is research confirming how grazing livestock fundamentally compromises the ability of water to flow properly through an ecosystem. Because livestock have degraded rangelands worldwide, water has been unable to replenish itself as it would in ecosystems left ungrazed. Because cows, sheep, and goats press on the land with the same weight as a tractor, watersheds have altered to the extent that precipitation cannot do what it would normally do in a properly functioning hydrological cycle.

Under ungrazed conditions, rainfall is held by soil vegetation and gradually spread across a watershed, infiltrating and replenishing groundwater at a relatively slow pace. When this happens, erosion is kept to a minimum and the soil's fertility is continually enhanced. With intensive livestock grazing, however, the infiltration process is drastically undermined. Surface flows increase, run-off leaches minerals from the soil and deposits them in oceans, and, most critically, the physical health of the soil is degraded.

With this basic physical alteration of the soil, the preconditions for persistent animal manure contamination of downstream freshwater sources are well established. What we're left to endure is therefore a kind of double whammy: more manure than the soil can accommodate hitting soil so damaged that precipitation carries that manure, as well as the microbes and chemicals in it, into the water supply we drink.[55]

A final point should complete this unsavory cycle of waste and degradation. Feeding livestock a steady diet of corn and soybeans means that the land requires much more water than it did before. Typically, producing crops for cows, chickens, and pigs requires a critical shift from endogenous to exogenous plants. Endogenous crops are crops that go dormant in the warmest months, when water demands are the highest. Exogenous crops do the opposite, extending their growing season over the periods when water demands are at a premium. Because soy and corn are exogenous, growing these crops for cows and for purposes other than as human food is an inherently wasteful aspect of conventionally produced meat.[56]

Naturally, efforts to mitigate the livestock-driven causes of water depletion and pollution are under way. Pragmatic strategies to make water use more efficient, improve irrigation, enhance water productivity, and manage manure more carefully are common themes in agriculture journals and ag school curricula. While it's important that we encourage efforts to do things such as aerate cow poop, create diets that minimize livestock excretion, and develop canal linings that better control irrigation, we must not forget that there's a much simpler, more empowering, and by far more effective answer to the problems these solutions address. As Peter Singer writes, "Vegetarianism is a form of boycott."[57]

Grass-fed, Free-range, and Other So-Called Solutions

Can we avoid such a boycott and still eat an environmentally responsible diet? One of the most common responses to the sad environmental consequences of meat production is to choose a supposedly safe alternative. Grass-fed beef is the current alternative of choice. There's no doubt that this mode of meat production is safer, more environmentally sound, more ethical, and, as far as it goes, more natural than conventional meat production. The digestive tract of a cow evolved to process grass, and grass is what it should eat.

As Michael Pollan convincingly demonstrates, not only is it healthier for humans to eat beef raised on grass (because of high omega-3s and low saturated fat), but the avoidance of corn and soy feed means doing away with the excessive pesticides, hormones, and fertilizers these crops require to feed billions of farm animals. The manure produced by a pastured cow is manure that—in the appropriate quantities—can be beneficial for the soil. The overall energy expenditure required to produce grass-fed beef is much lower than the energy needed to make feedlot beef—as mentioned, about ten times lower—and thus grass-fed means a large relative drop in energy application.[58]

Finally, for those concerned with the ethics of meat production, the process of raising a grass-fed versus a feedlot cow is immeasurably more humane. The grass-fed beast escapes what Michael Fox, a vice president of the Humane Society, calls "an immense slaughtering machine that causes great suffering to animals." (Of course, this is not to suggest that grass-fed cows aren't slaughtered!) All in all, grass-fed beef is clearly an improvement, one that you should exclusively pursue—if you must eat beef.[59]

But just because grass-fed beef is more favorable in relative terms does not mean that it's an inherently responsible choice. As John Robbins, the author of *Diet for a New America*, puts it, "I wouldn't get too carried away and think that as long as it's grass-fed then it's fine and dandy." There's much evidence to back him up. Grass-fed beef still comes from a cow, after all, and no matter how one massages the math, cows are comparatively inefficient converters of energy into nutrition. When you break it down, a bunch of protein is all we get out of the deal—no fiber, no real vitamins or minerals, no complex carbohydrates. This nutritional point is as true for grass-fed beef as it is for feedlot beef.[60]

Animals use most of this energy not to generate nutrients to keep us healthy and strong but to move around their bloated bodies and live their truncated lives while trampling the landscape, sending methane into the atmosphere, and endangering water supplies. The inadequacy of this conversion, even if it is more efficient than the feedlot option, is further highlighted by the fact that the land used to graze cattle in order to fatten grass-fed beef could (in most cases) be used to grow plant food for people using energy provided by the sun.[61]

Moreover, grass-fed cattle graze. Grazing animals to feed millions of people, as we've seen, degrades the land, water, and air. Grass-fed cows are indeed fed a more natural diet than conventional ones, but they still trample riparian zones and compact the soil into runoff-friendly cement, in the same way that conventional cattle do. As we've seen, grass-fed cows produce more methane than conventional cows, a gas that's much more potent than carbon in generating global warming.

Also, while cattle grazing might conjure up a picture of pastoral purity, the grass in many cases is irrigated from aquifers, and unless the beef is labeled "organic" as well as grass-fed, the grass can be covered with synthetic fertilizer and insecticides. One can only imagine how much more extensive such practices would become if grass-fed went to a global scale of production.

So all the many real benefits of grass-fed beef must still be weighed against Edward Abbey's assessment of cows: "They pollute our springs, and streams and rivers. They infest our canyons, valleys, meadows, and forests. They graze off the native bluestems and grama and bunch grasses, leaving behind jungles of prickly pear." No study I've seen convincingly shows that the exchange is worth it.[62]

Certainly there are impressive cases in which responsible ranchers (for both cows and pigs) effectively balance land-and-animal ratios in order to enhance the quality of the soil with a cyclical use of animal resources. From a global perspective, however, this arrangement unravels. The major problem is that the sustainable scenario works well only as a boutique endeavor. Scale is everything when it comes to raising animals to feed billions of people.

The specialized approach might be environmentally sound, and even profitable, for a few small-scale ranchers making grass-fed beef for privileged eaters worried about their omega-3s. However, this approach cannot (as far as I'm able to judge) produce enough grass-fed beef to replace the conventional beef consumed in dangerous quantities by the developed world's fast-food-eating masses. John Robbins has explored this problem of scale extensively and cannot get around the point that "to bring cows to market weight on rangeland alone would require each animal to spend not six months foraging, but several years, greatly multiplying the damage to our western ecosystems." To go all grass-fed would in essence slam us into a wall of shrinking resources.[63]

To be fair, maybe this line of attack misses a critical point. At a recent conference I attended in western New York, an organic farmer and I fell into a discussion about the land requirements for grass-fed beef. He argued quite convincingly that the land needed to graze 100 million grass-fed cattle could be made available if we converted land that is now exploited to grow feed into grassland. This proposal has theoretical merit, but there's little concrete evidence that such a system could keep up with rising per capita demand for beef and the projected population growth between now and 2060.

Does the equation work? No one has said, either way. Given the uncertainty, if we're going to think in land conversion terms, it would make much more sense either to grow plants for people on the reclaimed land or to conserve it by leaving it alone (thereby enhancing biodiversity) or to turn it over to solar operations and wind farms. All these options strike me as more achievable. Grass-fed beef, in my final analysis, is an effective alternative to feedlot beef. Still, we should eat less meat, even if it is grass-fed.

Another common response to the environmental argument against eating meat is to consume "free-range" chickens, pigs, and eggs. Not to be glib, but the term, when applied to chickens at least, is a complete joke. "Free-range" is a USDA designation that certifies that an animal has access to the outdoors. This stipulation, however, means virtually nothing. No provisions are made about the size of the outdoor area, the space created for each individual animal, the animals' ease of access to the designated outdoor space, or, perhaps most important, the overall quality of the animals' environment. Moreover, from an animal welfare perspective, few, if any, advantages are conferred to chickens by a generic free-range designation. As Charles Olentine, the editor of *Egg Industry* magazine, writes, "Just because it says free-range does not mean that it's welfare friendly."[64]

The everyday reality of free-range chicken farming is profoundly disturbing. A free-range chicken generally has 1 to 2 square feet of maneuverability inside a factory shed instead of the conventional 50 square inches. This might seem to be a generous expansion of space, but a chicken needs about 75 square inches just to stretch its wings—as if that alone were an acceptable standard of welfare. In most free-range egg farms chickens are packed into a shed so tightly that most cannot make it to the narrow passageway leading to that single patch of cement representing the great outdoors. Diseases spread more rapidly than in caged farms because "free-range" birds must trample through their own excrement rather than live in cages mercifully suspended above the floor of poop.[65]

Most free-range chickens (organic being the exception) endure the usual rounds of antibiotics, growth-promoting drugs, and industrial feed enhanced with animal by-products. In some cases the chickens become so top-heavy and fat from hormone injections, dense feed, and lack of maneuverability that they die of dehydration, because they cannot reach the water source located on the other side of a shed without toppling over.

Even the industry admits that "free-range" means little more than a token light at the end of an enormously long tunnel, and that most birds spend their lives trapped inside the "grow out facility" rather than stretching their wings and roaming the earth after grubs. In essence, there are no uniform standards for "free-range" as there are for organic foods. That said, if you do choose to eat free-range chicken, buy it organic and try to buy it from a supplier that does not use birds designed to gain weight fast. For instance, Cornish X chickens are engineered strictly for industrial production and should be avoided.[66]

The situation with free-range pork is another story, and an instructive one. The logistics of a pig's maneuverability mean that "free-range" pigs enjoy access to genuine outdoor space—paddocks, as the grounds are typically called. Although it's not in any way required, pigs should also be able to express their "natural behavior": eating grass, wallowing in mud, rooting for grubs, and playing with other pigs. No stalls or crates are permitted on free-range farms. However, unless free-range producers are certified (voluntarily) by an association such as Australia's Free Range Pork Farmers Association, farmers can freely use antibiotics to treat sick pigs, apply vaccinations, and even use growth promoters and hormones.

The "free-range" language is purposefully loose and can easily be manipulated to mislead consumers. For example, a producer can label his product "bred free-range" while keeping his pigs locked in a shed with a cement floor. Free-range pigs might eat vegetation during the day, but they usually need supplementary feed enhanced with protein from recycled animal products. Free-range feed, moreover, can be generic grain-based feed used by factory farms—feed that requires tons of fertilizer and insecticides to produce. There are very few organic free-range pig farms, owing to the fact that organic feed is very hard to find and, once found, is usually prohibitively expensive. Finally, as with cattle, pigs that are not properly managed can quickly degrade paddocks with their incessant trampling of a relatively small outdoor space. Like cows, they are heavy animals that do a poor job of converting feed into human nutrients.[67]

But all hope is not lost when it comes to the prospect of sustainable pig production. As the well-publicized cases of Niman Farms in Iowa, Polyface Farms in Virginia, and Berkshire Meats pork attest, several pioneers in agricultural sustainability have proven that pigs can be worked into a brilliantly balanced system of integrated farming. In these operations, farmers take advantage of pigs' natural behaviors to accomplish many agricultural tasks in a way that wastes very little while saving the farmer money.

Sowing native grasses and grazing pigs on rotated pastures allows the farmer to use the pigs as free fertilizing machines. The free organic fertilizer provided by the pigs builds up soil quality for farmers to sow grain that is then fed to the pigs. By rotating the pigs' paddocks—accomplished by moving the troughs and water supply—farmers literally subcontract to animals the labor-intensive tasks of mulching and slashing. Happy pigs, best of all, make their own beds, acquire much of their own food, play, and then, when the abattoir puts an end to the fun, are supposed to yield exceptionally succulent meat.[68]

As with grass-fed beef, if you are going to eat pork, this is the only justifiable route to take: buying from a small operation, preferably run by someone you know, and trusting that operation to follow the eco-correct rules of low-impact pig farming. But still, if a substantial reduction in meat consumption does not take place, we're unavoidably back to the question of scale. It's tempting to look at such cases of environmentally successful pig farming and argue that all pig farming could be this way. But can we say this with complete intellectual honesty? One could begin by asking if the resources, labor, expert knowledge, patience, and land exist for the world to convert to such forms of pork production while maintaining the same rates of meat consumption.

We don't have the answer to this hypothetical question, but for the sake of argument, let's say it is theoretically possible to make such a transition. Would we then be prepared to accept the presence of pig farms and slaughterhouses in our communities? Would we be content to use land to grow pigs rather than using it to grow grain, farm wind, or lie untouched? Would there be ways to keep pigs from congregating around natural bodies of water, fouling the streams with manure, and damaging watersheds? Perhaps most important, would taking the scale of these operations to another level—something that would have to be done in order to meet global pork demand—preserve the delicate balance that works so well on these exceptional small-scale farms? Aren't we left with the same conundrum that grass-fed beef leaves us with, namely, that this will work, but only for a small number of privileged consumers? As conscientious eaters, are we content to accept this reality?

A final note draws on very recent evidence to downplay the popular enthusiasm for the free-range alternatives. When I was finishing the research for this chapter, a report came out highlighting the danger of assuming that free-range pork (and chicken too, but pork has much better documentation) is the answer to conventional feedlot pork. The study, funded by the pork industry and published in *Foodborne Pathogens and Disease*, found that naturally raised, antibiotic-free pigs contained higher rates than conventionally raised pigs of the antibodies for three common and dangerous food-borne pathogens. Free-range pigs had almost five times as much *Toxoplasma gondii*, more than half had *Salmonella* (compared with 39 percent of conventional pigs), and, perhaps most distressing, 2 of the 616 studies tested positive for *Trichinella spiralis*, a parasite that agricultural scientists thought had been completely eliminated from the pork supply. In fact, it was the supposed elimination of this pathogen that led chefs to start cooking pork pink, as *Trichinella spiralis* was the parasite that spawned the conventional wisdom that we should cook pork to the consistency of a tire.[69]

What are we to make of this study? One irony is hard to escape: when farm animals are returned to "natural" conditions, they encounter the very same wilderness-related problems that led farm-ers to corral them into feedlots in the first place. Indeed, the authors of the report believe that the free-range pigs contracted higher rates of parasites as a result of their interaction with wild animals and, oddly enough, domestic cats, which can carry these parasites. I read widely on the legitimacy of this argument and it seems quite sound.

The most insightful way of interpreting it came from a blogger named Sara Davis, a rancher of whom I otherwise know nothing. Despite having no apparent scientific expertise on the matter, she concludes with a very insightful analysis: "It is important to remem-ber that many production practices that come under fire, such as indoor rearing and antibiotics, were put into place to increase food safety and/or animal welfare in response to increasingly inten-sive animal production. Merely removing these practices without addressing the reasons they were implemented in the first place does not necessarily bring about the benefits to humans or animals envisioned by consumers who purchase based on a 'free-range' label."[70]

The point is an elegant one in that it reminds us that just as turning weeds into crops to feed human beings is an unnatural act of manipulating the natural world to serve our needs, so is raising animals to kill for our diet. Much as most of us would not eat weeds, there are risks in allowing meat to go wild. Fact is, the domestication of meat once served a nutritional need. It no longer does, and we continue to pursue it at our great environmental peril. Free-range is a smart compromise that might work for a few, but as this parasite study suggests, as it's currently practiced, it offers no fail-safe solution to the world's meat problems.

Another Compromise

So can meat play an integral role in the golden mean? It can, but with strict qualifications. As much as I would like to push a completely meatless diet, I know that such a change is virtually impossible to achieve on even a small scale. Fortunately, isolated examples of environmentally effective meat production offer rays of hope that it is possible to work pork, chicken, and beef into sustainable systems with a global reach. The bottom line, however, is that conscientious eaters must radically reduce current rates of consumption if this goal is to be achieved. Environmentalists who ignore the ecological costs of producing meat are in denial of one the greatest threats to the world's ecosystems and to the prospect of eating ethically.

As responsible consumers, we really have no choice but to confront the reality bluntly articulated by World Watch: "It has become apparent that the human appetite for animal flesh is a driving force behind virtually every major category of environmental damage now threatening the human future." Unlike so many other environmental issues, our response here can be direct and personal. As Gidon Eshel, a geographer at Bard College, writes, "However close you can be to a vegan diet and further from the mean American diet, the better you are for the planet."[71]

In the end, the only environmentally viable kinds of meat production are the emerging alternatives to conventional factory production—grass-fed beef, free-range organic chicken, and free-range pork being prime examples. However—and this a big however—it will work only when kept small and integrated into midsized sustainable farms that place the bulk of their emphasis on growing plants to feed people. In order for this transition to happen on a much larger scale, citizens of developed nations, who do lead by example, must be prepared not only to buy all their meat from sustainable alternative suppliers, but to do so about once a month. This may not happen all at once—as PETA's Wayne Pacelle has noted, "Changing one's dietary habits is a process, not an event"—but it must happen nevertheless.[72]

5

The Blue Revolution: Ecological Aquaculture and the Future of Floating Protein

Aquaculture is the future. — JASON CLAY

Consider, if only for a moment, the gas bladder. This unassuming organ, perfected by millions of years of evolution, enables fish to float. Wedged between spine and stomach, the gas bladder is a hidden pressure gauge instructing fish to absorb gas when ascending and to release it when sinking. It's also a hidden biological treasure. By keeping a fish's body density lower than water density, the gas bladder enables fish to seek food without expending the energy required by a land mammal to haul itself across a pasture.

The ability to float effortlessly negates the need to undertake such energy-hogging endeavors as standing, walking, and running. All these forms of mobility are internal energy sinks for terrestrial creatures, but not for fish. A fish is ecologically honed to translate the majority of its caloric intake into ample flesh that's edible, usually tasty, rich in protein, and flush with heart-healthy oil. This streamlined translation, if responsibly managed and harnessed by humans, has the potential to improve the environment while generating more protein with fewer resources. The key to this noble quest is the responsible farming of fish, a process also known as aquaculture. This chapter makes a case for why we need much more of it.

Fish in a Barrel

Aquaculture as a formal practice is over three thousand years old. Only in the past twenty-five years, however, has it grown into a major supplier of human protein. In 1970 aquaculture provided a mere .7 kilograms of fish per year per person; by 2002 that figure had jumped to 6.4 kilograms. This nearly ninefold increase over the short course of a generation ranks aquaculture as the fastest-growing method of producing food worldwide. This trend is with us for good.[1]

Needless to say, aquaculture's skyrocketing popularity has little to do with widespread appreciation for the beauties of the gas bladder. Instead, as most fish eaters are somewhat aware, marine fish stocks worldwide are declining rapidly. Fishermen reap without sowing—that's the inherent nature of fishing—but when the reaping outpaces natural increase, the obvious result is depletion. The FAO reported in 2004 that 75 percent of commercial fish stocks are "overused, collapsed, or in a state of repair." In stark contrast to the livestock that proliferate across the landscape, today's fish are in the process not just of being depleted but of actually approaching mass extinction. This is no joke. A group of prominent ecologists has warned that all major fish species will be totally ruined in our lifetime if current rates of extraction continue. To be more precise: major fish stocks are on pace to collapse by 2048.[2]

The reasons for these declines aren't hard to discern. Weapons typically deployed by commercial fishermen to maximize harvests turn the ocean into a barrel of water. The fish industry relies on state-of-the-art vessels equipped to travel the oceanic globe while holding 3000 tons of fish. They sail the ocean blue armed not with hook and line but with satellite navigation systems, computer-imaging devices, and hulking bottom trawls that scrape the sea floor to churn up and harvest anything that happens to be in the way. Despite increasingly stringent rules on catch limits, the international scramble to abscond with what little remains of marine life proceeds with flagrant disregard for the rule of law. The Northwest Atlantic Fisheries Organization, which requires European Union fishing vessels to host independent observers, found in 2002 that ships routinely targeted illegal fish, including American cod, despite the supposed deterrent of direct oversight. According to the reporter Charles Clover, who spent time on these ships, the damning reports "simply gather dust in a drawer in Brussels."[3]

The environmental consequences of scouring the seas are every bit as dire as those perpetrated by conventional livestock ranching. "Nothing," writes Dr. Sylvia Earle of the National Geographic Society, "has been more damaging to the health of the ocean than the large-scale taking of wild fish and other marine life." The documented impact of by-catch on marine biodiversity confirms Earle's assessment. "By-catch" is a term referring to the aquatic life accidentally hauled up by marine trawlers and seines. According to some estimates, roughly 85 to 95 percent of the fish caught by commercial enterprises are considered by-catch. Very little of it survives when summarily tossed back into the sea. Stephen Sloan, a former chairman of the Marine Advisory Fishery Commission, writes that "for every pound of shrimp [people] eat, nine pounds of juvenile game fish are killed." In one especially egregious case, Norwegian fishermen in 1986 and 1987 discarded as by-catch 80 million codfish because they were too small to sell. Charles Clover calls by-catch "a fact of life for fishermen," one that leads to the depressing upshot that we end up eating only about *10 percent of all marine life that's killed in order to feed us.* Given the harsh reality of by-catch, eating fish taken from the ocean is, with a few notable exceptions, such as the careful monitoring of wild salmon, a venal environmental sin.[4]

Never has the time been better for viable alternatives. Unfortunately, as a sustainable replacement scheme, aquaculture as a whole has thus far been a bust. Frantically trying to satisfy exploding first-world demand for resource-intensive species such as salmon, halibut, and shrimp—species that too many of us demand on high-end menus—commercial operations have fouled the environment in ways all too reminiscent of the terrestrial feedlots explored in the last chapter. The excessive application of antibiotics to reduce diseases spawned by overcrowded tanks or cages, mismanagement (or no management) of fish waste, minimal and unstandardized regulatory measures, uncontrolled outbreaks of disease (namely sea lice), and the necessity of feeding carnivorous species food that's harvested from the ocean are all factors exacerbating the degrading ecological impact of conventional aquaculture.

Like typical land-animal feedlots, aquaculture operations can easily succumb to the worst habits of industrial food production. They can burn excessive fossil fuels, turn natural ecosystems into controlled areas of exploitation, cultivate stocks without managing the waste, and contribute to global warming at almost every stage of production. High-input/high-output aquaculture systems in essence have proven themselves to be no different from any other industrial operation that disregards recycling, fails to pay for environmental damage, and generally places short-term profit ahead of long-term sustainability. It's an all-too-familiar story.

And it's becoming increasingly well known. Recent press coverage has highlighted the errors of aquaculture's ways, and the popular message has seriously damaged aquaculture's current reputation and perhaps its future prospects. Take as just one example the *New York Times*'s recent treatment of aquaculture. The salvos began in 2005 with a lead editorial explaining that aquaculture might hold promise as a sustainable form of production but was ultimately bound by "sobering limitations." Pleading for strict environmental regulations, the editors explained how farmed fish "frequently escaped into the wild, creating a kind of genetic pollution." It noted how carnivorous species of fish "are fed protein from wild fish, a practice that does nothing to reduce our dependence on an overfished ocean."[5]

On December 14, 2007, we learned how lice in fish farms are endangering wild salmon. One day later a 2500-word piece on fish farming in China made aquaculture appear to be an activity more appropriate for the ninth circle of hell than for coastal Asia. A 2008 article on Chilean farmed salmon vividly recounted an outbreak of "infectious salmon anemia," the intensive use of antibiotics, and conditions so unsanitary that the FDA rejected shipments from Chile. In November 2008 the *Times* ran a poignant piece on the decline of orca whales. The cause was the decline of wild salmon, which were being depleted by sea lice that had escaped from an aquaculture farm. All in all, bad—often disgusting—news for the dominant systems of aquaculture.[6]

The *Times* deserves credit for drawing public attention to these critically important problems. But one point that's easily lost in this thorough environmental critique is that aquaculture is not a homogenous industry. Instead, it's a wide range of systems, many of which have the potential to be highly sustainable operations that can collectively revolutionize how the world produces and consumes protein. When monocultural aquaculture dominates the press, we forget that beyond the aqueous feedlot lurks a variety of inspiring alternatives.

As we'll see, scientists are beginning to explore, producers are beginning to embrace, and organizations are beginning to support methods of aquacultural production that integrate commercially and environmentally sound principles and that have the potential to meet substantial demands for animal protein. Creative combinations of agriculture and aquaculture, the farming of more herbivorous than carnivorous fish, shellfish farming, fish polyculture, and even something called aquaponics are promising alternatives that run counter to the dominant feedlot model. They collectively foretell a bright future for sustainable protein, one we can support with our consumer choices.

Protein That Floats Above the Competition

Defenders of sustainable livestock production might read this chapter and protest (with some justification) that the symbiotic, nutrient-recycling, low-input, low-impact, and sustainably integrated nature of responsible fish farming can just as likely be achieved with beasts that roam land. It is certainly true that every aqueous example of ecological integration potentially has its terrestrial counterpart. As mentioned in the previous chapter, Polyface Farms is one. Niman Farms is another. Berkshire Meats is a third. Perhaps you know of a local farmer who fits the bill. And thus my initial reaction to this objection is generally to agree, to support every example of responsible animal husbandry out there, and to note that a sound global system of food production will surely create space for a diversity of enlightened endeavors. In fact, it must. So there's no reason that ecological animal farming and ecological fish farming cannot supplement, or even complement, each other in the global quest to meet the protein needs of 10 billion people. There's no fundamental dispute between protein that floats and protein that walks.

That said, there are still inherent ecological advantages to farming fish rather than farming mammals. As already suggested, there are the physical properties of fish. Not only do fish float, but they also have higher flesh-to-bone ratios than mammals. In addition, they've not been subjected to nine thousand years of direct human meddling with their genetic selection. The tools that evolution has bestowed upon fish are tools that epitomize a level of efficiency and genetic diversity that domesticated land animals simply don't maintain. Land animals have been swindled into laziness, homogeneity, and inefficiency by human domestication. Fish, however, have instinctively mastered the science of resource maximization. Note that only .01 percent of all tuna hatchlings live to maturity. This startling figure reminds us that the survivors of the fish world are by nature well-oiled machines capable of surviving on fewer inputs relative to the amount of meat that fattens around their bones. Fish farming capitalizes on this comparative physical advantage, thereby enabling fish to maximize resources for us.

Another reason that fish enjoy an inherent advantage over cattle is that aquaculture operations are more easily incorporated into areas that are unsuited for other forms of food production. "Aquaculture," writes Andrea Katz in a journal published by the Swedish Royal Academy of Sciences, "[can] make effective use of available resources that might otherwise go to waste." The FAO agrees, noting that "such systems often are within the reach of a wider range of resource-poor producers." Oceans, lakes, ponds, and rivers can readily be improved with the careful integration of environmentally sound aquaculture operations.[7]

A land-animal facility, no matter how sustainable, is still a facility that requires significant capital and increasingly precious acreage—and a lot of it—relative to other forms of production. Freshwater aquaculture enjoys a distinct advantage when it comes to land conversion, because it's easier and cheaper than animal husbandry to insinuate into preexisting agricultural systems (rather than expanding into mangrove forests or wetlands). Thus it's more likely to emerge as a popular option among a relatively large number of farmers. Dr. Adrian Collins, of Australia's Agency for Food and Fibre Sciences, explains: "There is potential for producers to diversify into aquaculture without major changes to their farm businesses." He adds, "Aquaculture can provide the opportunity for producers to not only maintain their existing cotton or cane enterprises, but to also diversify production by establishing facilities on unused or unsuitable land."[8]

Higher yields from less space are another bonus for the fish option. An aquaponics operation—a contained aquaculture system in which plants grow in the same water that fish inhabit—can produce somewhere near 50,000 pounds of tilapia and 100,000 pounds of vegetables every year from a single acre of space. By contrast, one grass-fed cow fed on "unimproved" land will need around 8 acres of grassland. Not only that, but the cow will have to occupy that land for about two years before it reaches slaughter weight, and then only about 50 percent of the beast will become marketable beef. The results of these figures are eye-opening. Over the course of a year, *aquaponics will generate about 35,000 pounds of edible flesh per acre while the grass-fed operation will generate about 75 pounds per acre.*[9]

True, this is an extreme comparison, and it must be stressed that these numbers are only ballpark figures. They do not take into account a variety of external factors such as location, type of grass, and the amount of feed added to the aquaponics operation. But still, it seems safe to say that on balance, aquaponics appears to be the far less resource-demanding and more productive of these two sustainable alternatives to conventional production.

There's a final, admittedly less scientific reason that I have more faith in the future of aquaculture than in a global transition to sustainable animal husbandry. As I've noted on several occasions throughout this book, we've inherited an agricultural history that to an extent limits what we can do. Economists often refer to a concept called "path dependency," and I think it's a useful one for understanding our current agricultural situation. It's basically the idea that once a bad behavior becomes habitualized, it's hard to collectively throw matters into reverse, back up, and pursue a more sensible option. Of course, real improvements can and do happen; otherwise there'd be no point in grappling with the agricultural issues explored in this book. But the fact remains: altering the course of an established practice on a global scale is far more daunting than attempting to develop a new system from scratch. Aquaculture, which has been a large commercial endeavor for only a few decades, is in its infancy. As a result, we have—as with genetic engineering—a rare opportunity to bring it to maturity according to a stringent set of environmental standards.

Scientists and policymakers are becoming increasingly aware of the opportunity to mass-produce floating protein through sound ecological principles. Dr. Barry A. Costa-Pierce, a professor of fisheries and aquaculture at the University of Rhode Island, has been especially vocal in this regard. "I support the rapid expansion of aquaculture worldwide," he writes, "but believe that expansion must be accomplished by promoting an alternative aquaculture development model: an 'ecological aquaculture' model." As Costa-Pierce puts it, mixing agriculture, animal husbandry, and aquacultural operations has already established viable aquaculture habitats in parts of Asia, ones that "closely resemble natural ecosystems." He'd like to see these operations scaled up into family farms that incorporate aquaculture into a diverse system of production. It is a vision about as hopeful, decentralized, and broadly applicable as one is likely to find in the contentious debates over how to feed the world animal protein without destroying the earth.[10]

Polyculture's Potential

Aquaculture might be commonly associated with coastal and oceanic fish farms that trash the environment, but as Costa-Pierce suggests, there's more to it. Aquaculture is at its very best when integrated into complementary forms of production, which is to say that it thrives when it becomes polyculture. Fish farming is more productive in the long term, healthier, and more environmentally sound when entwined with related endeavors and designed to respect the ecosystem.

While it is true that recently established salmon and shrimp farms have fallen victim to the short-term temptations of monoculture, isolating themselves as polluting aqueous CAFOs, the industry as a whole offers a wealth of cases that confirm the benefits of enlightened polyculture models. With the right incentives in place, backed by an agriculturally literate consumer public making modest dietary changes, the chances that integrated aquaculture will become the standard model of global protein production significantly improve.

Plus commercial fish farming is young. Aquaculture "alternatives" are—again, with the right support, incentives, and regulations—poised to become conventional modes of production. The leading pioneers of modern aquaculture/polyculture systems have been working to develop and promote an ideal of what the "conventional alternative" might look like. It's an ideal that's increasingly being put to the test and, although not enjoying the same publicity as land-dwelling "protein machines," one that offers examples of ecological integration that will brighten the day of even the grumpiest food skeptic.

Why do we know so little about these developments? Indeed, it seems fair to say that most consumers concerned with the environmental ethics of food production have not heard much about the prospects of *sustainable* aquaculture. We've been put off by unsavory stories of shrimp farming in Thailand. Our stomachs have turned in response to the horrors of farmed Chilean salmon. Tilapia exports from China have earned too many black marks. Laurence Hutchinson, a founding member of the Organic Aquaculture Initiative and a master builder of ecological fish facilities, offers an additional reason: "When we travel, we are able to observe the diverse territorial environment around us. The aquatic environment is not so accessible or easy to investigate. It has long been overlooked."[11]

His point suggests that the time is ripe to peek under the waters of the world and examine the models that people like Hutchinson and others are actively pioneering. Not everything we see will inspire hope for a sustainable future. The current drawbacks to sustainable aquaculture go well beyond shrimp and salmon and their unhealthy reliance on fish-based feed, excessive antibiotics, and unsustainable methods of eliminating waste (basically, letting it drift into the ocean). Regrettably, much of world's water used in aquaculture today (around 70 percent) is in Asia, and most of that water is fouled. In many ways, this is aquaculture's saddest inheritance.

However, we should not declare defeat because of this pervasive environmental condition. One thing to keep in mind as I elaborate upon systems in developing countries is that while the water might be foul and the regulations lame, the blame for these conditions cannot be laid at the feet of small-scale aquaculture itself, whose operations, as we'll see, are based on sound ecological principles. A virtual lack of environmental laws in many Asian nations has enabled big industry to pollute the air, soil, and water to such an extent that developed countries have become rightfully wary of coming within smelling distance of edible products from, say, China. Aquaculture has been a victim of this broader degradation.[12]

Therefore, what matters most as I survey current aquaculture operations is that we take home the lessons of ecological symbiosis central to these systems, and that we do so while imagining how they could transform fish farms closer to home, in places where regulations and active public interest better frame the production of food.

Old Harbingers of a New Revolution

The ideal aquaculture system is a freshwater operation that not only produces fish or shellfish in a sustainable fashion but actually improves the quality of the ecosystem in which it operates. Theoretically, it can accomplish this feat because it relies on an integrated design that arranges carefully chosen plants, fish, and shellfish to regulate the system in a self-sustaining fashion. The farmer essentially works to maintain a habitat that capitalizes on basic biological processes, and if he's successful (something that takes time and expertise), his role in producing fish gradually diminishes over time. Of course, a large-scale fish farm will always demand human participation, just as it will always demand inputs, but an important point to keep in mind is that an aquaculture operation that works according to ecological principles can produce a great deal of edible biomass in a small space with little labor. The skilled farmer conducts rather than dictates the performance.

A well-balanced fish farm begins with an honest source of energy: the sun. The sun powers the growth of aquatic plants, algae, phytoplankton, and bacteria that feed on nutrient-rich water to create the nutritional foundation of an aquatic habitat. The next stage involves "algal grazers" and phytoplankton consumers called zooplankton. These barely visible organisms prevent the foundation of the system—algae and related organisms—from overcrowding the pond's resources. Several larger organisms are responsible for consuming zooplankton. These include nymphs, crustaceans, fish fry, and freshwater shrimp. It is upon these creatures, in addition to crayfish, dragonfly nymphs, mussels, eels, and minnows, that mature fish eventually feed. They then fatten and emit the waste that the zooplankton consume. Thus the cycle spins within a poly-cultural system: fish feed on plants and small animals while plants feed on the sun and the waste that fish generate. Around the core of these symbiotic relationships food webs of varying complexities evolve, minimizing the need for external pest control, disease man-agement, or other aggressive human interventions. This scenario, in essence, is the platonic ideal of fish farming.[13]

Nobody, of course, is anywhere near consistently achieving it on a commercial scale. Aquaculture systems that mirror the natu-rally calibrated cycles of undisturbed ecosystems are more fantasy than reality. We shouldn't be discouraged. As I've said, farming of any sort interrupts nature. Nevertheless, the versatility and broad genetic diversity that polycultural fish farming exploits mean that it makes much more sense to let fish float than cows trample. The intricate and flexible nature of an aqueous food web allows fish farmers to experiment with and develop a menu of ecological rela-tionships unavailable to land farmers. The examples that follow—all of them from developing countries—only touch the surface of the many aquacultural options producers are starting to grow into commercially viable ventures. As such, they are harbingers of an animal protein revolution that ethical producers and consumers of animal flesh will have no choice but to explore as population grows, land shrinks, and, one hopes, marine stocks recover.

Although currently a rarity on North American menus, carp are tenacious fish popular in diets throughout the world. Farmers in Asia have long exploited a number of productive connections between traditional agricultural waste and carp aquaculture. An integrated earthen carp pond is a productive receptacle for recycled farm refuse, including grass, cow manure, rice bran, vegetable refuse, pig dung, and even banana peels. Complementing this array of waste is an equally wide array of species. One kind of carp, common carp, consume these inputs and produce feces that stimulate the production of algae, which in turn another breed of carp, usually silver or bighead carp, will eat.

Yet another layer of diversity can be woven into the pond by incorporating crustaceans. Mollusks, for example, feast on the feces of silver and bighead carp and in so doing filter the water while providing food for a carnivorous breed of carp called black carp. A strategic combination of bottom feeding, surface feeding, filtering, and macro-vegetation-eating species thereby heightens the approximation of "natural" systems while reducing the need for environmentally costly external inputs. As Jinyun Ye, a Chinese authority on carp aquaculture, explains, "Major carps are cultured together at a ratio determined by the quantity and quality of the natural food available in the pond."[14]

The Chinese in particular have shown how human-managed multilayered ecosystems can become remarkably sustainable and productive at relatively low cost. They can generate about 1000 pounds of fish per acre annually and demand only minimal inputs. Farmers who can afford to buy feed pellets (processed from agricultural waste and a small amount of fish meal) have seen yields increase tenfold while keeping their operations "semi-intensive" (that is, not exploitative of the environment) rather than stepping over the line to more wasteful "intensive" systems. Of course, the cautious use of processed feed could be said to compromise the habitat's sustainability. However, consider the possible tradeoff and you'll see that the modest environmental cost of increasing fish harvests through feed supplements would be greatly mitigated by a consumer transition from cows to fish. Such a prospect, given Asia's long history of aquaculture, is by no means a long shot. As Ximing Guo, a shellfish geneticist at Rutgers University, explains, "If given a choice, most Chinese people prefer to eat fish."[15]

The ecology of these operations is carefully nurtured. Specialized aquaculture systems in Asia have, according to Andrea Katz, "made progress toward meeting the growing demand for protein derived from sources which will not exacerbate soil erosion." This emphasis on land conservation can be seen in the way fish farmers often integrate fish into surrounding stands of mulberry and bamboo plants, which, among other benefits, secure the soil along pond banks.[16]

With mulberry trees, farmers have been able to use leaves to fuel the rapid growth of silkworms (sericulture). Silkworm excretion and detritus provide both feed to the fish and fertilizer for fish food. Fish also feed on silkworm pupae. It takes roughly 8 kilograms of silkworm waste and 2 kilograms of pupae to produce 2 kilograms of fish—an impressive feed conversion ratio typical of a well-ordered fish farm. Pond wastewater feeds nutrients to the trees, whose root systems filter the water of impurities before ushering it back into the pond. The fortunate farmer even gets a little silk out of the deal. A similar flow of nutrients drives a bamboo-fish operation, with pond mud fertilizing a bamboo plot and bamboo by-products feeding and fertilizing the fish farm. Again the conversion rates are noteworthy. A single hectare of bamboo waste can produce 500 kilograms of fish. Mature bamboo can be used for a wide range of purposes, including firewood, fencing, and poling for plants. Waste is there, but it's minimal.[17]

Asian systems also effectively capitalize on rice-fish relationships to produce commercial-grade Nile tilapia and ample quantities of common carp. A standard arrangement places fish ponds on opposite ends of a rice field, connecting the ponds with shallow canals that fish use to swim among the rice paddies when they're submerged. Water comes from irrigation, springs, or groundwater and fish are held in the system with bamboo screens. Fish that float through rice fields serve several critical functions, including weed and insect control, fertilization, and maintenance of pond pH balance. Many farmers supplement the system with taro root, beans, and eggplant sowed on the banks of the refuge ponds. Others add azolla, a kind of aquatic fern, to promote atmospheric nitrogen fixation, thus reducing the need to dump in external fertilizer. In many rice-fish arrangements, no added feed is necessary beyond a few handfuls of kitchen scraps. When it's time to harvest rice, farmers slowly drain the field, allowing fish to retreat to their refuge ponds. Nutrient-rich fishpond water has led to 15 to 50 percent increases in rice yields while producing fish and other vegetable crops that can be taken to market.[18]

A fascinating study undertaken by three scientists for the FAO explored the impact of polyculture on the life of a single fish farmer living in the Philippines. The sixty-six-year-old farmer confirmed that achieving sustainable systems takes time, skill, and insight. Among the many things he had learned were that incorporating carp into his rice crop doubled his rice yield, controlled for insect pests, and even minimized unwanted weeds, because, as he came to realize, carp burrowed into the pond bottom and dredged up weeds. Over the years he worked to maximize his resources in ways that only the most careful observation allowed. He lined his agricultural plots with burned rice straw, introduced golden snail eggs as feed for carp after noticing that carp ate eggs that fell in by accident, periodically introduced ducks to eat the snails if they proliferated, submerged crops for three hours to end insect infestations, controlled for other pests with gliricidia trees, and fed fish rice flowers to counteract the often sharp flavor imparted to tilapia by pig manure. The operation never required intensive inputs but nonetheless remained "a source of continuous income" for this innovative farmer.[19]

Small-scale or semi-intensive fish farmers working in India have made similarly noteworthy strides toward tapping the wide variety and productive potential of inland aquaculture. Favoring mainly carp, Indian aquaculture relies more heavily on chicken manure than cow or pig manure as a cheap and readily available organic fertilizer. Chicken manure produces more phytoplankton and thus creates a more nutritionally rich ecosystem. Higher levels of phytoplankton help ensure that ammonia levels do not reach dangerous percentages, because phytoplankton feed on ammonia to acquire the nitrogen they need to grow. Supplementary feed is required to increase yields, and Indian fish farmers have pioneered a "bag feeding method" whereby they submerge sacks of de-oiled rice bran, cottonseed cake, and groundnut cake into their ponds. Ever conscious of "feed conversion ratios," other farmers argue that the bag systems lead to too much nutrient loss and prefer instead to broadcast a light film of floating feed pellets. However it's distributed, feed comes from local and recycled material.[20]

Indian fish farming tends heavily toward the use of multiple species of fish at once. High levels of phytoplankton demand that farmers stock a single pond with as many as six carp varieties in order to ensure that the oxygen-hogging phytoplankton do not proliferate to the point of suffocating fish. Moreover, while farmers might favor carp, they've been relatively eager to experiment with breeding techniques and new species, including Nile tilapia, silver-striped catfish, and prawns. Plants are also amenable to a variety of uses. Of special interest to Indian fish farmers is azolla. As in Chinese

rice systems, it fixes nitrogen and thus acts as a natural biofertil-
izer capable of releasing nutrients at a rate that's ideal for slow and
steady algal growth rather than intensified blooms.[21]

Indian fish farmers have successfully innovated with integrated
fish-horticulture systems as well. The gist of this approach is to
exploit pond embankments, which are usually left uncultivated, as
grounds to grow fruits and vegetables. The rewards to come from
this kind of aquaculture are many. Nutrient-rich pond mud serves
as fertilizer for the crops, manured pond water flows through and
feeds crops, and residue from the fruits and vegetables provides
additional food for fish. Throughout the process, the pond's architecture is improved, because (as with mulberry and bamboo in
Asian systems) embankments, which are always susceptible to erosion, are made stronger by deep plant root systems. Through this
method, fish farmers throughout India have grown everything from
papaya, bananas, and coconuts to radishes, cucumbers, and okra,
all the while harvesting high yields of carp and tilapia.[22]

Polyculture has found an especially productive niche in Nepal.
Nepal contains a great of deal of land that cannot be cultivated
because of its steep terrain. As a result of the country's geography,
farmers have embraced aquaculture as the "most promising means of
intensifying the utilization of available cultivation areas and improving conditions in rural areas." Most operations are currently designed
to raise grass carp. As a testament to the adaptability of aquaculture
to local conditions and tastes, fish farmers in Nepal have learned how
to use the dung of the locally preferred source of meat—duck—to fertilize fish ponds. When this fertilizer source is not readily available,
farmers resort to Napier grass as the exclusive nutrient input in polyculture systems. Grass carp have taken to the fast-growing tropical
grass and on this input alone "can produce a reasonable yield."[23]

Innovative farmers are also experimenting with incorporating
Nile tilapia into their ponds. A 2003 report conducted by Sustainable Aquaculture for a Secure Future concluded that "Nile tilapia is

an excellent candidate to be polycultured with grass carp to utilize the natural foods derived from plants fed to grass carp." With the nation's "uncultivated land [as] the only refuge for much of Nepal's wildlife," farm-raised tilapia becomes critical to feeding local residents while preserving the region's biodiversity.[24]

A final example is Bangladesh, where the aquaculture situation reveals both the versatility and the multifaceted potential of polyculture fish farming. Embodying the adage that necessity is the mother of invention, residents of this deeply impoverished country practice what might be called homestead seasonal aquaculture. Basically, any hole in the ground will do. Indeed, residents make temporary fish ponds out of canals, irrigation ditches, and washing and bathing pits. Fertilizer primarily consists of chicken and cow dung; additional feed comes in the form of azolla, grass, sweet potatoes, rice bran, and duckweed. A "season" can be as brief as three months—as long as it takes for fish to reach "table size." Naturally, most of the tilapia and carp harvested through these scaled-down operations are used for subsistence purposes only. However, with farmers able to produce up to 100 kilograms of fish on a 500-square-meter pond in a few months, the potential for expanding into commercial operations remains high. No matter how much fish is produced, though, the broad flexibility of polyculture is on display in these homestead ponds of the developing world.[25]

Aquaculture's False Start?

Between 1970 and 2000, the contribution of aquaculture to the world's supply of fish and shellfish rose from 4 percent to 33 percent. In the 1950s, global production of fish from aquaculture was less than a million tons; today it is over 60 million tons. The vast majority of this burgeoning supply has come from the developing nations described above. Unfortunately, most of this production derives not from small-scale innovative operations but from huge factory fish farms, highly concentrated monocultural operations lacking environmental oversight and caring very little about the long-term sustainability of their production methods.

I'd like to think, in light of the overview above, that the factory farms do not represent the norm of aquacultural production but rather reflect what we might call aquaculture's false start. If this is the case, consumers have a responsibility to stop supporting them by avoiding farm-raised salmon and shrimp or freshwater fish (tilapia and catfish) imported from nations with low environmental standards. This act alone might not undo factory fish farming, but it would be an excellent start.

At the same time, we must not allow the increasingly well-publicized cases of environmental degradation to obscure the long-term potential of the polycultural freshwater systems that have been operating on a small scale across China and India for centuries. Noninvasive and semi-intensive, these systems thrive on being decentralized, highly flexible, relatively nonpolluting, and supportive of innovation based on the accumulation of indigenous knowledge.

While it would be untenable and most likely unsustainable to scale up such operations in order to serve global markets (something the poor water conditions throughout Asia also obviate), these impressive examples of ecological aquaculture provide us with an opportunity to rethink the principles upon which the future of protein will develop in other places. At the least, we should seek information about where our fish comes from and adjust our dietary habits to eat more fish farmed according to the ideals of sustainable polycultural production. Our choices in this vein may be limited now, but in being vigilant and proactive about our fish consumption, we can help these kinds of underappreciated systems find larger markets in the developed world. Fortunately, as the following section will show, this process may already be under way.

A *Five-Gallon Bucket and a Pickup Truck*

Aquaculture experts in the developed world have by no means over-looked the ideals underlying the freshwater polycultural models that prevail in the quiet corners of the developing world. In fact, over the past decade or so, they've started to discuss the future of fish farming explicitly in terms of resource management and ecological impact. In 1996 the World Food Summit agreed "to promote the development of environmentally sound and sustainable aquaculture well integrated into rural, agricultural, and coastal development." The Food and Agriculture Organization encouraged producers, governments, NGOs, and consumers to turn their attention to "significant opportunities for widening development perspectives toward alternative, more sustainable increases in food supplies." The Code of Conduct for Responsible Fisheries, adopted in 1995 by the FAO, is bound to leave any green advocate feeling warm and fuzzy. These are all just words, of course, but they're words that bode well for regulated commercial operations around the globe.[26]

In the United States, the recent history of aquaculture suggests why it makes sense to be optimistic about the international rhetoric on sustainable aquaculture. By no means has U.S. aquaculture as a whole been a model steward of the environment. As we've seen, industrial aquaculture has been a mess, even going so far as to taint the reputation of fish farming as a whole. Nevertheless, several other aquaculture systems began to go commercial in the 1960s, and all things considered, what's developed thus far has avoided the environmental stigma marking shrimp and salmon production.

It perhaps goes without saying that the media generally do not write features about how a particular industry isn't environmentally perfect but, all things considered, is doing pretty well in the green department. As a result, only the most actively engaged consumer of fish has any appreciation for the sustainable options that have evolved over the past thirty years. The reason that this brief history of eco-correct fish farming matters is that—again, unlike cattle—it provides the basis for a future commercial takeoff.[27]

Examples are global, but the United States provides an especially clear picture of the wide range of relatively clean aquaculture systems in operation across the developed world. Of course, the United States is hardly on the verge of a polycultural revolution. However, if its current aquacultural operations have not fully embraced the integrated approach central to polyculture, they do have the potential to do so. The current state of aquaculture, both marine and freshwater, is at least predisposed to making polyculture a standard aspect of commercial fish production. The U.S. National Research Council set the tone for this hopeful orientation in 1998. Promoting an "ecosystem approach" to aquaculture, it elaborated its reasons for doing so: "[This approach] values habitat, embraces a multispecies perspective, and is committed to understanding ecosystem processes."[28]

If, as Barry A. Costa-Pierce writes, "environmental groups have done a service to both society and global aquaculture by pointing out the ecological and social effects of aquaculture," it is up to consumers and producers to bridge rhetoric and reality. Consumers who have the power to switch their protein from farmed salmon, shrimp, and halibut to tilapia, catfish, trout, and shellfish farmed in countries with sound environmental laws must do so in order to become loyal advocates of protein production that's sustainable, polycultural, and supportive of biodiversity.[29]

One can already see etched into the American landscape the outlines of a popular turn toward environmentally sound protein production. William A. Wurts of Kentucky State University points to the emergence of local aquaculture enterprises that begin with "a 5-gallon bucket and a pickup truck." Throughout the eastern half of the state, farmers interested in "diversifying farm enterprises" are doing so with small-scale and sustainable channel catfish farming that integrates aquaculture and agriculture in order to serve local markets. These "low management systems" do not require mechanical aeration, are not energy-intensive, and are amenable to the incorporation of filter fish and freshwater mollusks in order to keep water purified and stocks well-balanced. Lest one think this level of production insignificant, Wurts adds that if 90,000 farmers in Kentucky incorporated a 2-acre fishpond into their existing operations, they would produce as much catfish as the entire southeastern United States did in 1993—over 440 million pounds. Theoretically at least, the industry could thrive as a decentralized, locally oriented endeavor.[30]

Of course, this is not how the industry is currently structured. Instead, it's large, concentrated, and for the most part monocultural. Catfish come from expansive farms in western Kentucky, Louisiana, Mississippi, and Alabama. They live in 10- to 20-acre recirculating ponds that are 3 to 6 feet deep. Big as these farms are, however, their impact on the environment remains moderate. Catfish need minimal added fishmeal (about 2 percent) for their feed, require few drugs, are native to the southeastern United States, and, owing in part to strict state water pollution standards, swim in relatively clean earthen ponds.

Catfish have no need for an effluent discharge pond, enjoy an enviably high feed conversion ratio, and are amenable to biological control methods to manage disease (for example, using black carp to prey on snails that carry dangerous bacteria). The Monterey Bay Aquarium, an advocate for socially responsible fish consumption, ranks catfish as a "best choice" option, while the Blue Ocean Institute, another environmental watchdog group, considers it worthy of a coveted "green fish" label.[31]

All catfish sold in the United States comes from domestic sources, so the consumer does not need to fret about confusing them with potentially unsafe foreign imports. Finally, in terms of land use, all catfish raised in the United States are produced on 174,000 acres of land, a mere speck of the southern landscape. It's for all these reasons that Craig Tucker, the director of the National Warmwater Aquaculture Center, has deemed catfish farming "one of the most environmentally friendly forms of aquaculture there is."[32]

What the American South is doing with catfish, the Gulf Coast and eastern seaboard are beginning to do with oysters and mussels. The benefits of shellfish aquaculture are only now coming to be appreciated, but what we're learning is that farmed shellfish may be one of the most environmentally pristine foods we can slurp down. Almost 95 percent of oysters and mussels are farmed, and there's no need whatsoever for fertilizer, added feed, insecticides, or antibiotics. It's a largely self-supporting system that's open to a range of polycultural combinations. Oysters are especially ameliorative because they serve as filters able to "scrub" impressive amounts of nitrogen and other sediments from polluted ocean water. A single oyster filters 15 gallons of water a day, and an entire bed of them—as scientists have learned from an operation they studied off the coast of Rhode Island—can filter up to 100 million gallons of ocean water daily.[33]

Shellfish farms tend to improve species biodiversity by supporting the growth of eelgrass, juvenile fish, and a wide variety of crabs. As with catfish, production is accomplished in relatively little space. An oyster farmer on the West Coast of the United States cannot help but brag, "We produce ten times as much protein per acre in water [as] we can on land." This is accomplished because a single acre of the ocean floor accommodates up to 500,000 oysters, which is how oysters typically congregate. A final bonus that comes from shellfish aquaculture is the potential of shellfish to sequester carbon in their shells and as a result lower the emission of global warming gases. The continued growth of this industry must be supported by government incentives and consumer demand alike.[34]

Rainbow trout production has become admirably sustainable as well, a couple of caveats notwithstanding. Idaho produces the vast majority of farm-raised trout in the United States. Like shellfish and catfish, trout can be produced abundantly in especially dense concentrations without causing environmental degradation. A single gallon of water yields 10 to 15 pounds of fish. Most trout are grown in the watershed of the Middle Snake River using freshwater flow-through systems called raceways. The fish are omnivorous and demand feed (usually made with anchovies and menhaden) that contains about 20 percent fish meal and oil—and this, of course, is trout's big drawback. The encouraging news on this score, however, is that farmers are gradually lessening the meal/oil content (it's dropped 50 percent since the 1980s) and scientists are currently experimenting with feed that's entirely plant-based. Improved feed, moreover, has enhanced the already exceptional feed conversion rates of trout—an important factor, given that the feed is partially fish-based.[35]

Further mitigating the negative impact of carnivorous feed is the fact that trout wastewater discharge (minor compared to that of farmed salmon) is strictly and heavily regulated according to standards set by the EPA; many facilities are tested weekly. It is indeed true that some trout farmers will spike water with doses of testosterone in order to alter the sex of male fish, which don't fatten as well as females, but this disturbing practice is not environmentally threatening enough to counter the high ranking of trout farming by both Blue Ocean and Monterey. The advantages that these organizations cite to justify their advocacy of trout include the preservation of freshwater systems (water is never depleted), the lack of harm to biodiversity caused by trout farming, the fact that trout are native to the region, and the extremely low input of drugs needed to control for disease.[36]

To this growing select list of fish farmed sustainably in the United States we can add tilapia. Most of the world's tilapia is produced in or around Asia. As we've seen, a considerable portion of this production is undertaken in small facilities practicing polycultural methods. However, tilapia that's exported from China comes from unregulated and unremorseful factory farms that cannot be trusted. U.S. farm-raised tilapia, however, is another story. Tilapia feed in the United States is virtually all plant-based, and these fish, like rainbow trout, enjoy a relatively high conversion rate of feed into body weight. Tilapia also earn high marks for being grown with minimal drugs in closed recirculating systems (rather than in pond cages), an arrangement that also helps reduce chances that the fish, which are nonnative and potentially invasive, will escape into the wild.[37]

Tilapia farms emit relatively small amounts of effluent, and if they fail to maintain those emissions, farmers run afoul of strict EPA regulations, which are enforced by permits required from a National Pollution Discharge Elimination System. Another advantage enjoyed by tilapia farming is its openness to polyculture; fish farmers have made great progress combining tilapia with catfish, shrimp, or aquatic plants reminiscent of the smallholder operations in China and India. Finally, tilapia farms do not cut into mangrove forests or disrupt the natural flow of nutrients in precious wetlands. Instead, they occupy land that once served the purpose of conventional agriculture, including, appropriately enough, ranching.[38]

As this brief overview suggests, there are genuine reasons to be optimistic about the future of protein in the developed world. Of course, no system is perfect. A pessimist could easily highlight the pitfalls of environmentally aware aquaculture—the use of external feed, the modest chemical input, the importation of nonnative species, the moderate waste—and then dismiss the entire project as an inadequate source for global protein. This would be a grave mistake. What stands out much more clearly in aquaculture systems that are well regulated and attuned to ecological principles is how—again, with the proper incentives—the industry could move much more aggressively into polycultural production.

One of the more regrettable aspects of aquaculture research in the United States and other advanced countries is the way in which government and industry have focused almost all their efforts (and money) on finding ways to expand salmon and shrimp aquaculture. Indeed, the Bush administration in 2005 pushed a plan to make 3.4 million square miles of coastal waters available to aquacultural production. The proposal was clearly a boon for salmon and shrimp farming but potentially devastating to the environment, leading one biologist to remark that it would be like "putting industrial hog farms in national parks."[39]

Supporters of expanded shrimp and salmon systems justify their argument based on the depletion of wild species and thus make their case appear to be an environmental one. The only thing that can prevent this kind of deception is an informed public. It is thus especially critical that consumers be wary of forming blanket opinions on "aquaculture" and instead remain attuned to the underlying variety of this potentially clean way of growing protein. Perhaps the most encouraging counterexample to salmon and shrimp farming that we should demand from our noble fishmongers is one that moves sustainable aquaculture in an even cleaner direction: aquaponics.

Fish Without Ponds + Vegetables Without Soil = the Future

In the early 1980s, a graduate student and his mentor at North Carolina State University undertook an experiment. They built a tilapia fish tank below the floor of a greenhouse that was actively growing tomatoes, lettuces, and herbs. The system was closed and all the water recirculated, with fish waste slowly irrigating vegetables that were grown in "sand-cultured hydroponic vegetable beds." The plant root systems in sand beds filtered the incoming water, leeched out nutrients, and sent the water back to the fish below. The only addition to the system was protein-enriched vegetable plant feed given to the fish. No drugs or pesticides were applied. It was in many respects much like the small operations that prevailed throughout Asia, but in this case no soil was involved in the process. Plants do not need soil; they just need nutrients. If this experiment caught on, the scientists realized, they might be able to solve aquaculture's biggest problem: how to systematically recycle the waste.[40]

What happened in North Carolina raised eyebrows. Compared to pond aquaculture, fish production increased, operating costs dropped, and, perhaps most notably, evaporation was minimal. In fact, the researchers' water consumption ended up being 1 *percent* of that needed to produce the same tilapia yields in traditional pond culture. What these men had stumbled upon was an aqueous example of radical polyculture. It was clean. It was conservative. It was productive. Perhaps it could reshape the future of food. In any case, aquaponics—the growing of plants and animals in a recirculating environment—was now on the still obscure map of possibilities for the sustainable production of both vegetables and fish in the same man-made habitat.[41]

This work did not go unnoticed. In the early 1990s, two fish farmers in West Plains, Missouri, Tom and Paula Speraneo, decided to try their hand at aquaponics after learning about the successful experiment at NC State. They stocked a 500-gallon tank with tilapia and channeled fish waste to hydroponic vegetable beds cultured in a layer of gravel. Then they placed the entire operation inside a greenhouse run exclusively on solar energy, added Purina fish chow, tested constantly for pH balance, and waited for results. The operation proved to be, according to one agricultural specialist, "practical, productive, and wildly successful." Indeed, the couple quickly expanded the operation to include six 1200-gallon tanks, called "nodes," that covered less than a tenth of an acre.

Fish yields swelled—tilapia are hardy fish—but what really surprised the Speraneos was the explosion of vegetables that emerged from so little space. The couple grew tomatoes, salad greens, bedding plants, basil, and cucumbers, generating 45 to 70 pounds of vegetables for every pound of fish grown. News of the Speraneos' success sent thousands of interested growers flocking to S & S Aqua

Farms, and the couple, responding to overwhelming demand, ended up writing an aquaculture design manual (price: $250) that is now used by fish farmers worldwide.[42]

The rise of aquaculture, if only as a subculture of food production, was unofficially under way. The next link in the aquaponics chain was a professor of plant biology at the University of the Virgin Islands named James Rakocy. Over the past eight years, Rakocy has become a living legend in the aquaponics world. In the late 1990s he and a team of researchers designed a commercial-scale aquaponics system by taking the Speraneo model to another level. It has since become a model of aquaponics production. Using four 7800-liter tanks, Rakocy stocked them densely, with 77 Nile tilapia per cubic meter and 154 red tilapia per cubic meter, and churns out fish flesh. Because production is staggered, a harvest takes place roughly every six weeks.

Rakocy and his colleagues began their experiments using basil and okra as the cultivated vegetables. The outcome was again almost an embarrassment of riches: 4.16 metric tons of Nile tilapia, 4.78 metric tons of red tilapia, basil yields triple those of field-grown basil, and okra yields eighteen times greater than those grown in soil. The system generated $134,245 in revenue. This output was impressive in itself, but was even more so given that it was accomplished on about one twentieth of an acre of space with no external inputs except floating fish pellets, occasional doses of iron, and the gentle application of calcium hydroxide and potassium hydroxide to keep pH levels balanced. Rakocy now runs an annual summer institute in St. Croix for aspiring aquaculturalists, publishes widely on the topic, and travels regularly to Southeast Asia to study the methods of the small-scale fish farmers who pioneered the principles of aquaponics three thousand years ago.[43]

Today commercial aquaponics, which is less than twenty-five years old, remains relatively obscure. Nevertheless, it has become an agricultural endeavor supported by a growing network of entrepreneurs, nonprofit institutions, and university programs. In the United States, the Freshwater Institute in Shepherdstown, West Virginia, has become a crucible of aquaponics information. The institute, which is run by the Conservation Fund, focuses especially on bringing cold-water recirculating systems to the impoverished residents of Appalachia. Operations designed by the institute have tended to grow Arctic char and trout mixed in with cooking herbs, lettuce, and plants endemic to wetlands. Employees run an "aquaponics demonstration program based on a Speraneo-style gravel-cultured system" and offer technical assistance and a range of educational materials to local fish farmers.[44]

Joining the Freshwater Institute in pioneering efforts to promote aquaponics is Cabbage Hill Farm, a nonprofit farm located in Mount Kisco, New York, just outside New York City. The organization is dedicated to promoting small-scale and sustainable systems of food production, and its members are strong advocates of aquaponics as part of a larger program of local and responsible food production. Because the principles of aquaponics can be taught through inexpensive aquaponics units, many agri-science programs at land-grant colleges offer courses in aquaponics. In light of this exposure, anyone interested in learning how to grow fish and vegetables in the same circulating medium needs only access to an Internet search engine to get started.[45]

IF AQUACULTURE IS in its infancy, aquaponics is newborn. Thus far operations have distinguished themselves by being relatively small, capable of integration into diverse farms, amenable to arid regions and areas without much access to fresh water, and, at least the way they're now evolving, prone to a modest independent business structure rather than a grand corporate arrangement. It takes about $18,000 to purchase a startup kit for a commercially viable aquaponics operation; costs of production do not include a steady stream of drugs and fertilizer, and the land and labor requirements are

minimal. These qualities place the emerging aquaculture industry in sharp contrast to the multinational conglomerates producing farmed salmon and shrimp destined for global markets. These
qualities also make aquaponics attractive to entrepreneurs with an
interest in fish, vegetables, local markets, sustainability, and profits.
Given the ecological and economic viability of aquaponics, food
would be significantly more just if this unique form of aquaculture
became the future of floating protein.

6

Merging Ecology and Economy: Perverse Subsidies, Rational Incentives, and the Path to Fair Trade

As long as the commodity title remains untouched, the way we eat will remain unchanged. —MICHAEL POLLAN

As I hope is clear by now, scaling down food production and eating local fare is not in and of itself going to feed the impending 10 billion in a sustainable way. Thus, in the quest for a model of global food production that feeds the masses in an environmentally sane manner, I've proposed the alternative of an agricultural golden mean. Of course, the idea of a golden mean is hardly mine—truth be told, it's Aristotle's—but I believe in the notion that a rational and achievable middle ground exists between the extremes of abundance and deficiency. Although Aristotle never got around to applying the idea of the golden mean to food, the concept seems like an appropriate one to help make sense of that underappreciated, ubiquitous, and certainly unvirtuous environmental minefield known as perverse subsidies.

Now, I'll admit that when I read the word "subsidies," my first reaction is to take a nap. But don't start snoozing yet. It's important for food activists to understand subsidies, because they're the hidden cause of many of the problems we currently face. If the answer to our food problems lies somewhere between industrial-scale production and the small-scale local farms locavores insist we support—as the golden mean suggests—then it's essential that we completely restructure the price supports, tariffs, tax breaks, and other economic incentives that currently dictate the global production of food. It's the only way we can realistically envision a global system of supplying food that honors sustainability while fostering clean air, soil, and water.

A Perverse Problem

A subsidy is any form of governmental financial assistance dedicated to an endeavor that would probably not be able to succeed without that assistance. Subsidies can be direct or indirect, centered on production or on consumption, or designed to promote imports or exports. Environmentally speaking, they can serve innumerable beneficial purposes. The government, for example, can offer tax incentives to reduce harmful greenhouse gas emissions. Perverse subsidies, however, are government-led economic incentives to promote forms of production that are environmentally wasteful. They've been said to "wreak havoc on the environment all over the world."[1]

To understand exactly how perverse subsidies undermine the quest for a sustainable global food system, we must first take stock of where we've been. Thus far, my proposal for achieving the golden mean of global food production has been based on five fundamental changes in the way we think about and consume food. To recap:

First, we must stop fetishizing food miles. The distance food travels certainly matters, but it is a relatively minor factor in the overall quest for ethical and sustainable food. Instead, consumers must pay attention to the wide variety of energy inputs present at every major stage in a product's route from farm to fork. Of course, with little hard data, our power as everyday consumers is limited when it comes to making life-cycle assessment calculations. That said, we should demand that consumer advocacy groups stop peppering us with a spectrum of environmental labels and work to create a universal efficiency scale that labels our food according to its overall energy efficiency.

Second, we must dissolve the dichotomy that now exists between organic and conventional products. It's not that we should reject organic foods. But we cannot accurately understand agricultural methods and their environmental impacts until we see them along a continuum rather than segregated into two poorly defined categories. To think that going organic is the answer to our agricultural ills, or that "conventional" agriculture is the sole cause of those ills, is to overlook the deeper complexity of food production.

Third, despite the well-coordinated campaign against agricultural biotechnology, we must remain open to the proven potential of genetically modified crops to achieve sustainable goals such as boosting levels of production on less land. GM crops do not have to be limited to corn and soy. Instead, with the right incentives, a range of crops can foster biodiversity by preserving wetlands and rainforests from exploitation.

Fourth, to ensure that the earth does not fall prey to the environmental degradation caused by cattle, we must radically scale down our consumption of meat derived from land-based animals. Meat from animals that are fed grain—that is, GM corn and soy—should be banned from the diet of every legitimate environmentalist, while the more environmentally sound alternatives, such as grass-fed beef and truly free-range organic chicken, must be eaten in the strictest moderation.

Fifth, we should make farm-raised fish (mostly fresh-water and domestic) our main source of animal protein. Ocean biodiversity is in tragic decline, and aquaculture offers something of a solution. "Aquaculture," however, is an umbrella term covering a wide variety of production methods and philosophies. We should forgo any fish farmed in nations with lax environmental standards (such as China), all farmed salmon and shrimp, and any fish deemed "Avoid" by groups such as the Monterey Bay Aquarium and the Blue Ocean Institute. Environmentally sound alternatives include farmed shellfish and farm-raised tilapia, rainbow trout, catfish, and carp from countries with acceptable regulations.

Now back to those perverse subsidies. Perhaps the most frustrating aspect of the broad program I have outlined is that the structure of our current food system will not allow us to act on these five recommendations to the extent we'd like to. The way the world produces food has developed and solidified around decades of artificial incentives. These distorting global inducements to overproduce and ignore pollution might have made sense when they were initiated in the 1930s, in response to a severe economic crisis, but they are now a primary reason that we lack the necessary information to make ethical culinary choices. Subsidies, in short, leave the environmentalist in the dark.

Indeed, perverse subsidies have an underappreciated impact on the information made available to environmentally concerned consumers. The impact involves two related developments. First, when polluting forms of production are financially supported—that is, when the environmental costs are subsidized rather than kept aboveboard—the problem itself is effectively hidden from view. For example, if a coal company is allowed to dump ash waste in the local river without cost, rather than paying to dispose of that waste safely or figure out how to reduce it, then (barring a high-profile media exposé) the average concerned consumer will probably never recognize the problem. (Labor or energy costs, by contrast, are something most consumers know something about, because they are the variable costs of doing business. If these costs were totally subsidized, though, they'd be largely removed from public discussion.) Thus, the coal company can duplicitously praise "free-market principles" when in fact it is buttressed by government support that erases the environmental cost. Furthermore, if the environmental cost is erased and so made a less likely factor of public outrage, then there's simply no perceived need for so much of the new information that the environmentalist requires in order to eat a truly ethical diet.

A brief consideration of the information we lack is sobering. We have no systematic access to LCA measurements; we can't discern what food comes from tilled land versus low- or no-till land; we have no idea what kind or how much of a certain dangerous chemical an organic or a conventional farm uses; we don't know which food came from diverse farms that produce high yields on less land; we don't know which products were grown with fertilizer that enhances uptake and which ones were larded with the cheap stuff; we don't know to what extent pesticides were decreased on a farm when GM crops were employed; we don't know what "free range" means for a particular product; we don't know the feed conversion rates of the grass-fed cows from which our beef came; we don't know if farmed fish came from a polycultural tank or a monocultural cage. And so on. In so many ways we're staring into a black hole, perceiving almost nothing about the precise methods and underlying ecologies of growing and processing the food we see in the market, be it a farmer's roadside stall or an endless Wal-Mart aisle.

This failure to acquire the requisite information leaves our reformist ideas as just that: ideas. But if we truly hope to consume food in a way that transforms ideals into reality, we must initiate programs that compile and disseminate this admittedly far-flung information. Needless to say, it will never be possible to obtain perfect data about the inner workings and ultimate efficiencies of something as vastly complex as a global food system. That said, the history of food labeling in developed countries offers real hope that with enough consumer agitation, those who produce and sell food will one day be required to label their products with a universally applied, internationally sanctioned Global Green rating that incorporates as many measures of efficiency (including transportation) as is reasonably possible. If we can list every ingredient on a can of soup, along with a wealth of nutritional data, we can certainly contemplate a reliable label that provides a basic environmental assessment of food.

Of course, there's political reality. The internecine battles over such a system would surely be legion, the regulatory apparatus immensely baroque, and I imagine the introduction of these proposals into international politics would be like sending raw meat into a grinder. But no matter how many well-heeled lobbyists block the door of reform, one thing is beyond dispute: we'll have a difficult time making our food system more transparent, accessible, and environmentally responsible if we fail to dismantle the subsidies that our government and governments throughout the world currently impose in order to foster a myopic notion of economic growth. It's this notion, after all, that keeps activist consumers less informed than they should be, mollified with the balm of cheap food, and literally forced to participate in a food system that's inherently corrupt and degrading to the natural world.

Hence the problem: perverse subsidies actively and aggressively work against every proposal offered in this book, and for that matter against every food reform idea of environmental worth. Of course, informed consumer activism will always be critical to the larger quest of producing food responsibly. As the food activist Mark

Winne writes, "Not a single social or economic gain has been made in the past fifty years without the instigation and participation of an active and vociferous body of citizens." But with global food production currently shaped by powerful government incentives designed to lay waste to the environment and hide the costs, informed and activist-minded consumers find their good intentions that much harder to achieve.[2]

To shed some light on perverse subsidies, this chapter will demonstrate the environmental damages they cause, suggest practical methods of dismantling these supports, and discuss how rational incentives might replace them. I know it's an ambitious goal, but until we make progress toward it, our current actions will continue to be mere gestures.

Subsidized Insanity

Estimates vary, but two leading authorities on perverse subsidies, Norman Myers and Jennifer Kent, conservatively peg the annual cost of global subsidies at the mind-numbing sum of $1.5 trillion—a level that enables these supports to "inflict grandscale injuries on our environments." The United States is responsible for about a fifth of this figure, with about $315 billion supporting production that systematically pollutes.[3]

In the most basic sense, then, subsidies not only allow but practically beg farmers to use excessive amounts of fertilizer, to spray pesticides and insecticides with abandon, to ruin the topsoil with intense monoculture, to tap out aquifers and build irrigation systems, to send millions of cattle to trample federally owned land, to expand relentlessly into rainforests and wetlands, and to abandon the ameliorative effects of crop diversification.

Adding insult to injury, the widespread environmental damage caused by factory farming—eutrophication, soil depletion, erosion, water contamination—is paid for by you and me. According to Myers and Kent, "A typical American taxpayer forks out at least

$2000 a year to fund perverse subsidies, and then pays another $2000 through increased prices for consumer goods and services or through environmental degradation." This is to say nothing of the uncalculated (and perhaps incalculable) health-care costs related to the unhealthy environment and food that emerge from these supports.[4]

In the United States (which, again, accounts for 21 percent of all subsidies) the injustice of perverse subsidies pervades every sector of the agricultural economy, but it's especially flagrant in the live-stock industry. As we've seen, the American West is being trampled by 20 million beef cattle roaming and degrading 2 million square kilometers of federal land. The 100,000 ranchers who lease these lands pay less than a third of the land's market value. As Myers and Kent explain, "American taxpayers have been subsidizing ranchers to overgraze these rangelands at a charge of just $1.61 a cow, less than it costs to feed a cat." Without the price supports, the market cost for grazing on private land is around $10 a cow.[5]

According to the U.S. Government Accountability Office, the federal government doles out at least $144 million a year in man-agement costs to graze livestock on federal land but collects only $21 million in grazing fees. The difference—$123 million—comes from the fleeced taxpayer, who has not only paid welfare to the west-ern rancher but has inadvertently supported considerable environ-mental degradation in the process. By virtue of being a tax-paying citizen, the U.S. environmentalist is automatically forced to con-done soil erosion, the killing of wild animals that threaten livestock, and damage to riparian zones. That so much of this beef goes to fast-food restaurants only makes the injustice more insulting.[6]

This subsidy-driven distortion reverberates far beyond cattle, coursing throughout the agricultural supply chain. Feeding these cows once they're pulled off the range and shunted into CAFOs is largely made possible by "subsidized cow chow." We're talking primarily about corn, a commodity that, as Michael Pollan has revealed, is coddled in the wealth of external support. In 2005 the federal government subsidized grain to the tune of $20 billion, thereby confirming Pollan's assertion that "the perverse economics of agriculture" had allowed corn to undertake "its final triumph over the land and the food system."[7]

Final triumph might be an overstatement, but there's no doubt that overproduction of corn as a result of perverse subsidies has led to widespread problems with acute environmental consequences. Most notably there's the incorporation of high-fructose corn syrup into most of our processed food and the transformation of corn into ethanol fuel, which is often cynically portrayed as an environmentally efficient alternative to fossil fuel (even though it takes 50 gallons of oil to grow an acre of corn).[8]

Beyond these conspicuous misappropriations of resources are the hidden environmental costs of producing corn for cattle feed. As we've seen, the extensive application of cheap nitrogen fertilizer, pesticides, insecticides, and fumigants, as well as the channeling of agricultural biotechnology into the wasteful venture of corn production, have resulted in extensive environmental damage and threaten to narrow down the foundation of the world's food supply to a few commodities.

Another resource threatened by perverse subsidies is water. Monocultural production gulps water, a lot of water, and the federal government has diligently ensured that the tap of this increasingly precious resource flows hard. Nowhere has this generosity been more evident than with the Central Valley Project in California. This initiative, which irrigates the San Joaquin and Sacramento valleys, is the largest federal water supply program on record in the United States. It began in 1936 with the express intention of transforming the desert into fertile cropland by manhandling the regions' rivers and aquifers.

Decades of adding and stirring in California have cost the American people over $3.6 billion for this one project, only $1 billion of which agribusiness was required to pay back (over the course of fifty years). By 2002 only 11 percent of that $1 billion had been paid off. But the water continues to flow unabated. So for a little over a million bucks, monocultural systems in California have enjoyed unlimited access to water that cost the taxpayers over thirty times more. In some cases (as if it could not get any more ironic), agribusiness has turned around and sold excess water back to the public at inflated prices.[9]

This endless funding of factory farms that produce thirsty monocultural crops in a region that was once a desert has contributed directly to declines in biodiversity (especially migratory birds), polluted over 700 miles of rivers (owing to runoff), burned untold gallons of fossil fuel to produce the requisite fertilizers and pesticides, and further perpetuated bad agricultural habits. The Environmental Working Group calls the project "an audacious attempt to change nature and a clear example of the inevitable environmental degradation." The factory farmers in the valley, unfortunately, call it a living.[10]

One might be tempted to rationalize agricultural crop subsidies as the necessary payoff to keep struggling farmers in business. After all, we can't let down the American yeoman or undermine anything so sacred as the family farm. Such a justification, however emotionally laden, would be misplaced, because the vast majority of agricultural subsidies go to a handful of large corporations. According to Myers and Kent, "Half of the rangelands are utilized by just 2 percent of the permit holders, these grand scale operators who make a fortune from the taxpayer." It's difficult to feel sorry for these recipients.[11]

The Environmental Working Group has shown that with corn subsidies, the top 2 percent of the beneficiaries in recent years received 30 percent of the subsidies, while the top 10 percent got 71 percent. Making this concentration more troublesome are the underlying political interests shaping appropriations in the nooks and crannies of the legislative labyrinth. Forty-two percent of all agricultural subsidies doled out between 2003 and 2005 went to districts with representation in the House Agriculture Committee. A single representative from Nebraska hauled home 5 percent of the pork, a clean $1.7 billion. He was reelected, but the family farm, I'm guessing, wasn't much on his mind.[12]

The environmentally damaging impact of domestic agricultural subsidies is only the most blatant case of a broader problem. To better appreciate the collective consequences of perverse subsidies, one only has to examine the arbitrary support of fisheries offered by governments around the globe. As we've seen, wild fish stocks are in freefall—it's a pressing environmental problem shared by the entire world. One might reasonably anticipate that such a decline would send a clarion call to governments to end, if not reverse, this dangerous race to the bottom.

To the contrary, governments have only intensified their perverse subsidies, underwriting ocean depletions as supplies rapidly dwindle. Rather than create incentives to conserve, governments are encouraging competing fleets to vacuum up what little is left of the oceans' natural stocks. Between 1970 and 1998 subsidies paid for the expansion of global fishing fleets from 585,000 to 3.5 million, in addition to scoop nets capable of holding 400 tons of fish, the most technologically sophisticated radars and sensing devices on earth, and even housing facilities for fishermen and programs that promote export deals for fishing companies. What all this means in the United States is that a fishing venture can spend $124 billion to catch fish over the course of a year, sell that catch for $70 billion, and count on the federal government to pick up the $54 million difference. "It's time," writes one conservation group, "to cut the bait." Unless you're a subsidized fishing operation, it's hard to disagree.[13]

The scope of perverse subsidies extends well beyond fields and oceans and reaches deep into the world's rainforests. In Brazil, subsidized deforestation dates back to the 1970s. The primary motivation to support the destruction of this rare crucible of megabiodiversity was the desire to graze cattle. Economists have long shown that these subsidies allowed ranchers to earn only a quarter of their costs while, as Kent and Myers put it, making "a commercial killing." Ranching subsidies soon led to extensive crop supports throughout Brazil, as others wanted in on the largesse. Farmers in Rondônia got $163 million ($3200 a person) to plant crops that were mostly sold to producers of cattle feed.[14]

The bright side of this sad history is that Brazil has recently come to realize that it makes little sense to hack down its most precious natural and economic resource. Plus the government has seen that it ultimately cannot afford the subsidies. So, quite wisely, it has scaled back subsidies that threaten rainforests. As encouraging as this development may be, subsidized deforestation remains an entrenched economic reality undermining biodiversity across Central and South America, and even in West Africa and Southeast Asia. It's hard to stop the onslaught of cattle, especially with global governments behind them.[15]

A final distortion that this rigged system of subsidized food production perpetuates is negating comparative ecological advantage. An environmentally sound food system is one in which productive endeavors naturally gravitate to geographical locations where the impact on resources is minimized. In other words, producers produce in the right places. It is this very reality, as we have seen, that makes the idea of global locavorism so hard to embrace. Geography is not democratic. Growing water-intensive crops in a desert, grazing cattle in a cleared rainforest, and planting drought-resistant crops in a wetland are examples of environmentally illogical decisions—unless, of course, subsidies render them "logical." And indeed, this is often what happens.

As Paul Roberts explains in *The End of Food*, "institutionalized overproduction" has played a direct role in shaping not only what and how we produce but also "where we make our food, especially our meat." Subsidies have pushed grain prices so artificially low, for example, that ranchers can move their operations away from the regions where feed is produced to regions that offer the best financial incentives to graze. They then "ship the below-cost feed," thereby unnecessarily extending food miles while using subsidized feed to fatten subsidized cows on subsidized lands. This is just one example among many where the environmental logic of natural comparative advantage plays no role in the critical ecological decision about where to situate cattle in the landscape. Subsidies, in other words, literally negate the significance of geography, leaving big producers to set up shop wherever the incentives to do so are the greatest.[16]

Perhaps no one has better captured the multifaceted distortions and disruptions caused by perverse subsidies than Paul Hawken, the author of *The Ecology of Commerce*. He writes: "The government subsidizes energy costs so that farmers can deplete aquifers to grow alfalfa to feed cows that make milk that is stored in warehouses as surplus cheese that does not feed the hungry." As depressing as Hawken's remark might be, there's a hopeful aspect to take away from it. The inherent illogic of the economic arrangement he describes might, once fully exposed, spur average consumers to action. Perverse subsidies are antithetical not only to the responsible production of food but also to the basic principles of a market economy, and so are crying out to become not a cause for a nap but a cause du jour. Surely if we can become worked up about "eat local," "buy organic," and "compost happens," there must be enough fire and brimstone left over for a catchy antisubsidy phrase that at least places the issue on the back of our cars.[17]

Externalities

Once properly exposed, subsidies are—with enough consumer awareness and resistance—bound to shame large producers into righting the rules of the game so as to eliminate the merest whiff of a word that's pretty close to socialism in the public mind-set: welfare.

Organizations such as the Environmental Working Group have already done a remarkably effective job of outing subsidy addicts by compiling and making available comprehensive data on who's getting what from whom, how much, how often, and where it's going. As EWG packages it, information offers empowerment, pure and simple. Unsubsidized neighbors can now check up on their subsidized neighbors. For a cohort of swaggering recipients who traditionally espouse the virtues of rugged individualism and survival of the fittest, the corporations (and farmers) revealed by these embarrassing numbers appear like a bunch of effete fat cats rather than the rock-ribbed capitalists or yeoman farmers they purport to be.[18]

The subsidy data carry even more weight when we consider that several countries have joined Brazil in starting to dismantle their own expensive subsidy programs. New Zealand, for example, has cut all agricultural subsidies, a decision that's resulted in the proliferation of farms growing increasingly diverse products serving global markets. Indonesia, alarmed by the impact that excessive nitrogen runoff was having on its natural resources, slashed fertilizer supports by 90 percent. Bangladesh and the Philippines went further, drawing them down to zero. With India and China now feeling the economic heat of expensive subsidies, they're also making moves to reduce these costly expenditures.[19]

One might hope that the United States and Europe are taking note of these liberalizing trends, or at least that their consumers are. After all, if consumers can force powerful retailers to buy local produce, they can certainly marshal enough outrage to pressure those same retailers into rejecting subsidized food. Of course, no supermarket could fully act on this demand (the shelves would be practically bare), but even a well-placed symbolic gesture against subsidized products would politicize the message that food producers have no natural right to a free lunch, especially not at our expense, nor at that of the environment.

Developing the means to stigmatize subsidy recipients is thus a powerful public relations tactic. This time around, though, we must ensure that the market principles we seek encompass the ecological principles we respect. Such a convergence is accomplished not through cheap corporate greenwashing but rather through real sacrifice—a word to which we in the environmentalist movement should probably pay more heed. Requiring food producers to swallow the full cost of production, *environmental costs included*, is essential to achieving genuine reform. To express this idea in the language of an economist, producers must be expected to internalize externalities, an externality being a cost otherwise shared by all (such as polluted water near a cattle ranch), and the internalizing process being a way of saying to the polluter, "You pay for it."

Paul Hawken explains, "We cannot return to the era of local markets, but we can regain control of the larger markets by enforcing the payment of costs—total costs." The goal here is not to beat corporations into humble submission. Instead, it's to encourage them through financial incentives to produce in ways that restore rather than destroy natural resources. Entrepreneurial innovation in the interests of preserving the environment is best achieved through some variation of a Pigouvian tax—that is, a tax that corrects for the negative side-effects of a market activity. Call it economic tough love.[20]

Removing agricultural subsidies might seem far from the average environmentalist's list of concerns. But the stakes are simply too high to overlook this issue. As Michael Pollan has made clear, "as long as the commodity title [billions of dollars in agricultural subsidies] remains untouched, the way we eat will remain unchanged." As we've seen, when the cost of harming the environment is not borne by those doing the harm, and when this process is underwritten by subsidies, what results is a powerful connection between food production and environmental degradation. The entire arrangement is structured by conscious design and rooted in over eighty years of practice. If an agribusiness operation can ruin topsoil, pollute rivers, and churn greenhouse gases into the atmosphere while generating profit, it will. After all, profit is exactly what a corporation is designed to achieve. And if environmental costs can be written off, rest assured, they will be.[21]

But if food producers were required to pay for the negative environmental effects they create, and if this were accompanied by the elimination of perverse subsidies, the landscape of food production would be transformed. Under their own economic logic, corporations would have to adapt and innovate to produce goods in a way that minimizes or reverses damage to the environment. The possibilities to grow green, live green, and eat green would expand exponentially. Farmers are ingenious people when it comes to adaptation, and there's no telling what they'd pioneer once the field of competition was leveled.

In such a context, food producers would treat the health of the environment like a savings account rather than a holiday bonus. And this more conservative ecological view would materialize not because of any sudden awakening to the noble virtues of environmentalism, but rather because of the old-fashioned logic of economic incentive and self-interest. As Paul Hawken writes, "Businesses must—*must*—be able to make money sustaining living systems, or global restoration will never happen."[22]

The decisions to create transparency, internalize environmental costs, and undermine perverse subsidies would together reverse the effect whereby producers who have no immediate stake in the survival of a resource plunder it to their own advantage, sometimes called "the tragedy of the commons." In turn, it would replace the tragedy of the commons with the triumph of collective environmental stewardship. This ideal, anyway, is what we must demand of those who produce our food, even as we strive to eat less meat, buy more of the right kind of fish, eat more vegetables and fruit, and work to learn about farms with healthy LCAs.

With these changes, our "foodsheds"—the local areas where food is grown, processed, and marketed—would not only broaden geographically but make room for average consumers, as opposed to being sanctuaries for the rare and privileged. Hawken calls this arrangement the basis of a "restorative economy," and it's one that "tries to achieve a market in which every transaction provides constructive feedback into the commons." Self-interest is preserved, but it's placed in a long-term perspective, one in which healthy air, soil, and water—everyone's life support—are essential components of self-interest.[23]

If the future I envision sounds far-fetched, do note that momentum is on the side of reform. Many companies have been chomping at the bit as economists and environmentalists knock around these themes. A substantial portion of them, in fact, have decided not to wait for the transformation to take place but to stick out their necks and lead by example. These "pioneer restorative companies" have already done the right thing by voluntarily eschewing subsidies and paying their own environmental costs (or avoiding them altogether) in the spirit of a green ethos.

The foodie press has lionized these ventures, as have locavores. Their underlying assumption has been that the beauty of these renegade operations—say, Polyface Farms, mentioned in Pollan's *The Omnivore's Dilemma*—is in their unique emphasis on localism. However, what also distinguishes them is that they are making sacrifices in order to unilaterally eliminate passive subsidies. The primary reason ecological farming is so costly and risky is that it competes with agribusiness, which benefits from welfare. So the removal of that welfare should turn the eco-alternatives into the future norm. It would be a norm, moreover, that would have no problem producing Berkeley microgreens for the midwestern masses. Yes, the allure of the "alternative" would disappear—but isn't that what we want?

Let me elaborate on this social aspect of the larger argument. Common examples of pioneer operations often involve meat. Although I have spent much of this book questioning the long-term sustainability of any sort of meat production, the fact remains that the polycultural production of beef, chicken, and pork represents a far more responsible use of resources than conventional methods do. These smaller producers pass some of their higher costs on to consumers willing to spend more money on meat produced in an environmentally friendly fashion. What inevitably results is a food distribution system predicated on privilege. Microgreens at Chez Panisse become expensive cultural capital rather than a healthy item that the average person might pick up in the yuppie-chow aisle at Wal-Mart.

However, if "big ag" had the big subsidy rug pulled out from under it, and if it were required to pay for the environmental costs of production, its economic advantage would quickly diminish. Indeed, it would yield to microgreen producers, who could now eye bigger markets of nonelite consumers. Without the required support of the culinary privileged to stay afloat, the microgreens grower could finally look beyond Berkeley.

It's exciting to imagine the ways in which agricultural production would adjust to the demise of conventional agribusiness. Although it's obviously hard to predict, perhaps the most conspicuous change would be a sharp trend toward more and more midsized and large sustainable farms located in regions of natural comparative advantage. These farms would practice more responsible agricultural habits while serving markets larger than small farms reach. It's these very operations, after all, that were pushed out when subsidies began to intensify after the 1930s. With the playing field thus leveled and the price supports withdrawn, farmers would move away from monocultural production toward a more plant-based system of diversified agriculture, because the market would push them in that direction.

It's fun to fantasize about such an agrarian shift, but I'm aware that between fantasy and reality there's the brick wall of politics. The specific externalities that governments could tax in order to foster this broad transition are open to endless debate. Most advocates of a Pigouvian taxation scheme, however, would probably agree that the environmental impacts of the following things should be internalized by agribusiness producers: nitrogen runoff, pesticide usage, water application, greenhouse gas output, damage to surrounding biodiversity (such as wetlands or rainforests), and effluent emissions from animal farms. More controversially, one could also push for a transport tax for goods shipped on airplanes that are carrying food alone, a tax on soil erosion, and a tax on the energy used to process food from one form into another—that is, a tax on the supply chain.

Of course agribusiness will violently oppose all these proposals on the grounds that they represent an intrusion by big government into the affairs of business. Instead of caving in to this deceptive argument, however, environmentalists must be prepared to turn the tables and remind agribusiness that it's inherently uncapitalistic to ignore the true cost of producing something and ask the government to pick up the tab with taxpayer dollars. It would also be a good idea to have those embarrassing EWG figures on hand, just to add some polish to our point.

As eloquent as the arguments may be, they may still not be enough to sway special-interest groups. At the least, powerful lobbies will work to ensure that any imposed taxes are low enough for producers to pass costs on to consumers rather than to switch gears and innovate along green lines. In response to this pressure, governments must be prepared to add to Pigouvian taxes a set of agricultural incentives geared toward promoting environmental sustainability. With subsidies eliminated (or at least contained), the prospects for such support would be economically feasible.

As Myers and Kent explain, "There would be a huge stock of funds available to give a new push to sustainable development—funds on a scale that would be unlikely to become available through any other source." Granted, this is not very free-market-sounding. Yes, it actually sounds like a subsidy. But a temporary incentive is different from a permanent boost. And indeed temporary subsidies for farmers converting operations to become more sustainable are a form of governmental assistance that in no way compares to the systematic welfare of perverse subsidies.[24]

Once again the list of options is open to debate, but here are a few rational subsidy suggestions that developed governments might spend their saved revenue to support: increased yields on less land with fewer inputs (an indirect subsidy for GM crops); increased diversification of crops; aquaculture (especially aquaponics); techniques that preserve topsoil (seed drilling); fertilizer schemes that maximize nitrogen uptake; wind and solar energy to power processing at any stage of production; train and ship transportation (which is much more efficient than air freight); and general agricultural research into sustainable farming (for example, rewarding ag schools that pursue genuinely sustainable schemes).

Throughout American history not a single industrial or agricultural endeavor has taken off without sustained government support at its start. It cannot, and should not, be any different with high-yielding sustainable agriculture. As the famous agricultural ecologist Gordon Conway explains, "Agricultural innovation...cannot be left simply to market forces." Although he was speaking about developing countries, the point holds true for developed countries that have chosen to restructure their agricultural systems to achieve a noble goal.[25]

Recall the proposals summarized early in this chapter: producing less meat, fostering clean aquaculture, placing food miles in perspective, cautiously accepting GM technology, and thinking beyond the organic/conventional dichotomy. Now think about these things in the context of an agricultural landscape unburdened by perverse subsidies, structured with taxes on externalities, and encouraged by beneficial economic incentives. They suddenly seem much more realistic. The obstacles to obtaining accurate information would slowly fall, the artificial engine of monoculture would be shut down, and the following prediction by Gordon Conway would be that much closer to realization: "Properly designed, suitable approaches to food production and to forestry and fishery management can reverse land degradation, reduce pollution from agrochemicals, remove pressure on national parks and reserves, conserve biodiversity and, at the same time, increase food security."[26]

The Environmental Justice of Trade

The developed world must lead these efforts. To do so, it is critical that we do not retreat into narrow localities and focus exclusively on the sustainability of our tiny foodsheds. One of the more myopic tendencies of the locavore movement is the failure to juxtapose the food situation at home with that in developing countries. There are plenty of bitter condemnations of the importation of "modern" agriculture into indigenous systems—this is a common critique delivered by NGOs. And there are many quite legitimate screeds against bioprospecting by wealthy nations. As we've seen, this antiglobalization rhetoric is a common justification for locavore action.[27]

But lost in these angry denunciations is a much more basic form of environmental injustice: *if poor countries do not develop the resources and infrastructures to mass-produce their own food and a surplus to trade, the developed world will have to donate that food to them.* In order to do this, we'll have to exhaust every inch of available land to produce the 860 million tons a year that the developing world will need by 2020.

The only way the developing world can even remotely begin to achieve the growth, income, and employment necessary to produce its own food is through trade. Now is not the time to retreat into locavore isolationism. To the contrary, we must scale up and reach out with our sustainable dreams, and the only way to do so is through trade that is simultaneously open, regulated, and fair. Trade is essentially a matter of basic environmental justice, one that considers the world's foodshed as important as the one in our backyard.[28]

Eliminating perverse agricultural subsidies and internalizing external costs are once again necessary prerequisites for change. Here's why: when the developed world supports the monocultural proliferation of selected crops under conditions not naturally suited to their growth (as we do in the United States), it directly undermines countries that *do* enjoy the proper conditions for growth and might otherwise capitalize on them. The disadvantaged countries, which are now unable to export their products because they cannot compete with subsidized grain, have no choice but to grow crops that are *not* suited to their natural conditions. This scenario, of course, leads to a reliance on an arsenal of harmful and expensive inputs—fertilizers, pesticides, and irrigated water. It's also why we here in the United States grow cotton in the Arizona desert.[29]

Another reason that it's so critical to destroy perverse subsidies and internalize externalities before forging global trade agreements is that doing so helps prevent the systematic exploitation of poor countries by wealthy ones. As we have seen, a corporation that can profit at the expense of the environment is bound to do so. "Eco-dumping" is a major problem when it comes to globalized exchange. Nations that lack strict environmental regulations (mostly poor nations) often become "pollution havens" for wealthy multinational corporations. In this sense, the lack of environmental laws in poor countries represents a hidden environmental subsidy that enables the big guys to come in, produce goods on the cheap, foist the externalities onto the indigenous population, undercut prices globally, and then, when the well runs dry, bid farewell and move on to the next impoverished country.

Thus, before countries trade, an international regulatory agency must first ensure that the trading plane is level, and that one country will not attract trade or investment from others by lowering the environmental bar. The best way to enforce this is for other nations to agree to impose a tariff on goods exported from an offending country until that country's anti-environmental subsidies are slashed. Such collective policing of rogue nations has the added benefit of creating harmonized environmental regulations among more and more nations.[30]

Unfortunately, the track record of international "free trade" agreements has thus far been notably weak on environmental issues. The North American Free Trade Agreement (NAFTA) and several World Trade Organization (WTO) trade pacts have tended to discourage harmonizing regulations by placing corporate "rights" ahead of environmental justice. For example, one power these agreements grant companies is the right to sue a nation that denies them permits to do business on the grounds of environmental degradation. Other trade agreements, including the Central American Free Trade Agreement (CAFTA) and the Free Trade Area of the Americas (FTAA), also lack sufficient regulations to prevent eco-dumping practices that would threaten biodiversity, add to global warming, and foster bioprospecting. In some cases the foreign corporations can even keep poorer countries from instituting stricter environmental laws designed to protect their natural resources and quality of life.[31]

In essence, the burden of proof for environmental disagreements weighs disproportionately on the developing country, which has to make the case that the proposed environmental regulation is not a hidden form of protectionism. Although the decision to favor environmental concerns over corporate profits might slow down rates of global trade, the right of nations to create strict environmental standards must be not only protected but also required by trade arrangements that penalize and isolate nations whose trade fosters environmental degradation. The problem, then, is not with "free trade," but with the failure to hold it to enlightened standards.[32]

Given the threat of corporate bullying, future regulations must be airtight. As the World Bank environmentalist Herman Daly explains, we must ensure that "trade meets the goals of environmentally sustainable development." If not, these free trade agreements will further push critics to the fringe position of dismissing global trade altogether, as so much of the locavore camp now does. For those living in privileged food enclaves, the quest for local self-sufficiency, especially when contrasted with the many injustices of globalization, will always hold tremendous appeal. However—and I say this with all due respect—it's a cowardly choice.[33]

I make this assessment because it's hard to stress just how detrimental such isolationism would be to the global environment in the long run. Unfortunately, we're looking at yet another dichotomy in the food wars. There seems to be a prevailing sense among advocates of sustainable agriculture that free trade and environmental responsibility are incompatible. As the authors Ted Nordhaus and Michael Shellenberger write, "Environmentalists believe conservation [of rainforests] and economic development are different issues." Thus locavores almost categorically oppose free trade while advocates of the status quo support it. Lost in the middle ground is a more reasonable point to consider.[34]

"Environmentalism" is a broad term encapsulating many themes and controversies, but if there's a timeless truth to this relatively young movement, it's this: it requires wealth. Indeed, both an environmental ethos and concrete environmental improvements correlate positively (and overwhelmingly) with economic growth. And economic growth, of course, increases with trade. Hence the critical upshot: while global trade often does lead to eco-dumping and other forms of environmental damage, the larger point is that *trade as a whole can improve the global environment.*[35]

To reiterate, the most important reason that trade relationships must be nurtured is that trade produces wealth and wealthy nations are, without exception, environmentalist nations. We can highlight every black mark along the path of free trade—and we should, as these exposés only urge us to adopt stronger environmental standards—but the fact remains that we are moving inexorably toward a global community that increasingly agrees that it's better to save the planet than it is to trash it.

The flip side to this axiom is that poverty perpetuates environmental degradation. There are many reasons for this correlation. Citizens in impoverished regions are burdened with immediate needs that downplay concerns for the long-term health of the environment. At the same time, they have few reasons not to destroy the commons for food, water, and energy. One only needs to look for confirmation at the underlying justifications behind decisions to allow poachers to hunt tigers to extinction in India, to build an oil pipeline through the Amazonian rainforest in Brazil, and to construct the Three Gorges Dam in China.

Poorer countries are also less inclined to privatize property. As James M. Sheehan, a scholar at the Mackinack Center for Public Policy, writes, "Logically, the less common property there is, the less pollution will be tolerated by a society of individual property owners." His opinion reflects the views of many prominent economists, including Gene Grossman and Alan Krueger of Princeton University, who found that "economic growth tends to alleviate pollution problems once a country's per capita income reaches about $4000 to $5000 US dollars."[36]

Indeed, the world's leading environmentalists, humanitarians, and economists have come out in favor of global trade as a viable approach to alleviating poverty and its counterpart, environmental destruction. Per Pinstrup-Andersen, the former head of the International Food Policy Research Institute, insists that properly regulated trade can be a "win-win proposition" for both trade partners and the environment. Gordon Conway freely acknowledges the inevitable short-term problems that global trade creates for many developing countries, but he believes that "in the long run, the expectation is that freer trade will provide widespread incentives and opportunities from which the poor will significantly benefit."[37]

The bioethicist and vegan advocate Peter Singer, after a careful analysis of free trade principles, concludes that "a free market should have the effect not only of making the world as a whole more prosperous, but more specifically, of assisting poorer nations." He quotes an Oxfam International report that makes this arresting statement: "History makes a mockery of the claim that trade cannot work for the poor." The report adds, "Participation in world trade has figured prominently in many of the most successful cases of poverty reduction—and, compared with aid, it has far more potential to benefit the poor."[38]

Food Miles

My argument in this chapter brings us back to where this book started: food miles. To highlight the overarching significance of food miles with a final concrete example, we can look to the current trade relationship between the UK and sub-Saharan Africa (SSA). UK residents spend over £1 million daily on produce imported from SSA. Seventy percent of the green beans grown in Kenya go to the UK, and 87 percent of the UK's green bean imports come from five African countries. Overall, almost half of the imports arriving in the UK by air come from SSA. Locavores in England have made food-mile assessments that cast all these figures in the light of environmental waste. In fact they are extremely promising statistics for the future of sustainable global trade for at least three reasons.[39]

First, as life-cycle assessment has revealed, the emissions from air-freighted African produce are relatively minuscule, in part because a great deal of African produce is carried in the belly holds of passenger flights. If the UK banned African imports, it would reduce emissions by no more than .1 percent. Moreover, only 1.5 percent of all produce from Africa arrives in an airplane. "In the big picture," write James MacGregor and Bill Vorley of the International Institute for Environment and Development, "the environmental cost of international food transport is trivial compared with UK domestic 'food miles.'"[40]

Second, not only would ending the trade between the UK and SSA reduce emissions by a negligible amount, it would eliminate farming jobs for over a million Africans. From a food-miles perspective, air-freighted produce might be "the epitome of unsustainable consumption," but from a poverty and development perspective, "the inclusion of sub-Saharan Africa in these high value markets has been a success story." An emphasis on LCAs would help ensure that an antidevelopment food-miles approach does not become widespread among consumers in wealthy nations, as it would then penalize developing countries by endangering the livelihood of their farmers.[41]

Third, conditions in SSA are far riper for sustainable agriculture than they are in the UK. Throughout the developing world, 80 percent of farming is already organic. While figures are not available for all of Africa, it is safe to assume that compared with the UK, where 96 percent of farming is industrialized (only 4 percent organic), African countries rate higher on the scale of comparative advantage. This comparison takes on added resonance in light of the fact that per capita carbon dioxide emissions are 9.2 metric tons in the UK and 1 metric ton in Africa (the global average is 3.6 metric tons). From another angle, SSA and other developing countries, as MacGregor and Vorley note, have considerable "carbon credit," so much so that "unallocated aviation emissions could accrue to African countries in a bid to stimulate trade." Finally, Europe is water stressed; most of SSA is not.[42]

Capitalizing on comparative advantages and achieving scale economies in an unencumbered and sustainable system of global food trade would benefit developing and developed countries alike—but only if fatal pitfalls are avoided. Donor nations working through international organizations such as Aid for Trade must be willing to prioritize, enact, and fund policies designed to foster a sustainable, global, and profitable system of trade in food.

GRANTED, THESE ISSUES are arcane, sometimes difficult to grasp, open to many interpretations, and by no means fodder for the foodie press. For all these reasons, they're not likely to top the agenda of the nearest locavore meeting. In fact, they're the furthest thing from the locavore mind. This must change. We must come to terms with the fact that we cannot eat ethically until the global food system is altered to provide genuinely ethical choices. Eating local, as long as these global conditions remain unmet, is a form of denial. And as concerned consumers, we're better—and bigger-thinking—than that.

Conclusion: The Golden Mean

Much of the advice on eating ethically that now exists is far too confident and incomplete in light of the options before us. It assumes that it is *already possible* for the world to eat an environmentally responsible diet. But, as should be clear by now, it's not. Over the past decade or so, largely under the guidance of locavores, we have searched for precise guidelines for how to eat. In undertaking this important mission, we have identified the right goal—sustainable food production—while jumping the gun on how to pursue it.

What we thus often end up doing is swallowing whole a bumper-sticker mantra—eat local, buy organic, support fair trade, damn Frankenfoods—without fully examining the effect of universalizing these impassioned imperatives. It rarely occurs to us as we contemplate our personal dietary values that the current options might be inadequate, or even counterproductive. The virtue we currently feel as a result of our green culinary decisions is, I fear, often a false virtue.

In light of this claim, this brief conclusion summarizes the alternative solutions we have discussed. As this overview will remind us, however, our job as consumers is not what it used to be. It is, in essence, less to make the right choices among the current range of food options, and more to advocate for changes that would help develop a sound twenty-first-century food system, one in which our collective choices might actually matter. Only then can "just food," as in it's nothing more than food, become "*just* food," as in food we can rightly associate with the justice of sustainability.

Beyond Food Miles

Food miles matter. But they should not be stressed at the expense of other energy inputs that are equally, if not more, important to the overall energy cost of making food. There is no doubt that buying local brings to consumers many tangible and intangible benefits. But we should not delude ourselves into thinking that the relatively easy decision to support the regional foodshed is automatically an environmentally superior choice. Life-cycle assessments remind us that when a wider range of factors is considered—the conditions under which a food was produced, access to water, processing techniques, the form of energy employed, and so on—transportation amounts to a small piece of the pie (about 11 percent of a product's energy cost).

Sure, it feels righteously green to buy a shiny apple at the local farmers' market. But the savvy consumer must ask the inconvenient questions. If the environment is dry, how much water had to be used to grow that apple? If it's winter and the climate is cold, was the apple grown in an energy-hogging hothouse? Is the local fish I'm ordering being hunted to extinction? The smart consumer will realize that in many cases it's more efficient to buy that apple from a faraway place where the press on precious resources was lower, or a fish from a sustainable farm located on the other side of the country. Distance, in other words, is just a minor factor to consider. In overemphasizing food miles, we have missed important opportunities to think more critically about the fuller complexities of food production.

Beyond Organic and Conventional

It is a common stance in the food wars to declare undying loyalty to organic agriculture. I've made my sympathies for organic production clear, but this kind of extremism is harmful. Dispensing with the organic/conventional framework is not only intellectually honest, it provides opportunities for progress. Most important, we can begin to sketch out alternative systems in a quest to seek what I've been calling the golden mean of agricultural production. If the golden mean is an idea that divests food of its ability to become a symbol for a certain kind of identity, it drives home the point that sustainability is a concern that transcends politics and ideologies. A viable global food system attuned to producing goods in a sustainable way would, as proof of its very success, decidedly not lend itself to a polarizing set of unrelated political ideals. It would simply be what it is: a sustainable food system that, in a perfect world, we could trust to deliver food we could eat without anxiety.

There are several general criteria that any model for global sustainable agriculture must to some extent incorporate as meaningful steps toward genuine environmental sustainability. None of them, I should stress, are necessarily geared for either large or small farms. In fact (although I would never argue that farm size should be formally dictated), they are criteria conducive to reviving the diversified midsized farm.[1]

A broad pattern of regionally integrated, technologically advanced, middle-size farms might very well be the best general answer to our food problems. Midsize agricultural operations situated in the same relative area of the world and linked through efficient transportation systems could provide the layout for an optimally efficient blueprint of sustainable and safe food production. The following criteria—ones best explored in the absence of the small organic/big conventional dichotomy—are designed to be flexibly and creatively applied to a wide range of agricultural contexts.

If it's not a smorgasbord, it is at least a menu with a growing list of appealing options.

A Judicious Use of Biotechnology

Biotechnology is a cultural minefield. However, to support biotechnology is not necessarily to support its current applications. Genetically modified crops are now employed primarily to boost yields for corn, cotton, and soy, all heavily subsidized and industrialized crops that rarely make it into the mouths of people. Instead, a more rational approach to genetic modification technology would be to support its application to essential food crops in developing countries, as the Gates Foundation is now doing. Flood-tolerant rice, drought-tolerant sweet potatoes, salt-tolerant cassava, and high-yield millet are fundamentally different beasts from the GM corn and soy being poured into Cargill silos and made into high-fructose corn syrup and cattle feed.

GM varieties have the potential to feed more people—mostly poor people—with less land expansion and reduced pesticide application. With a little imagination, one can also see how such technology—technology, by the way, that is solely responsible for the production of insulin and many other life-saving drugs—could become a handy green tool on a midsize, diversified farm in the developed world.

As it now stands, we're mired in a situation in which agribusiness employs biotechnology to grow staple commodities to feed cows (and cars) while advocates of agroecology and organic methods battle what they call Frankenfoods tooth and nail. But there's hope. Discussing "the way forward" when it comes to food production, Gordon Conway explains that it "lies in harnessing the power of modern technology, but harnessing it wisely in the interest of the poor and hungry and with respect for the environment." His attitude is one well worth adopting and, in small increments, is catching on.[2]

A Judicious Use of Chemicals

We've seen the importance of this point throughout Chapters 2 and 3. Still, the lesson is worth repeating: it's not the poison, it's the dose. A genuine embrace of this aphorism would go a long way toward fostering a rational approach to chemical use in modern agriculture. One of the most common dichotomies characterizing today's food wars is that between synthetic and natural chemicals used for fertilization and pest control. In many respects, this polarization represents yet another red herring, one that can lead consumers to reach unproductive conclusions.

Recently I was fortunate enough to hear a round table of experts discuss the issue of public perceptions of chemicals, safety, and food production. An associate director of the Food Policy Institute at Rutgers, William Hallman, explained that a disturbingly large percentage of the consumers he surveyed preferred that their food be "chemical free." An interesting desire, Hallman quipped, if only because it suggests that consumers want to eat products that do not exist. Another panelist, Mary Bohman, a USDA scientist interested in scientific literacy related to food issues, cited extensive research proving that the general public lacks the proper scientific grammar to make responsible evaluations of chemical use in agriculture. Popular opinions about chemicals confirm that far too many socially conscious consumers automatically see chemicals as inherently dangerous.

These are discouraging conclusions. After all, we will never resolve our food crisis if we do not resolve our crisis of scientific illiteracy. It requires, for example, a basic sense of what bioaccumulation is in order to evaluate the danger of a particular herbicide. Similarly, one must have some grasp of how DNA works to understand how GM corn is altered to contain the gene for pest resistance. It is only when we demystify "chemicals" in the public mind that we can start to make sound judgments about these contentious issues and argue for the right kind of stringent regulation.

Achieving a competent level of popular scientific understanding, moreover, does not necessarily require a major educational campaign. Instead, it demands that we change the way we discuss these matters in the public arena. We must learn to talk sensibly about food, committing ourselves to accepting more complexity, less radicalism, and the wisdom of compromise.

Reduced Tillage

Although the plow is an iconic symbol of agricultural progress, tillage is harmful to the soil. Farms that rely more heavily on GM crops tend to radically decrease tillage practices, primarily because they control weeds with herbicide-resistant crops and the application of relatively safe herbicides. By contrast, organic farmers, who reject synthetic herbicides as a rule, as well as GM crops, have to till heavily in order to control weeds. The soil that organic farmers work so diligently to keep natural and healthy ends up being tilled and thereby rendered more susceptible to wind and water erosion. This is not to suggest that we should do away with organic agriculture; that would be self-defeating. But it is a reminder that organic is by no means our sole savior in the face of industrial agriculture.

The more techniques farmers can use to lessen the disturbance of the soil, the better. Reduced tillage and, ideally, nontillage practices preserve the soil's microbial nutrients, enhance local water quality, lessen fertilizer usage, increase biodiversity, limit agricultural sprawl, and sequester more carbon, thus reducing greenhouse gas emissions. One can go in circles, of course, within the organic/ conventional paradigm, arguing in return that reduced tillage, for all its benefits, means more herbicides. But this tradeoff, according to David Pimentel, the Cornell entomologist, pioneer of integrated pest management, and environmental activist, might be worth it. As he says, "I'd take chemicals over soil erosion any day."[3]

Given the long-term benefits of preserving topsoil, it makes more sense, I would argue, to worry about tillage habits than about organic classification, farm size, or the distance food travels to land on your plate. As the plant biologist Pamela Ronald summarizes her justification for spraying herbicides and reducing tillage: "There are clear advantages to conventional growers and to the environment." These advantages should be realized.[4]

Integrating Livestock and Plant Crops

It's commonplace to note the horrors of industrial meat production. Excessive inputs of conventional grain, antibiotics, growth hormones, and equally excessive outputs of manure and dangerous, chemical-laden runoff are now well known. There's no defending these methods. Organic, grass-fed meat production, however, is not a surefire antidote to the evils of industrialized beef, chicken, and pork. While the immediate inputs are certainly far fewer, this approach demands excessive amounts of terrain, reminding us of Victor Davis Hanson's remark that grazing is "a foolhardy thing to do if you wish to save the land."[5]

The unfortunate fact of the matter is that if we are to have a fighting chance of hitting the sustainability benchmark, we must radically reduce our meat intake. We should eat meat in the most moderate amounts, from a wide range of animals and sources, and not very often.

Instead of subsidizing the costs of grazing and grain production, it would make much more environmental sense for governments or other certifying agencies to reward farms that keep only as much livestock as is necessary to partially fertilize that farm's or a comparably sized farm's range of plant crops. The experts call this plan "enhanced nutrient management." Such a built-in limitation to livestock expansion would be a welcome start in reducing the supply of meat and reversing the tremendous ecological problems caused by its overproduction.

Once again, it is worth noting how the organic/conventional debate obscures this option. Conventional systems consume massive amounts of chemicals and grain to feed livestock that in turn produce dangerous concentrations of manure. Organic systems consume vast acreages of land to graze grass-fed animals and grow what is often lower-yielding organic feed for their diet (using imported manure!). They do this while insisting that humans can eat all the meat we want so long as we transfer land now used to grow grain for conventional livestock over to native grasses for organic animals to graze. Neither plan is sustainable. The organic assumption is unrealistic, and both plans refuse to acknowledge that meat production must be seriously curtailed. Adherence to one form of production or another, however, has thus characteristically stifled the search for a better way.

Freshwater Aquaculture

Conventional aquaculture, like commercial meat production, has come in for its share of well-earned condemnation. Exposés of Asian aquaculture systems in particular have gone a long way toward tarnishing the reputation of fish farming in general. But once again we must be prepared to draw some fine lines beyond the organic/conventional distinction. There is currently no way to mass-produce ocean fish consistently and sustainably—conventionally or organically. The USDA is starting to label farmed salmon "organic," and the designation would demand that no more than 25 percent of salmon feed comes from wild fish (wild fish, that is, that are not considered overfished). The development has infuriated environmentalists. Fortunately, freshwater systems offer a way around this debate, and much more hope for an ecologically sustainable way to produce animal protein.[6]

Unlike their saltwater counterparts, freshwater systems can be contained and integrated into agricultural landscapes as part of poly-cultural production. When handled properly, wastewater from fresh-water farms can irrigate surrounding crops, the waste residue from those crops can be dumped into the ponds to make zooplankton for fish to eat, and bottom layers of pond sludge caused by fish waste can be used to mulch crops. Freshwater aquaculture has the added benefit of producing animal protein from proportionally less feed, owing in large part to the fact that fish do not have to hold themselves up or maintain a consistent body temperature.

Two thirds of today's farm-raised fish in the United States come from freshwater systems. Because the proper incentives are not in place, and because so many large fish producers are allowed to bypass environmental costs, very few of these systems happen to be sustainable. But—and this is what matters—with the right inducements in place and with the end of perverse subsidies, they certainly could be. The organic movement has come late to the game of freshwater fish farming, but it is working diligently to take this fledgling industry in a sustainable direction. In many ways the effort makes great sense. The organic emphasis on diversification and closed-loop resource management is perfectly consistent with the quest to integrate aqueous and land-based farming systems.

We should expect to see many more examples of organic farmers incorporating contained aquaculture in their operations, especially as the environmental problems of meat become more publicized. We can encourage these innovative developments through consumer choice.

Again, though, we must not fall into the trap of labeling organic the *only* viable approach to sustainable aquaculture. Organic aquaculture is a legitimate practice on a small scale, providing an important consumer alternative. But if freshwater aquaculture as a whole is going to expand and intensify to the point that it provides protein for millions of consumers who have shifted away from red meat and chicken, many tools of conventional production will have to drive that intensification. For example, scientists are currently pursuing genetic modifications to fish species that reduce disease and increase fish yields. As the staunch Australian environmentalist

Richard Roush reminds us, "If improving sustainability and reducing the environmental footprint is the goal, we need to be prepared to use the best tools we have."[7]

THESE TOOLS ARE out there, they're being refined and perfected, but they ultimately await our collective support. Thinking critically about food and coming to terms with the reality that, as much as we might wish otherwise, food is not simple are brave steps toward providing that support. As we expand our food horizons, we can hold tight to the local, and we should. At the same time, though, we must see our eating choices as undeniably, inevitably global.

Notes

Introduction: From the Golden Age to the Golden Mean of Food Production

1 Gordon Conway, *The Doubly Green Revolution: Food for All in the Twenty-First Century* (Cornell University Press, 1999).

2 Julie Guthman, *Agrarian Dreams: The Paradox of Organic Farming in California* (University of California Press, 2004), 175; Wendell Berry, "A Standing Ground," from *The Selected Poems of Wendell Berry* (Counterpoint, 1999), 73.

3 Interview with Nina Fedoroff, January 8, 2008; "nature's misfits" is from J. G. Hawkes, "The Origins of Agriculture," *Economic Botany* (April 1970): 131.

4 Pamela C. Ronald and Raoul W. Adamchak, *Tomorrow's Table: Organic Farming, Genetics, and the Future of Food* (Oxford University Press, 2008), 32; Richard Manning, *Against the Grain: How Agriculture Has Hijacked Civilization* (North Point, 2004), 8, 24, 29, 119; Victor Davis Hanson, *Fields Without Dreams: Defending the Agrarian Idea* (Free Press, 1996), xi. Not to make too much of this point, but it's hard not to notice that the most vigorous advocates of a romanticized agricultural ideal have never had to make a sustained living from the land. Michael Pollan is a journalist; Wendell Berry is a poet; Alan Chadwick, who started the UC Santa Cruz Farm and Garden Program, was a Shakespearean stage actor before becoming a plant biologist; Jose Bove, the supposedly simple French farmer whose fame comes from having ransacked a McDonald's, is an activist who grew up in Berkeley.

5 Paul H. Ehrlich and Anne H. Ehrlich, "The Biggest Menace?," letter to the editor, *New York Review of Books*, February 14, 2008, 57.

6 Vandana Shiva et al., eds., *Manifestos on the Future of Food and Seed* (South End, 2007), 77.

Chapter 1: Food Miles or Friendly Miles?

1 Jane Black, "What's in a Number: How the Press Got the Idea That Food

Travels 1,500 Miles from Farm to Plate," *Slate*, September 17, 2008, www.slate.com/id/2200202.

2   This sign was observed at Bishop's Orchards market in Guilford, Connecticut, on a box of local tomatoes, May 13, 2008. The tomatoes were, I should note, delicious.

3   Gilbert Gillespie et al., "Farmers' Markets as Keystones in Rebuilding Local and Regional Food Systems," in C. Claire Hinrichs and Thomas Lyson, eds., *Remaking the North American Food System: Strategies for Sustainability* (University of Nebraska Press, 2007), 81.

4   It also doesn't hurt that a farmers' market is a place where our altruistic behavior happens to be on public display, a social-psychological factor that cannot be discounted as at least a subconscious reason for filling up the hemp bag with local heirlooms. On the significance of food and public virtue, see Julia Whitty, "The 13th Tipping Point," *Mother Jones*, November/December, 2006, 48.

5   Mikkel Thrane, "Environmental Impacts from Danish Food Products," in Neils Halberg, ed., *Life Cycle Assessments in the Agri-Food Sector*, Proceedings of the Danish Institute of Agricultural Sciences Report, October 6–8, 2003, 85; Dominique Patton, "Food Miles or Green Spin?: Is It a Ploy to Protect UK Farmers?" *Business Daily*, March 19, 2007. It should be noted that, as a later chapter will show, this kind of commercial fishing of the depleted oceans is problematic no matter what kind of net is used. The point here is simply to show how LCAs can uncover important areas of unnecessary waste.

6   V. Neilson and T. Luoma, "Energy Consumption: Overview of Data Foundation and Extract of Results," in B. P. Weidema and M. J. G. Meeusen, eds., *Agricultural Data for Life Cycle Assessments*, vol. I, Agricultural Economics Research Institute (February 2000), 56; Jane Jordan, "Cutting the Distance Won't Save the Planet," www.thepigsite.com/articles/1986/food-miles-cutting-the-distance-wont-save-the-planet.

7   James E. McWilliams, "What If…New Challenges in Export Development," Studies Prepared for the World Export Development Forum, October 8–11, 2007, www.intracen.org/wedf/ef2007/Global-Debate/Individual-Papers/WEDF%20Pre-Debate%20Publication.pdf.

8   Clarisse Douaud, "Food Choices and Production Matter More than Food Miles," April 28, 2008, www.foodnavigator-usa.com/Financial-Industry/Diet-choices-and-production-matter-more-than-food-miles-study; Rich Pirog et al., "Food, Fuel, and Freeways: An Iowa Perspective on How Far Food Travels, Fuel Usage, and Greenhouse Gas Emissions," Leopold Center for Sustainable Studies, Iowa State University at Ames, www.leopold.iastate.edu/pubs/staff/ppp/food_mil.pdf; Christopher L. Weber et al., "Food Miles and the Relative Climate Impact of Food Choices in the United States," *Environmental Science and Technology*, April 16, 2008, abstract.

9   Landcare scientists are quoted in "Greener by the Miles," *Daily Telegraph*,

March 3, 2007, www.telegraph.co.uk/news/main.jhtml?xml=/news/ 2007/06/03/nrgreen03.xml&page=1. The study, undertaken by Caroline Saunders, can be found at www.wfa.org.au/PDF/NZ%20Food%20miles.pdf.

10 Gallon Environmental Newsletter, "Energy Use Comparison of Local and Globally Sourced Food," Research Report #285, www.cialgroup.com/ hrGLV12N05.htm; "Food and Agriculture," *Energy Bulletin*, June 4, 2007, www.energybulletin.net/30560.html; "Voting with Your Trolley," *The Economist*, December 7, 2006, www.decal.org/file/396.

11 David Foster, "Tangerines per Gallon," blog at http://chicagoboyz.net/ archives/5111.html.

12 Matt Mariola, "Over the Long Haul: Consequences of Local Versus Long-Distance Food," *Agriculture and Human Values* (forthcoming). I am grateful to Mariola for sharing an unpublished draft of his article with me. I might also add that, as a piece at www.ag.ohio-state.edu/~news/story.php?id=4724 shows, Mariola is a strong advocate of farmers' markets, even selling his own produce at one in Ohio.

13 Holly Hill, "Food Miles: Background and Marketing," National Sustainable Agriculture Information Service, Attra Publication #IP312 (2008).

14 Mariola, "Over the Long Haul," 7.

15 Lee Barter, "Efficiency, Not the Distance Traveled, Might Hold the Key to Supply Chain Sustainability."

16 Marion Stamp Dawkins and Roland Bonney, *The Future of Animal Farming: Renewing the Ancient Contract* (Blackwell, 2008), 71; "$100 Billion in Edible Food Wasted Each Year," www.kitchengardeners.org/2005/12/100_billion _in.html.

17 Niels Jungbluth, "Life Cycle Assessment for Stoves and Ovens," UNS Working Paper No. 16 (August 1997), 1–11, www.esu-services.ch/cms/fileadmin/ download/jungbluth-1997-WP16-LCA-cooking.pdf.

18 Clare Hinrichs et al., "Moving Beyond 'Global' and 'Local,' NE-185 Working Statement (October 2, 1998), draft available at www.ces.ncsu.edu/depts/ sociology/ne185/global.html.

19 Susanne Friedberg, "Not All Sweetness and Light: New Sociologies of Food," *Social and Cultural Geography*, 4, 1 (2003): 3–6; Robin H. Ray, "Anthropologist's Talk on Cheese Gives a Taste of Terroir," *MIT Tech Talk*, January 10, 2007, 7.

20 Hinrichs and Lyson, *Remaking the North American Food System*, 84, 99, 33.

21 Stan Cox, *Sick Planet: Corporate Food and Medicine* (Pluto, 2008), xi; James Gustave Speth, *Bridge at the End of the World: Capitalism, the Environment, and Crossing from Crisis to Sustainability* (Yale University Press, 2008), 194.

22 David S. Connor, "Expressing Values in Agriculture Markets: An Economic Policy Perspective," *Agriculture and Human Values* 21 (2004): 27–35; Petrini quoted in Vandana Shiva et al., eds., *Manifestos on the Future of Seed and Food* (South End, 2007), 18.

23   Marcia Ruth Ostrum, "Community Supported Agriculture as an Agent of
     Change: Is It Working?," in Hinrichs and Lyson, *Remaking the North American
     Food System*, 100; Shiva et al., *Manifestos on the Future of Seed and Food*, 6.

24   Clare Hinrichs, "The Practice and Politics of Food System Localization,"
     Journal of Rural Studies 19, 1 (January 2003): 33–45.

25   Patricia Allen, "Reweaving the Food Security Safety Net: Mediating Entitle-
     ment and Entrepreneurship," *Agriculture and Human Values* 16 (1999):
     120–122.

26   Russ Parsons, "Food Fight Grows Over the Cream of the Crop," *Los Angeles
     Times*, March 9, 2008, A1.

27   Ibid.

28   Allen, "Reweaving the Food Security Safety Net," 119.

29   Ibid.

30   Melanie Depuis and David Goodman, "Should We Go Home to Eat?: Toward
     a Reflexive Politics of Localism," *Journal of Rural Studies* 21 (2005): 360–363.

31   Ibid.

32   Amy B. Trubek, *The Taste of Place: A Cultural Journey into Terroir* (University
     of California Press, 2008), 72–77.

33   Patton, "Food Miles or Green Spin?"

34   Ibid.; James MacGregor and Bill Vorley, "Fair Miles? The Concept of 'Food
     Miles' Through a Sustainable Development Lens," *Sustainable Development
     Opinion*, International Institute for Environment and Development (2006),
     www.agrifoodstandards.net/en/filemanager/active?fid=75.

35   "Food with Integrity," *Business Week*, February 16, 2007); on Wal-Mart, see
     http://instoresnow.walmart.com/food-article_ektid44214.aspx and www.ethi
     curean.com/2008/07/06/walmart/; the agitprop on Bon Appétit Management
     is at www.bamco.com/page/14/farm-to-fork.htm.

36   Bon Appétit press release, www.bamco.com/news.24.htm; Jane Black, "In Trial
     Run, Chipotle Heads to the Farm," *Washington Post*, March 26, 2008, F01.

37   Hinrichs, "The Practice and Politics of Food System Localization," 33–45.

38   N. Hamilton, "Put Iowa Grown Foods on Your Table," *Des Moines Register*,
     February 9, 1998, 7A.

39   Black, "In Trial Run, Chipotle Heads to the Farm."

40   Samuel Fromartz, *Organic, Inc.: Natural Foods and How They Grew*
     (Harcourt, 2007), 108–144.

41   Jennifer Wilkins, "Eating Right Here: The Role of Dietary Guidance in
     Remaking Community-Based Food Systems," in Hinrichs and Lyson, *Remak-
     ing the North American Food System*, 174. On water supply rankings, see www
     .sustainlane.com/us-city-rankings/categories/water-supply.

42   Wilkins, "Eating Right Here," 171–172.

43   Ibid., 172.

44   P. Jones et al., "A Case Study of Local Food and Its Routes to Market in the
     UK," *British Food Journal* 106, 4 (2004): 328–335.

45 Gareth Edward-Jones et al., "Identifying and Managing Emissions from Farms and Food Chains," paper presented at the Carbon Footprint Supply Chain Summit, London, May 24–25, 2007, available at http://relu.bangor.ac.uk/documents/gejcarbonsummit.ppt.

46 Food and Agriculture Organization, *Livestock's Long Shadow* (2006), 126, www.fao.org/DOCREP/010/a0701e/a0701e00.htm.

47 United Kingdom Department for Environment Food and Rural Affairs, "Report of the Food Industry Sustainability Strategy Champions' Group on Food Transport," May 2007, www.defra.gov.uk/farm/policy/sustain/fiss/pdf/report-food-transport-may2007.pdf.

Chapter 2: Organic Panic

1 Eliot Coleman, e-mail correspondence with author, February 12, 2008.

2 The most recent examination of this case found yields in developing countries that were "roughly comparable"—but lower—and actually found higher yields in undeveloped countries. See www.i-sis.org.uk/organicagricul turefeedtheworld.php. Such studies do bode well for the future of organic farming, but they are rarely contextualized in a wealth of scientific data high-lighting more substantial cases of low-yielding organic crops. For example, even in a pro-organic book such as Leslie A. Durham's *Good Growing: Why Organic Agriculture Works* (University of Nebraska Press, 2005), the author writes that "out of sixty-six comparisons, organic yields were lower two-thirds of the time" (p. 43).

3 Holger Kirchmann and Megan H. Ryan, "Nutrients in Organic Farming—Are There Advantages from the Exclusive Use of Organic Manures and Untreated Minerals?," *Proceedings of the 4th International Crop Science Congress*, September 26–October 1, 2004, available at www.cropscience.org.au.; Gregory Conko and C. S. Prakash, "Can GM Crops Play a Role in Developing Countries?," *AgBioWorld*, December 13, 2004, www.agbioworld.org/biotech -info/articles/agbio-articles/gm-crop-role.html; Borlaug is quoted in Center for Global Food Issues, "High-yield Conservation Protects Biodiversity," www .highyieldconservation.org.

4 Pamela C. Ronald and Raoul W. Adamchak, *Tomorrow's Table: Organic Farming, Genetics, and the Future of Food* (Oxford University Press, 2008), 26–28. The 2007 University of Michigan study did admirably try to lay out statistically how organic agriculture could feed the world. It is, however, replete with problems that scientists have identified. An overview of the study is available at www.i-sis.org.uk/organicagriculturefeedtheworld.php. One problem is that it does not offer assurance that organic farming will be able to feed the world in 2050, when the world's population will have grown by 75 percent. Fuller critiques of the Michigan study can be read at www.ohiopma.org/pdfs/insight/organics/organic-abundance-report-fat.pdf and at http://gmopundit.blogspot .com/2007/07/two-sides-to-argument-that-organic.html.

5   Ronald and Adamchak, *Tomorrow's Table*, 26.

6   Ibid., 16; and Final Report to Defra [Department for Environment, Food, and Rural Affairs] for Project ISO205: *Environmental Burdens and Resource Use in Agriculture;* the final document is Mark Shepherd et al., *An Assessment of the Environmental Impact of Organic Farming* (Defra, 2003), 1–79; Center for Global Food Issues, "High-Yield Conservation Protects Biodiversity." On the increase in conventional yields on less land, see Paul K. Conkin, *A Revolution Down on the Farm: The Transformation of American Agriculture since 1929* (University of Kentucky Press, 2008), 149–151.

7   Ron Bailey, "Billions Served: Norman Borlaug Interviewed," *Reason* (April 2000), www.reason.com/news/show/27665.html. A. G. Williams et al., Final Report to Defra for Project ISO205: *Determining the Environmental Burdens and Resource Use in the Production of Agriculture and Horticulture Commodities* (Defra, 2006), 22. The Organic Research Centre's response to this study can be found at www.organicinform.org/newsitem.aspx?id=555.

8   Ronald and Adamchak, *Tomorrow's Table*, 16, 26; Rob Johnson, "The Great Organic Myths," *Independent*, May 1, 2008, www.independent.co.uk/environment/green-living/the-great-organic-myths-why-organic-foods-are-an-indulgence-the-world-cant-afford-818585.html; Craig Sams et al., "RSA Economist Debate—Organic Food Is a Con," *Economist*, June 21, 2005, www.lecturelist.org/content/view_lecture/1960; Cahal Milmo, "Organic Farming 'No Better for the Environment,'" *Independent*, April 19, 2007, http://casfs.blogspot.com/2007_02_01_archive.html.

9   Sams et al., "RSA Economist Debate"; Bob Goldberg, "The Hypocrisy of Organic Farmers," *AgBioWorld*, June 5, 2000, www.agbioworld.org/biotech-info/articles/biotechart/hypocrisy.html. Add to these problems the fact that composting manure concentrates heavy metals, a phenomenon that has been well documented by soil scientists. See http://attra.ncat.org/attra-pub/manures.html#rawman.

10   Bailey, "Billions Served"; Ronald and Adamchak, *Tomorrow's Table*, 109.

11   Bailey, "Billions Served"; International Food Policy Research Institute, "Green Revolution: Curse or Blessing?" (2002), www.ifpri.org/pubs/ib/ib11.pdf.

12   Gregg Easterbrook, "Forgotten Benefactor of Humanity," *Atlantic Monthly*, January 1997, 75–82.

13   Jason Clay, *World Agriculture and the Environment: A Commodity-by-Commodity Guide to Impacts and Practices* (Island, 2004), 50–52; Stan Cox, *Sick Planet: Corporate Food and Medicine* (Pluto, 2008), 88–92; Paul Roberts, *The End of Food* (Houghton Mifflin Harcourt, 2008), 216.

14   Jane E. Brody, "Strong Views on Origins of Cancer," *New York Times*, July 5, 1994, C1.

15   Rob Lyons, "The Truth About Organic Food," *Spiked*, January 9, 2007, www.spiked-online.com/index.php?/site/boxarticle/2691; Brody, "Strong Views on Origins of Cancer."

16   L. S. Gold, "Rodent Carcinogens: Setting Priorities," *Science* 258, October 9,

1992, 261–265; R. Doll and R. Peto, "The Causes of Cancer," Oxford Medical Publications (Oxford University Press, 1981), 1191–1312.

17 Finkel quoted in Nerissa Hannink, "Reporting on the GM Debate," *University of Melbourne Voice* 3, July 14–August 10, 2008, http://uninews.unimelb.edu.au/articleid_5277.html; Finkel, "Organic Food Exposed," *Cosmos* 16 (August 2007), www.cosmosmagazine.com/node/1567. Faidon Magkos et al., "Organic Food: Buying More Safety of Just Peace of Mind? A Critical Review of the Literature," *Critical Reviews in Food Science and Nutrition* 46, 1 (2006): 23–56.

18 Soil Association, "What's Your Poison?: The Soil Association Guide to Pesticide Residue in Popular Food," www.soilassociation.org/web/sa/saweb.nsf/ed0930aa86103d8380256aa70054918d/6b19f3eca09aabed8025708a00374e6d/$FILE/whats_your_poison.pdf; Dennis Avery, *Saving the Planet with Pesticides and Plastic* (Hudson Institute, 2000), 131.

19 Sams et al., "RSA Economist Debate"; Laura Pickett Pottorff, "Some Pesticides Permitted in Organic Gardening," Colorado State University/Denver County Extension Master Gardener (September 15, 2008), www.colostate.edu/Dept/CoopExt/4DMG/VegFruit/organic.htm.

20 Lyons, "The Truth About Organic Food."

21 Groth quoted in Alex Avery, *The Truth About Organic Foods* (Henderson Communications, 2006), 89; Pottorff, "Some Pesticides Permitted in Organic Gardening." It should also be noted that because many organic fertilizers, fungicides, and pesticides are considered "natural," they do not have to meet the same EPA standards and undergo the same regulatory scrutiny as synthetic products.

22 Julie Guthman, *Agrarian Dreams: The Paradox of Organic Farming in California* (University of California Press, 2004), 124. An extensive list of references on Chilean nitrate and fertilizer issues in general can be found at www.naturalnitrogen.com/_STUDIOEMMA_LIVE/images/files/References.pdf. According to one study, producing sodium nitrate through rock crushing and ore conveying uses more energy overall than conventional N fertilizer. However, sodium nitrate mining relies heavily on solar energy, whereas as N fertilizer uses natural gas. See www.naturalnitrogen.com/start/chilean. Sodium nitrate cannot be used as a main source of nitrogen, since some states limit it to 20 percent of overall fertilizer. For example, see Idaho: www.oneplan.org/Crop/OrganicFertilizer.shtml.

23 *Agrarian Dreams*, 175; Jorg Prietzel et al., "Cumulative Impact of 40 Years of Industrial Sulfur Emissions on a Forest Soil in West-Central Alberta," *Environmental Pollution* 131, 1 (November 2004): 129–144. A U.S. Department of Defense report on the dangers of sulfur dust can be found at http://chppm-www.apgea.army.mil/documents/SulfurInfoSheet.pdf; on sulfur and fish, at http://householdproducts.nlm.nih.gov/cgi-bin/household/brands?tbl=brands&id=2015055.

24 Wayland J. Hayes, Jr., *Pesticides Studied in Man* (Williams and Wilkins, 1982), 6. See also the Hazardous Substances Databank entry on copper sulfate: http://toxnet.nlm.nih.gov/cgi-bin/sis/search/r?dbs+hsdb:@term+@rn+7758-98-7.

25   Pesticide Information Profiles, s.v. "Copper sulfate," Extension Toxicology
      Network (EXTONET), Oregon State University, http://extoxnet.orst.edu/pips/
      coppersu.htm?; Banu B. Saleha et al., "DNA Damage in Leukocytes of Mice
      Treated with Copper Sulfate," *Journal of Food Chemistry and Toxicology* 42, 12
      (December 2004): 1931–1936; J. Razinger et al., "Antioxidative Responses of
      Duckweed (Lemna minor L.) to Short Term Copper Exposure," *Environmen-
      tal Science and Pollution International* 14, 3 (May 2007): 194–201.
26   M. A. Pavan et al., "Effects of Copper and Organic Fungicides on Coffee
      Seedlings at Nursery Conditions," *Arquivos de Biologia e Tecnologia* 31, 1
      (1995): 167–173; L. Van Zweiten et al., "Influence of Copper Fungicide
      Residues on Occurrence of Earthworms in Avocado Orchard Soils," *Science
      of the Total Environment* 329, 1–3 (August 15, 2004): 29–41; Sams et al., "RSA
      Economist Debate." The Pesticide Information Project can be found at http://
      pmep.cce.cornell.edu/profiles/extoxnet/index.html.
27   World Health Organization and Food and Agriculture Organization, "Data
      Sheet on Pesticides No. 24: Zinc Phosphide," (December 1976), www.inchem
      .org/documents/pds/pds/pest24_e.htm; Queensland government, "Mice
      Plagues in Northern Australia," www2.dpi.qld.gov.au/fieldcrops/7942.html.
28   M. J. McCoid and P. W. Bettoli, "Additional Evidence for Rotenone Hazards
      to Turtles and Amphibians," *Herpetological Review* 27, 2 (1996): 70–71; N.
      Lapointe et al., "Rotenone Induces Non-specific Central Nervous System and
      Systemic Toxicity," *FASEB* [Federation for American Societies of Experimen-
      tal Biology] *Journal* 18, 6 (April 2004): 717–719, www.fasebj.org/cgi/content/
      short/18/6/717; Larry Turner et al., "Risk Assessments for Piscicidal Formula-
      tions of Rotenone," Compliance Services International (June 29, 2007), 14,
      www.ecy.wa.gov/programs/wq/pesticides/seis/csirotenone_ra062907.pdf.
29   Ronald and Adamchak, *Tomorrow's Table*, 98; Pottorff, "Some Pesticides
      Permitted in Organic Gardening"; on pyrethrins, see Pesticide Information
      Profiles, s.v. "pyrethrin" Extension Toxicology Network (EXTONET), Oregon
      State University, http://extoxnet.orst.edu/pips/pyrethri.htm; L. G. Talent,
      "Effect of Temperature on Toxicity of a Natural Pyrethrin Pesticide to Green
      Anole Lizards," *Environmental Toxicology and Chemistry* 24, 12 (December
      2005): 3113–3116.
30   Lapointe et al., "Rotenone Induces"; National Garden Research Center,
      "Botanical Pest Controls," *Gardens Alive Catalog*, late spring 2008, www.iserv
      .net/~wmize/botan.htm.
31   National Garden Research Center, "Botanical Pest Controls."
32   Finkel quoted in Hannink, "Reporting on the GM Debate."
33   Quoted in Holger Kirchmann and Megan H. Ryan, "Nutrients in Organic
      Farming: Are There Advantages from the Exclusive Use of Organic Manures
      and Untreated Minerals?," paper presented to the 4th Annual Crop Science
      Congress, 2004, available at www.cropscience.org.au/icsc2004/symposia/
      2/6/828_kirchmannh.htm.

34   Avery, *The Truth About Organic Foods*, 22–23.

35   Ibid.

36   Kirchmann and Ryan, "Nutrients in Organic Farming"; Mullen quoted in press release, http://comdev.osu.edu/~news/story.php?id=4703. Also see X. P. Pang and J. Letty, "Challenge of Timing Nitrogen Availability to Crop Nitrogen Requirements," *Soil Science Society of America Journal* 64 (2000): 247–253.

37   Tom Bruulsema, "Productivity of Organic and Conventional Cropping Systems," speech delivered at OECD Workshop on Organic Agriculture, September 23, 2002, Washington, D.C.

38   Mark Measures, "To Compost or Not to Compost," Head Organic Development Systems Programme, EFRC [Energy Frontier Research Centers], www.organicaginfo.org/upload/Compost.MarkMeasures.pdf.

39   Kirchmann and Ryan, "Nutrients in Organic Farming"; James E. McWilliams, "Rusted Roots," *Slate*, September 8, 2008, www.slate.com/id/2198756. On the connection between composting and heavy metals, see http://attra.ncat.org/attrapub/manures.html.

40   Kirchmann and Ryan, "Nutrients in Organic Farming." Like the yields issue, the question of nutrient leaching is perpetually contested. For an overview of the competing schools of thought, see http://orgprints.org/4637/02/4637.pdf.

41   F. H. King, *Farmers of Forty Centuries: Organic Farming in China, Korea, and Japan* (Dover, 2004 [1911]), 193–196.

42   Kirchmann and Ryan, "Nutrients in Organic Farming."

43   Achim Dobermann, "Nitrogen Use Efficiency in Cereal Systems," Australian Society of Agronomy (2006), www.regional.org.au/au/asa/2006/plenary/soil/dobermannad.htm.

44   Keith Bradsher and Andrew Martin, "Shortages Threaten Farmers' Key Tool: Fertilizer," *New York Times*, April 30, 2008, www.nytimes.com/2008/04/30/business/worldbusiness/30fertilizer.html?partner=rssnyt&emc=rss; Roberts, *The End of Food*, 217.

45   Dobermann, "Nitrogen Use Efficiency in Cereal Systems."

46   Ibid.

47   Ibid.

48   Klaus Ammann, "Sustainable Food Security for All by 2020," Conference on Sustainable Food Security for All, September 4–6, 2001, Bonn, available at www.ifpri.org/2020conference/summaries.asp.

Chapter 3: Frankenfood

1   Daniel Charles, *Lords of the Harvest: Biotech, Big Money, and the Future of Food* (Basic Books, 2001), 249.

2   Pamela C. Ronald and Raoul W. Adamchak, *Tomorrow's Table: Organic Farming, Genetics, and the Future of Food* (Oxford University Press, 2008), 66; "Bad-Mouthing Biotech," *Wall Street Journal*, January 11, 2001, www.junkscience.com/jan01/biotech-wsj.html.

3   An excellent recap of the butterfly scandal can be found in Nina Fedoroff, *Mendel in the Kitchen: A Scientist's View of Genetically Modified Foods* (Joseph Henry Press, 1999), 200–210; M. J. Scribner, "Bt or Not Bt: Is That the Question?" *Proceedings of the National Academy of Sciences* 98 (2001): 11937–11942.

4   Per Pinstrup-Andersen, *Seeds of Contention: World Hunger and the Global Controversy over GM Crops* (Johns Hopkins University Press, 2001), 138–140; Fedoroff, *Mendel in the Kitchen*, 203–207; Scribner, "Bt or Not Bt."

5   Fedoroff, *Mendel in the Kitchen*, 206.

6   Richard Lewontin, "Genes in the Food!," *New York Review of Books* 48, 10 (June 21, 2001), www.nybooks.com/articles/14298.

7   Wargo quoted in James Gustave Spelth, *Red Sky at Morning: America and the Crisis of the Global Environment* (Yale University Press, 2004), 77.

8   Peter Pringle, *Food, Inc.: Mendel to Monsanto—The Promises and Perils of the Biotech Harvest* (Simon & Schuster, 2005), 135.

9   Fedoroff, *Mendel in the Kitchen*, 192.

10 Ronald and Adamchak, *Tomorrow's Table*, 35, 44.

11 Ibid., 37; Lloyd T. Evans, *Feeding the Ten Billion: Plants and Population Growth* (Cambridge University Press, 1998), 164.

12 Pringle, *Food, Inc.*, 117; Darwin quoted in Richard Dawkins, *A Devil's Chaplain: Reflections on Hope, Lies, Science, and Love* (Houghton Mifflin, 2003), 8. Howard laid out his ideas about nature's being the best farmer in *An Agricultural Testament* (Oxford University Press, 1943).

13 Peter Dreyer, *A Gardener Touched with Genius: The Life of Luther Burbank* (University of California Press, 1985).

14 Luther Burbank, *How Plants Are Trained to Work for Man* (Collier and Son, 1921), I, 27. Emphasis added.

15 Richard Manning, *Against the Grain: How Agriculture Has Hijacked Civilization* (High Point, 2004), 26; Lewontin, "Genes in the Food!"

16 Pinstrup-Andersen, *Seeds of Contention*, 47; J. Huang et al., "Plant Biotechnology in China," *Science* 295 (January 2002): 674–677; Jennifer A. Thomson, *Seeds for the Future: The Impact of Genetically Modified Crops on the Environment* (Cornell University Press, 2006), 15–16; J. Huang et al., "Economic Impacts of Genetically Modified Crops in China," *Proceedings of the 25th Conference of Agricultural Economists*, August 16–22, 2003, 1077.

17 Thomson, *Seeds for the Future*, 15–18.

18 Ronald and Adamchak, *Tomorrow's Table*, 38, 66–67.

19 Julie Guthman, *Agrarian Dreams: The Paradox of Organic Farming in California* (University of California Press, 2004), 170.

20 Thomson, *Seeds for the Future*, 32; Ronald and Adamchak, *Tomorrow's Table*, 58.

21 Nigel G. Halford, *Genetically Modified Crops* (Imperial College Press, 2003), 46–47; telephone interview with Jessica Adelman, public relations, Syngenta, June 16, 2008.

22 Fedoroff, *Mendel in the Kitchen*, 212; Halford, *Genetically Modified Crops*, 46.

23   Ronald and Adamchak, *Tomorrow's Table*, 72; Halford, *Genetically Modified Crops*, 46. F. Wu, "CAB Reviews," *Perspectives in Agriculture, Veterinary Science, Nutrition, and Natural Resources* 2, 60 (2007): 1–8.

24   Leonard P. Gianessi et al., *Plant Biotechnology: Current and Potential Impact for Improving Pest Management in U.S. Agriculture*, National Center for Food and Agricultural Policy (June 2002), 1–3, www.ncfap.org/documents/Herbi cideTolerantMaize.pdf.

25   A reasoned discussion on GM crops and pesticides can be found in Charles Benbrook, "Do GM Crops Mean Less Pesticide Use?", www.mindfully .org/Pesticide/More-GMOs-Less-Pesticide.htm; Jonathan Rauch, "Will Frankenfood Save the Planet?," *Atlantic Monthly*, October 2003, www.theatlantic .com/doc/200310/rauch; Jon Entine, *Let Them Eat Precaution: How Politics Is Undermining the Genetic Revolution in Agriculture* (American Enterprise Institute, 2005), 180.

26   Entine, *Let Them Eat Precaution*, 180; Pinstrup-Andersen, *Seeds of Contention*, 47; Jason Clay, *World Agriculture and the Environment: A Commodity-by-Commodity Guide to Impacts and Practices* (Island, 2004), 60.

27   Balfour quoted in Fedoroff, *Mendel in the Kitchen*, 246; Edward Faulkner, *Plowman's Folly* (Grosset & Dunlap, 1943).

28   David R. Montgomery, *Dirt: The Erosion of Civilizations* (University of California Press, 2007), 51.

29   Frank Valenzo et al., *National Carbon Accounting System: The Impact of Tillage on Changes in Soil Carbon Density with a Special Emphasis on Australian Conditions* (Australian Government, 2005), www.climatechange.gov.au/ncas/reports/pubs/tr43final.pdf.

30   Richard Fawcett and Dan Towery, *Conservation Tillage and Plant Biotechnology: How New Techniques Can Improve the Environment by Reducing the Need to Plow* (Conservation Technology Information Center, n.d.), 1, www.whybio tech.com/resources/tps/ConservationTillageandPlantBiotechnology.pdf; Kabir Zahangir, "Tillage or No Tillage: Impact on Mycorrhizae," *Canadian Journal of Plant Science* 85, 1 (2005): 23–29.

31   R. S. Fawcett et al., "The Impact of Conservation Tillage on Pesticide Runoff into Surface Water: A Review and Analysis," *Journal of Soil and Water Conservation* 49, 2 (1994): 126–134; Alison Laughlin and Pierre Mineau, "The Impact of Agricultural Practices on Biodiversity," *Agriculture, Ecosystems, and Environment* 55, 3 (October 1995): 201–212; R. Lal, "Soil Erosion Impact on Agronomic Productivity and Environmental Quality," *Critical Reviews in Plant Science* 17, 4 (July 1998): 319–464, www.informaworld.com/smpp/content~content=a713608206~db=all.

32   Donald R. Griffith and Samuel D. Parsons, "Energy Requirements for Various Tillage Planting Systems," Purdue University Cooperative Extension Services (NCR-202-W), www.extension.purdue.edu/extmedia/NCR/NCR-202-W.html; Steve Gibson, "No Till Small Grain," *Soil Quality Newsletter* 7(3A), 5.

33 Faulkner, *Plowman's Folly*, 12.

34 Paul K. Conkin, *A Revolution Down on the Farm: The Transformation of American Agriculture Since 1929* (University of Kentucky Press, 2008), 115–116.

35 Halford, *Genetically Modified Crops*, 41; Rachel Carson, *Silent Spring* (Houghton Mifflin, 1962), 43.

36 Interview with David Montgomery, March 10, 2008; figures are from Fawcett and Towery, *Conservation Tillage and Plant Biotechnology*, 1–6.

37 Ibid.

38 Fedoroff, *Mendel in the Kitchen*, 274; Fawcett and Towery, *Conservation Tillage and Plant Biotechnology*, 3.

39 Caroline Cox, "Glyphosate Factsheet," *Journal of Pesticide Reform* 108 (Fall 1998), www.dontspraycalifornia.org/Glyphosate%20Factsheet%202.htm.

40 Spectrum Chemical Fact Sheet, Chemical Abstract #1071836, www.speclab.com/compound/c1071836.htm.

41 Halford, *Genetically Modified Crops*, 42; Fedoroff, *Mendel in the Kitchen*, 274.

42 Harry Fountain, "On Not Wanting to Know What Hurts You," *New York Times*, January 15, 2006.

43 Pringle, *Food, Inc.*, 174–175; Fedoroff, *Mendel in the Kitchen*, 231; Halford, *Genetically Modified Crops*, 91; Ronald and Adamchak, *Tomorrow's Table*, 117.

44 David Bennett, "Glyphosate-Resistant Giant Ragweed Confirmed in Tennessee," *Delta Farm Press*, March 25, 2008, http://deltafarmpress.com/soybeans/resistant-weeds-0325/; Hager quoted in Mark Moore, "Weeds Rebound," *Farm Industry News*, December 1, 2007, http://farmindustrynews.com/crop-protection/herbicides/weeds-rebound/; Conkin, *Revolution on the Farm*, 116.

45 Moore, "Weeds Rebound."

46 Bennett, "Glyphosate-Resistant Giant Ragweed Confirmed in Tennessee."

47 D. B. Keetch et al., "Bt Maize for Small Scale Farmers: A Case Study," *African Journal of Biotechnology* 4 (2005): 1505–1509; Graham Brookes and Peter Barfoot, "GM Crops: The Global Economic and Environmental Impact—The First Nine Years, 1996–2004," *AgBioForum* 8 (2005): 187–196.

48 African Agriculture blog, http://africanagriculture.blogspot.com/2008/04/gm-maize-field-trials-show-20-yield.html; Australian government, *GM Crops in Emerging Economies: Impacts on Australian Agriculture* (March 2008), www.abareconomics.com/interactive/08_ResearchReports/gmcrops/htm/chapter_4.htm; David Tribe, "Why GM Soybeans and GM Corn Have Both Been a Success with Canadian Farmers," GMO Pundit blog, http://gmopundit.blogspot.com/2008/02/why-gm-soybeans-and-gm-corn-have-both.html; Brookes and Barfoot, "GM Crops: The Global Economic and Environmental Impact."

49 "Dicamba Resistant Soybeans to the Rescue?," Seed to Plate blog, www.seedtoplate.com/article-1181230191.html.

50 Benbrook quoted in "Independent Reports Yield Conflicting Conclusion on Environmental Effects," iGreens blog, www.igreens.org.uk/gm_soybeans.htm;

Lim Li Ching and Jonathan Matthews, "GM Crops Have Failed," *Isis* (December 15, 2001), www.mindfully.org/GE/GE3/GM-Crops-Have-Failed.htm.

51 John Storer, *The Web of Life* (The Devin Adnir Co., 1958), 36.

52 Interview with Nina Fedoroff, January 5, 2008.

53 Robert Paarlberg, *Starved for Science: How Biotechnology Is Being Kept Out of Africa* (Harvard University Press, 2008), 67.

54 Dennis Avery, "How High-Yield Farming Saves Nature," *Social Science and Public Policy* 44, 6 (2007): 137–140.

55 Paarlberg, *Starved for Science*, 123–124. It goes without saying that Paarlberg has his detractors. See this report by the UN: www.unctad.org/en/docs/ditcted 200715_en.pdf.

56 Ibid., 14–15.

57 Amy Trubek, *The Taste of Place: A Cultural Journey into Terroir* (University of California Press, 2008).

58 Interview with Roger Beachy and Ernest Jaworski, January 25, 2008.

59 Ibid.

60 "Reflections of a Science Pioneer," Monsanto, October 31, 2006, www.mon santo.com/features/rob_horsch.asp.

61 Paarlberg, *Starved for Science*, 169.

62 Ibid., 159–175.

Chapter 4: Meat—The New Caviar

1 Peter Singer, *Animal Liberation* (HarperCollins, 1975), 160; Brown is quoted in Jim Motavalli, "Across the Great Divide: Environmentalists and Animal Rights Activists Battle over Vegetarianism," *E: The Environmental Magazine*, January/February 2002.

2 Caroline Stacey, "Food Miles," *BBC Food*, June 19, 2008, www.bbc.co.uk/ food/food_matters/foodmiles.shtml; Ian Lowe, "Think You Can Be a Meat-Eating Environmentalist? Think Again," November 6, 2006, www.vegan sworldnetwork.org/topic_environment_meat_eating.php.

3 John Robbins, *Diet for a New America: How Your Food Choices Affect Your Health, Happiness, and the Future of Life on Earth* (Stillpoint, 1987), 97–122.

4 The Sierra Club report "That Stinks" is found at www.sierraclub.org/cleanwater/ that_stinks.

5 Ibid.

6 Singer, *Animal Liberation*, 167.

7 Lowe, "Think You Can Be a Meat-Eating Environmentalist?"

8 These figures come from a remarkable database compiled by the World Resources Institute: http://earthtrends.wri.org/searchable_db/index .php?action=select_countries&theme=8&variable_ID=192. A U.S. ton or "short ton" is 2000 pounds. A metric ton is 1000 kilograms or 2204.6 pounds.

9 Ibid.

10 Ibid.; Brown is quoted in Jim Motavalli, "Across the Great Divide." One might

think it is unfair for the developed world to tell the developing world how to manage food resources, but consider that "the China Health Project, a joint Sino-American undertaking, examined the health effects of changes in the Chinese diet since the economic reform of 1978 and concluded that the[ir] recent increases in breast cancer, colorectal cancer, cardiovascular disease and obesity are closely linked to increased meat consumption. Moreover, these disease changes occurred at a level of meat consumption that is only a fraction of the typical American or European intake." See "United States Leads World Meat Stampede," Worldwatch Institute, July 2, 1998, www.worldwatch.org/node/1626.

11   Food and Agriculture Organization, "Farm Animal Diversity Under Threat," *FAO Newsroom*, June 14, 2007, www.fao.org/newsroom/en/news/2007/1000598/index.html; Ken Midkiff, *The Meat You Eat: How Corporate Farming Has Endangered America's Food Supply* (St. Martin's, 2004), 76; Singer, *Animal Liberation*, 95.

12   Peter Singer, "The Ethics of Eating," *Chinadialogue*, April 30, 2006, www.chinadialogue.net/article/show/single/en/326-The-ethics-of-eating.

13   Food and Agriculture Organization, "Livestock a Major Threat to Environment," *FAO Newsroom*, November 29, 2006, www.fao.org/newsroom/en/news/2006/1000448.

14   Ibid.

15   Food and Agriculture Organization, *Livestock's Long Shadow: Environmental Issues and Options* (2007), 87, available at www.fao.org/DOCREP/010/a0701e/a0701e00.HTM; Paul Roberts, *The End of Food* (Houghton Mifflin Harcourt, 2008), 206.

16   FAO, *Livestock's Long Shadow*, 87.

17   Ibid., 89.

18   "Scientific Facts on Desertification," Greenfacts, www.greenfacts.org/en/desertification/; the definition of "desertification" is at www.unccd.int/knowledge/glossary.php.

19   FAO, *Livestock's Long Shadow*, 27–29; Joseph Romm, "The Desertification-Global Warming Feedback Loop," *Grist*, September 13, 2007, http://gristmill.grist.org/story/2007/9/12/152749/121.

20   FAO, *Livestock's Long Shadow*, 90–95.

21   Ibid., 95.

22   "Findings," *Harper's Magazine*, September 2008, 100; Amber Fields, "Fighting Cow Methane at the Source: Their Food," *Discover*, July 8, 2008, http://discovermagazine.com/2008/aug/08-fighting-cow-methane-at-the-source.

23   Midkiff, *The Meat You Eat*, 63.

24   FAO, *Livestock's Long Shadow*, 82, 103–105.

25   Ibid.; John Nowatzki, "Anhydrous Ammonia: Managing the Risks," North Dakota State University, August 2008, www.ag.ndsu.edu/pubs/ageng/safety/ae1149-1.htm.

26 FAO, *Livestock's Long Shadow,* 107.

27 Midkiff, *The Meat You Eat,* 90; the Pollan reference is in Peter Singer and Jim Mason, *The Way We Eat: Why Our Food Choices Matter* (Rodale, 2006), 61.

28 Sierra Club, "Tour de Stench: A Trip through CAFO Country in Western Kentucky," www.sierraclub.org/factoryfarms/tour_de_stench.

29 Motavalli, "Across the Great Divide."

30 Sustainable Development Networking Programme Bangladesh, "Desertifi cation," www.sdnpbd.org/sdi/international_days/wed/2006/desertification/index.htm; Ourplanet, "Pastures," www.ourplanet.com/aaas/pages/population03.html.

31 Erik Marcus, *Meat Market: Animals, Ethics, and Money* (Brio, 2005), 197.

32 FAO, *Livestock's Long Shadow,* 32; Marcus, *Meat Market,* 197.

33 BBC News, "World's Plants Under Pressure," November 1, 2002, http://news.bbc.co.uk/2/hi/science/nature/2385591.stm.

34 Singer and Mason, *The Way We Eat,* 233; Michael Williams, *Deforesting the Earth: From Prehistory to the Global Crisis* (University of Chicago Press, 2006), 461; for deforestation figures, see RRojas Databank, "World Development Indicators 2005," www.rrojasdatabank.info/wdi2005/env3.4.pdf; FAO, *Livestock's Long Shadow,* 27–29.

35 RRojas Databank, "World Development Indicators 2005"; FAO, *Livestock's Long Shadow,* 27–29.

36 George Wuerthner and Mollie Matteson, *Welfare Ranching: The Subsidized Destruction of the American West* (Island, 2002), 33–38.

37 FAO, *Livestock's Long Shadow,* 160; Howard P. Lyman, *Mad Cowboy: Plain Truth From the Cattle Rancher Who Won't Eat Meat* (Touchstone, 1998), 141.

38 Ourplanet, "Pastures"; Thomas L. Fleischner, "Land Held Hostage: A History of Livestock and Politics," in Wuerthner and Matteson, *Welfare Ranching,* 34.

39 Reynell Carew, "A Necessary Companion, or The English Interest Discovered and Promoted…" (Williams Budden, 1685), 15; Fleischner, "Land Held Hostage," 37–38.

40 Yong Zhong Su et al., "Influences of Grazing and Exclosure on Carbon Sequestration in Degraded Sandy Grassland," *New Zealand Journal of Agricultural Research* 46, 4 (2003): 321; Vaclav Pavel, "The Impact of Grazing Animals on Nesting Success of Grassland Passerines in Farmland and Natural Habitats: A Field Experiment," *Folia Zoology* 53, 2 (2004): 171–178, www.ivb.cz/folia/53/2/171-178.pdf.

41 Joy Belsky and Dana M. Blumenthal, "Effects of Livestock Grazing on Stand Dynamics and Soils in Upland Forests of the Interior West," *Conservation Biology* 11 (February 2002): 315–327; Jacobson is quoted in Motavalli, "Across the Great Divide."

42 Marcus, *Meat Market,* 198.

43   Ibid., 198; Andy Lamey, "Food Fight! Davis Versus Regan on the
     Ethics of Eating Beef," *Journal of Social Philosophy* 38, 2 (May 2007):
     331–348; James E. McWilliams, *American Pests: The Losing War on
     Insects from Colonial Times to DDT* (Columbia University Press, 2008),
     chap. 5.

44   Kathie Durbin, "Restoring a Refuge: Cows Depart, but Can Antelope
     Recover?" *High Country News*, November 24, 1997, www.hcn.org/
     issues/119/3790.

45   FAO, *Livestock's Long Shadow*, 126; Lyman, *Mad Cowboy*, 132.

46   Stacey, "Food Miles"; Lyman, *Mad Cowboy*, 132; Fred Pearce, "Water Scar-
     city: The Real Food Crisis," Yale University Environment 360, June 3, 2006,
     http://e360.yale.edu/content/feature.msp?id=1825.

47   Wuerthner and Matteson, *Welfare Ranching*, 65, 128.

48   Midkiff, *The Meat You Eat*, 47; Pimentel quoted in Pearce, "Water Scarcity:
     The Real Food Crisis"; Don Hinrichsen and Henrylito Tacio, "The Coming
     Freshwater Crisis Is Already Here," Woodrow Wilson International Center for
     Scholars, www.wilsoncenter.org/topics/pubs/popwawa2.pdf; Stephen Tyler,
     "Governance and Water Management in Asia: What Do We Need to Learn?,"
     in World Water Council, ed., *Proceedings of the Workshop on Water and Poli-
     tics*, February 26–27, 2004, Marseille, 115, available at www.worldwater
     council.org/fileadmin/wwc/Library/Publications_and_reports/Proceedings
     _Water_Politics/proceedings_waterpol_pp.115-196.pdf; David Pimentel
     et al., "Environmental and Economic Costs of Soil Erosion and Conservation
     Benefits," *Science* 267 (February 24, 1995): 1117–1123.

49   Marcus, *Meat Market*, 160–161; J. D. Paoloni et al., "Fluoride Contamination
     of Aquifers," *Environmental Toxicology* 18 (October 2003): 317–320.

50   Midkiff, *The Meat You Eat*, 46.

51   Ibid., 76.

52   FAO, *Livestock's Long Shadow*, 142–143.

53   Ibid.

54   Ibid., 153–156.

55   Canadian Ministry of Agriculture (Ontario), Food and Rural Affairs, "Water
     Quality and Pig Performance," www.omafra.gov.on.ca/english/livestock/
     swine/facts/91-071.htm.

56   FAO, *Livestock's Long Shadow*, 166.

57   Singer, *Animal Liberation*, 162.

58   Michael Pollan, *The Omnivore's Dilemma: A Natural History of Four Meals*
     (Penguin, 2006).

59   Motavalli, "Across the Great Divide."

60   John Robbins, "What About Grass-Fed Beef?," www.foodrevolution.org/
     grassfedbeef.htm.

61   Britt Bailey and Mark Lappe, eds., *Engineering the Farm: Ethical and Social
     Aspects of Biotechnology* (Island, 2002), 157.

62   Robbins, *Diet for a New America*, 7; Edward Abbey, *One Life at a Time, Please* (Henry Holt, 1978), 13.

63   Robbins, "What About Grass-Fed Beef?"

64   Quoted in All-creatures, "How Free Is Free Range?," www.all-creatures.org/articles/ar-howfree.html.

65   Ibid.

66   Video, *45 Days—The Life and Death of a Broiler Chicken*, www.chicken industry.com/cfi/videogallery. Other useful information on the reality of "free-range" can be found on the All-creatures website, www.all-creatures .org/articles/ar-howfree.html.

67   Melanda Park, "FAQs About Free Range," www.melandapark.com.au/organ ics.html; Free Range Pork Farmers Association, www.freerangeporkfarmers .com.au/; on animal products in pig feed, see AllAboutFeed, "EC Allows Feed Fodder to Contain Animal Protein," February 27, 2009, www.allaboutfeed .net/news/ec-allows-feed-fodder-to-contain-animal-protein-id2913.html.

68   For an overview of more sustainable pork options, see www.ucsusa.org/assets/ documents/food_and_agriculture/greener-eggs-and-ham.pdf.

69   Wondwossen Gebreyes et al., "Seroprevalence of *Trichinella, Taxoplasma*, and *Salmonella* in Antimicrobial-Free and Conventional Swine Production Systems," *Foodborne Pathogens and Disease* 5 (April 2008): 199–203, available at www.liebertonline.com/doi/abs/10.1089/fpd.2007.0071.

70   Sara Davis, "Pigs Raised Outdoors and 'Natural' Carry More Bacteria," Down to Earth blog, July 2, 2008, www.downtoearthblog.com/foodproduction/ pigs-raised-outdoors-and-natural-carry-more-bacteria/archives/121.

71   Editorial, "Meat, Now, It's Not Personal," *Worldwatch Magazine*, July/August 2004: 12; Eshel quoted in "Study: Vegan Diets Healthier for Planet, People than Meat Diets," www.news.uchicago.edu/releases/06/060413.diet.shtml.

72   Motavalli, "Across the Great Divide."

Chapter 5: The Blue Revolution

1   Food and Agriculture Organization, "The State of the World's Fisheries and Aquaculture I" (FAO Corporate Document Repository, 2006), 3–4; the entire two-part report is available at www.fao.org/DOCREP/009/a0699e/A0699E00 .HTM.

2   Taras Grescoe, *Bottomfeeder: How to Eat Ethically in a World of Vanishing Seafood* (Bloomsbury, 2008), 10; Stuart W. Bunting and Jules Pretty, "Aqua-culture Development and Global Carbon Budgets: Emissions, Sequestration and Management Options," Center for Environment and Society Occasional Paper, 2007, 2; John Tibbets, "Satisfying the Global Appetite," *Environmental Health Perspectives* 109 (July 2001): 318; Ralf Doering, "Investing in Natural Capital—The Case of Fisheries," in U. Sumaila et al., eds., *2005 North American Association of Fisheries Economists' Forum Proceedings*, Fisheries Center Research Papers 14, no. 1.

3   Grescoe, *Bottomfeeder*, 26; Charles Clover, *The End of the Line: How Overfishing Is Changing the World and What We Eat* (University of California Press, 2006), 166–168; FAO, "The State of the World's Fisheries and Aquaculture II," 5.

4   Earle quoted in Stephen Sloan, *Ocean Bankruptcy: World Fisheries on the Brink of Disaster* (Lyons, 2003), 114; Clover, *The End of the Line*, 93; Doering, "Investing in Natural Capital," 56.

5   Editorial, "The Limits of Agriculture," *New York Times*, June 10, 2005.

6   Cornelia Dean, "Lice in Fish Farms Endanger Wild Salmon," *New York Times*, December 14, 2007; David Barboza, "In China: Farming Fish in Toxic Waters," *New York Times*, December 15, 2007; Alexei Barrionuevo, "Salmon Virus Indicts Chile's Fishing Methods," *New York Times*, March 27, 2008; Cornelia Dean, "Saving Wild Salmon, in Hopes of Saving the Orca," *New York Times*, November 3, 2008.

7   Andrea Katz, "The Role of Aquaculture in Nepal: Towards Sustainable Development," *Ambio* 16 (1987): 222–224; U. Barg and M. J. Phillips, "Environmental Interactions," from Food and Agriculture Organization, "Environment and Sustainability," in *Review of the State of World Aquaculture* (FAO Corporate Document Repository, 1997), www.fao.org/DOCREP/003/w7499e/w7499e14.htm.

8   QFS [Queensland Fisheries Service] news release, "Freshwater Aquaculture by Cotton and Cane Farmers," Ausfish Australian Fishing Forum, August 16, 2001.

9   Interview with cattle owner David Todd, October 10, 2008; interview with Ray Cone, an aquaponics specialist, October 7, 2008; Steve Diver, "Aquaponics—Integration of Hydroponics with Aquaculture," AATRA Publication #IP163 (2006), http://attra.ncat.org/attra-pub/aquaponic.html.

10   Dr. Barry A. Costa-Pierce, "The 'Blue Revolution'—Aquaculture Must Go Green," http://oceancommission.gov/publicomment/novgencomment/costa_pierce_comment.pdf.

11   Laurence Hutchison, *Aquaculture: A Sustainable Solution* (Permanent, 2006), 12.

12   Grescoe, *Bottomfeeder*, 182.

13   Hutchison, *Aquaculture*.

14   Jinyun Ye, "Carp Polyculture System in China: Challenges and Future Trends," in Margaret Eleftheriou and Anastasios Eleftheriou, eds., *Aquachallenge Workshop, Beijing, China, April 27–April 30, 2002*; ASEM Science & Technology Workshops, No. 2, European Commission, October 2003, ftp://ftp.cordis.europa.eu/pub/inco2/docs/asemaquaprint041119.pdf.

15   Tibbets, "Satisfying the Global Appetite," 320–321.

16   Katz, "The Role of Aquaculture in Nepal," 222.

17   Kuanhong Min and Baotong Hu, "Chinese Embankment Fish Culture," in Food and Agriculture Organization, *Integrated Agriculture-Aquaculture: A Primer* (FAO Corporate Document Repository, 2001), www.fao.org/

DOCREP/005/Y1187E/yl187e09.htm; Frank Fermin et al., "The Case of Rice Fish Farmer Mang Isko," in ibid., www.fao.org/DOCREP/005/Y1187E/yl187e25.htm.

18   Bunting and Pretty, "Aquaculture Development and Global Carbon Budgets," 18; Catalino dela Cruz et al., "Rice-Fish Systems in Guimba, Nueva Ecija, Philippines," in FAO, *Integrated Agriculture-Aquaculture*, www.fao.org/DOCREP/005/Y1187E/yl187e24.htm; Catalino dela Cruz, "Rice-Fish Systems in Indonesia," in ibid., www.fao.org/DOCREP/005/Y1187E/yl187e19.htm.

19   Fermin et al., "The Case of Rice Fish Farmer Mang Isko."

20   Peter Edwards, "Inland Aquaculture: Comments on Possible Improvements to Carp Culture in Andhra Pradesh," Network of Aquaculture Centres in Asia-Pacific (September 2008), www.enaca.org/modules/news/article.php?storyid=1774&keywords=peter+edwards.

21   Ibid.

22   S. D. Tripathi and B. K. Sharma, "Integrated Fish-Horticulture Farming in India," in FAO, *Integrated Agriculture-Aquaculture*, www.fao.org/DOCREP/005/Y1187E/yl187e12.htm.

23   C. Kwei Lin et al., "Polyculture of Grass Carp and Nile Tilapia with Napier Grass as the Sole Nutrient Input in the Subtropical Climate of Nepal," in Aquaculture Collaborative Research Support Program, *Feeds and Fertilizers Research* 3 (January 2003), http://pdacrsp.oregonstate.edu/pubs/workplns/wp_10/10FFR3.html.

24   Katz, "The Role of Aquaculture in Nepal," 222–224; Diver, "Aquaponics," 5.

25   Modadugu V. Gupta, "Culture of Short-Cycle Species in Seasonal Ponds and Ditches in Bangladesh," in FAO, *Integrated Agriculture-Aquaculture*, www.fao.org/DOCREP/005/Y1187E/yl187e13.htm.

26   Barg and Phillips, "Environmental Interactions."

27   Dennis Bell, "Advice to the Catfish Industry," *Farm Press*, February 17, 2006, http://deltafarmpress.com/news/060217-catfish-environment; Nick Romanowski, *Sustainable Freshwater Aquaculture: The Complete Guide from Backyard to Investor* (University of New South Wales Press, 2007), 9–11; Committee on Assessment of Technology and Opportunities for Marine Aquaculture in the United States, *Marine Aquaculture: Opportunities for Growth* (National Academy Press, 1992), 20–63.

28   S. M. Garcia, "The Ecosystem Approach to Fisheries" (FAO Corporate Document Repository, 2003), 6, www.fao.org/DOCREP/006/Y4773E/y4773e03.htm.

29   Costa-Pierce, "The 'Blue Revolution'"; Doering, "Investing in Natural Capital," 53.

30   William A. Wurts, "Small-Scale and Home-Use Channel Catfish Farming in Kentucky," *World Aquaculture* 35, 8–9, www.ca.uky.edu/wkrec/SmallScaleHomeUse.htm; William A. Wurts, "Sustainable Channel Catfish Farming,"

World Aquaculture 26 (2005) 54–59, www.ca.uky.edu/wkrec/Sustainable
CatfishFarming.htm.

31   For the Monterey Bay Aquarium on catfish, see www.montereybayaquarium
      .org/cr/SeafoodWatch/web/sfw_factsheet.aspx?gid=34; for the Blue Ocean
      Institute on catfish, see www.blueocean.org/seafood/seafood-search-result
      ?keyword=catfish.

32   Bell, "Advice to the Catfish Industry."

33   For the Blue Ocean Institute on oysters, see www.blueocean.org/seafood/
      seafood-search-result?dropdownlist=Oysters&keyword=Type+in+your
      +search; East Coast Shellfish Growers' Association pamphlet, www.ecsga.org/
      pages/BenefitsBrochure.pdf.

34   Sam Spiewak, "Largest Oyster Restoration in California," *Point Reyes
      Light*, August 12, 2006, www.ptreyeslight.com/cgi/news_archive_2006
      .pl?record=166.

35   For the Blue Ocean Institute on trout, see www.blueocean.org/programs/
      seafood-search-result?dropdownlist=Trout&sushi=n&keyword=.

36   Ibid.

37   For the Blue Ocean Institute on tilapia, see www.blueocean.org/programs/
      seafood-search-result?dropdownlist=Tilapia&sushi=n&keyword=.

38   Ibid.

39   "Creating an Aquaculture of Life," *Grist: Environmental News and Commen-
      tary*, www.grist.org/news/daily/2005/06/08/4/index.html.

40   Diver, "Aquaponics," 5–6.

41   Ibid.

42   Ibid., 7–9.

43   Ibid., 9–10; James E. Rakocy, "Pond Culture of Tilapia," Southern Regional
      Aquaculture Service, Publication #280 (July 1989), http://aqua.ucdavis.edu/
      dbweb/outreach/aqua/280FS.PDF.

44   Diver, "Aquaponics," 8.

45   For more on Cabbage Hill Farm, see www.westchestergov.com/PARKS/pdfs/
      AquaponicsPresentation1-23-03.pdf.

Chapter 6: Merging Ecology and Economy

1   Tom Philpott, "I'm Hatin' It: How the Feds Make Bad for You Food Cheaper
      than Healthful Fare," *Grist*, February 22, 2006, www.grist.org/news/main
      dish/2006/02/22/philpott.

2   Mark Winne, *Closing the Food Gap: Resetting the Table in the Land of Plenty*
      (Beacon, 2008), 149.

3   Jason D. Scorse, "Subsidies: The Good, the Bad, and the Ugly," *Grist*, March
      8, 2007, www.grist.org/article/subsidies-the-good-bad-and-the-ugly; this page
      contains a link to Norman Myers with Jennifer Kent, "Perverse Subsidies:
      Taxes Undercutting our Economies and Environments Alike," International
      Institute for Sustainable Development (1998), xvi.

4   Myers and Kent, "Perverse Subsidies," xiii. An important clarification is needed here: Myers and Kent are probably discussing subsidies in which growers are paid not to produce. This kind of subsidy raises food prices because the supply is artificially kept low. Subsidies may also lower food prices. This primarily happens when the costs of production, like environmental costs, are subsidized. In this case the cost of food goes down for the consumer, but the hidden costs—health problems, environmental problems—rise.

5   Norman Myers and Jennifer Kent, *Perverse Subsidies: How Tax Dollars Can Undercut the Environment and the Economy* (Island, 2001), 49–50.

6   The GAO figures are from "Fiscal Costs of Federal Public Lands Livestock Grazing," www.sagebrushsea.org/pdf/factsheet_Grazing_Fiscal_Costs.pdf.

7   Charles Abbott, " 'Green Pay,' Not Crop Subsidies, US Activists Ask,' " Common Dreams.org (May 9, 2006): www.commondreams.org/headlines06/0509-03.htm. Michael Pollan, The Omnivore's Dilemma: A Natural History *of Four Meals* (Penguin, 2007), 48–49.

8   Angel Gonzalez, "Seeding the Way to Better Biofuels," *Seattle Times*, November 21, 2007, http://seattletimes.nwsource.com/html/biotech/2004026594_biotechcrops21.html.

9   The Environmental Working Group (EWG) has compiled comprehensive statistics on agricultural subsidies. For a history and overview of California water subsidies, see http://archive.ewg.org/reports/Watersubsidies/printerfriendly.php.

10   Ibid.

11   Myers and Kent, *Perverse Subsidies*, 50.

12   See the EWG Farm Subsidy Database: for corn subsidies, http://farm.ewg.org/farm/progdetail.php?fips=00000&progcode=corn&page=conc; for commodity subsidies to districts represented by the House Agriculture Committee, http://farm.ewg.org/sites/farmbill2007/agcomm.php.

13   Myers and Kent, *Perverse Subsidies*, 152–153; Stephanie Nebehay, "WWF Urges Reform of $15 bln Fishing Subsidies," Reuters, October 26, 2001, www.planetark.org/dailynewsstory.cfm/newsid/12993/newsDate/26-Oct-2001/story.htm; report from Oceana, "It's Time to Cut the Bait," www.oceana.org/north-america/what-we-do/stop-overfishing-subsidies.

14   Myers and Kent, *Perverse Subsidies*, 165–167.

15   Ibid.

16   Paul Roberts, *The End of Food* (Houghton Mifflin Harcourt, 2008), 122.

17   Paul Hawken, *The Ecology of Commerce: A Declaration of Sustainability* (Collins, 1993), 93; Myers and Kent, "Perverse Subsidies," xviii.

18   See EWG's farm subsidy database, http://farm.ewg.org/farm/.

19   Laura Sayre, "Farming Without Subsidies," The Rodale Institute (March 20, 2003): http://newfarm.rodaleinstitute.org/features/0303/newzealand_subsidies.shtml; http://epi.yale.edu/AgriculturalSubsidies.

20   Hawken, *The Ecology of Commerce*, 79–81. The Pigouvian tax is named after the English economist A. C. Pigou, who wrote *The Economics of Welfare* in 1920.

21 Michael Pollan, "Weed It and Reap," *New York Times*, November 4, 2007, www.michaelpollan.com/article.php?id=89.

22 Hawken, *The Ecology of Commerce*, 89.

23 Ibid.

24 Myers and Kent, "Perverse Subsidies," xxiii.

25 Gordon Conway, *The Doubly Green Revolution: Food for All in the Twenty-First Century* (Cornell University Press, 1999), 39.

26 Ibid., 37.

27 See virtually anything written by Vandana Shiva, starting perhaps with *Manifestos on the Future of Food and Seed* (South End, 2007).

28 Conway, *The Doubly Green Revolution*, 34. "Fair trade," as it's conventionally understood, means that workers receive a fair wage.

29 Daniel Griswold et al., "Ripe for Reform: Six Good Reasons to Reduce U.S. Farm Subsidies and Trade Barriers," Center for Trade Policy Studies, September 5, 2005, 1–4, www.freetrade.org/pubs/pas/tpa-030.pdf.

30 James M. Sheehan, "Free Trade Is Green Trade," Competitive Enterprise Institute, June 1, 2000, http://cei.org/gencon/019,03111.cfm.

31 Deborah James, "Free Trade and the Environment," Global Exchange, n.d., www.globalexchange.org/campaigns/wto/Environment.html.pf.

32 Ibid.

33 Sheehan, "Free Trade Is Green Trade."

34 Ted Nordhaus and Michael Shellenberger, *Break Through: From the Death of Environmentalism to the Politics of Possibility* (Harcourt, 1991), 57.

35 Daniel K. Benjamin, "Is Free Trade Good for the Environment?," *Property and Environment Research Center Reports* 20, 1 (March 2002), www.perc.org/articles/article262.php; Phil Goff, "Fair Trade and Free Trade—Two Sides of the Same Coin," New Zealand government, July 5, 2008, www.beehive.govt.nz/speech/fair+trade+and+free+trade+%E2%80%93+two+sides+same+coin.

36 Sheehan, "Free Trade Is Green Trade"; Gene M. Grossman and Alan B. Krueger, "Environmental Impacts of a North American Free Trade Agreement," in P. Garber, ed., *The Mexico-U.S. Free Trade Agreement* (MIT Press, 1993), 35.

37 Andersen is quoted in the film *Silent Killer: The Unfinished Campaign Against Hunger*, www.silentkillerfilm.org/interview_andersen.html; Conway, *The Doubly Green Revolution*, 38.

38 Peter Singer and Jim Mason, *The Way We Eat: Why Our Food Choices Matter* (Rodale, 2006), 154.

39 James MacGregor and Bill Vorley, "Fair Miles? The Concept of 'Food Miles' Through a Sustainable Development Lens," *Sustainable Development Opinion*, International Institute for Environment and Development (2006), www.agr.unipi.it/labrural/Didattica/corso-social-and-environmental-assessment-of-food/fair-miles-kenya-vegetables.pdf; James MacGregor and Bill Vorley,

"Fresh Insights: Fair Miles? Weighing Environmental and Social Impacts of Fresh Fruit Exports from Sub-Saharan Africa to the UK," International Institute for Environment and Development (October 2006), 3, www.research4 development.info/PDF/Outputs/EcoDev/fairmiles2.pdf.

40 MacGregor and Vorley, "Fair Miles?"

41 Ibid.

42 Nicholas Stern, "The Economics of Climate Change," *Stern Review* (2006); Delphine Strauss, "French PM Calls for European Carbon Levy," *Financial Times*, November 13, 2006; MacGregor and Vorley, "Fair Miles?"

Conclusion: The Golden Mean

1 Julie Guthman, *Agrarian Dreams: The Paradox of Organic Farming in California* (University of California Press, 2004).

2 Pamela C. Ronald and Raoul W. Adamchak, *Tomorrow's Table: Organic Farming, Genetics, and the Future of Food* (Oxford University Press, 2008), ix.

3 Elizabeth Finkel, "Organic Food Exposed," *Cosmos* 16 August, 2007), www .cosmosmagazine.com/node/1567.

4 Ronald and Adamchak, *Tomorrow's Table.*

5 Victor Davis Hanson, *Fields Without Dreams: Defending the Agrarian Idea* (Free Press, 1996), 16.

6 Juliet Eilperin and Jane Black, "USDA Panel Approved First Rules for Labeling Farmed Fish 'Organic,'" *Washington Post*, November 20, 2008, www .washingtonpost.com/wp-dyn/content/article/2008/11/19/AR2008111903787 .html.

7 Finkel, "Organic Food Exposed."

Acknowledgments

A historian writing about current events is a lot like a fish struggling out of water. In the course of researching and writing this book I've found myself especially dependent on the emotional and intellectual dedication of many gifted individuals. I particularly wish to acknowledge the generosity of my good friend Benjamin A. Hicklin, who stimulated my thoughts and challenged my analysis at every turn; my editor, Asya Muchnick, whose guidance revealed a remarkable ability to grasp the whole picture while managing the finest details; and my agent, Jim Hornfischer, who more than anybody else taught me how to transform ideas into a book. A wonderful year I spent as a fellow in the Agrarian Studies Program at Yale provided me with the time and the intellectual community to sharpen many of my arguments. I'm especially grateful to Jim Scott for creating a stimulating atmosphere dedicated to meaningful dialogue about agricultural issues. My home base at Texas State University continues to offer an ideal professional environment. In the course of writing this book I've benefited greatly from discussions with Margaret Menninger and Ken Margerison. One could not ask for better colleagues. My loving family continues to somehow put up with my long hours of researching and writing, and even longer hours talking about the finer intricacies of food production. It is to my daughter Ceci that I dedicate this book.

Index

About the Author

James E. McWilliams is an associate professor of history at Texas State University at San Marcos and a recent fellow in the Agrarian Studies Program at Yale University. His articles have appeared in the *New York Times, Slate, Washington Post,* and the *Times* of London, among other publications, and he is the author of three previous books and a contributing writer at the *Texas Observer.* He lives in Austin, Texas.

Reading Group Guide

JUST FOOD

WHERE LOCAVORES GET IT WRONG AND HOW WE CAN TRULY EAT RESPONSIBLY

by

JAMES E. McWILLIAMS

The *Just Food* Index

Number of people on earth today: almost 7 billion

Number of people who will live on earth in 2050: 9.5–10 billion

Percentage increase of food needed to feed the world in 2050: 60

Insecticides, herbicides, fungicides, rodenticides, and biocides
added to the environment each year, in pounds: 5–6 billion

Gallons of gasoline required to make enough fertilizer
for one acre of conventionally grown corn: 30

Percent of global warming gas emissions from
all transportation worldwide: 13.5

Percent of global warming gas emissions from livestock: 18

Amount of antibiotics fed to cows each year: 25 million pounds

Calories of fossil fuels required to produce
one food calorie of grain: 0.4–0.7

Calories of fossil fuels required to produce one
food calorie of free-range beef: 3

Calories of fossil fuels required to produce one
calorie of conventionally raised beef: 33

Pounds of grain required to make one pound of beef: 16

Number of cattle currently on earth: 1.3 billion

Number of chickens raised and slaughtered
each year, worldwide: 45 billion

Percentage more land than the earth has that would be required if everyone ate as much meat as Americans do: 67

Percentage of U.S. grain used for animal feed: 80

Amount of carbon dioxide emitted in the production of nitrogen fertilizers: 41 million metric tons

Percentage of the earth's dry land area currently being occupied by cows, pigs, sheep, and chickens: 66

Percentage of soil erosion in the United States which is caused by cattle: 85

Amount of water required to make a hamburger: 2,400 liters

Factor by which methane is more efficient at trapping heat than carbon dioxide: 21–24 times

Amount of methane emitted by livestock each year: 86 million metric tons

Percentage of fish caught by commercial fishing that is by-catch (thrown back, dead): 85–95

Amount of edible grass-fed beef flesh produced per acre of land in a year: 75 pounds

Amount of edible fish flesh produced per acre of land in a year using aquaponics: 35,000 pounds

Gallons of ocean water a bed of farmed oysters can filter and clean each day: 100 million

Corn subsidies that go to the top 10 percent of U.S. corn producers: 71 percent

A Conversation with
James E. McWilliams

Why is the idea of eating locally so appealing to so many people?

The idea of eating locally produced food has intuitive appeal: support the local economy, build community relations, and, by cutting back on "food miles," save the planet. Ultimately, it's a simple and, in general, pretty good idea. But—and this is the premise of my book—there's more, much more, we can do to achieve a sustainable food supply capable of feeding the impending billions an environmentally responsible diet.

Why shouldn't we all be locavores?

We should, but only up to a point. The major problem with the locavore movement, as I see it, is the fact that it stresses locality at the expense of many other propositions that could bring us closer to achieving a sustainable agricultural system. Most notably, if we obsess over food miles, we miss a critical point: the energy expenditure for transportation is small—roughly 10 percent of a food's overall energy cost. By buying local, we may be supporting methods of production that are more energy intensive than they are in places far away. What if a region is water stressed? What if the climate requires hothouses? What if the local beef is produced in an energy-hogging factory farm? If an environmentally sound diet is the goal, there are many cases in which it makes sense to buy from afar—that is, to buy from places where production methods and comparative advantages are low enough to counteract the cost of transportation. The upshot: we need to learn more about the "life cycle" of our food products rather than assume distance is the only measure of sustainability.

How did your thinking change as you were researching and writing this book?

My thinking—and more notably my behavior—changed dramatically with respect to meat. Basically, and much to the dismay of my fifth-generation Texan wife, I became a vegetarian. While my decision had something to do with ethical concerns over animal suffering, the main reason I gave up grilling land-based animals was that I reached the conclusion that it was impossible to be a meat-eating environmentalist. I'm not terribly happy about this realization. I love meat, but there's no way around the inefficiencies of meat production. Compared with plants and certain kinds of fish, meat requires more energy per pound to produce. This claim is true for free-range and grass-fed animals as well as for conventional ones (although to a lesser extent). Farm animals use most of their energy to stay warm and upright. Only 40 percent of their weight is transformed into meat. Conventionally produced animals demand corn-based feed. This feed not only requires massive fertilizer and pesticide inputs, but it's spiked with antibiotics and vaccines. Grass-fed cows emit four times more methane than corn-fed ones (and methane is an exceptionally potent greenhouse gas). Grazing cows trample land, cause soil erosion, ruin riparian zones, and require "manure lagoons" to manage their effluent waste. These lagoons leak. A variety of environmental and health problems result. The lagoons smell. Local residents suffer health problems. I could go on. But, yes, no more meat for me. More than any other argument I make in the book, it's this one—stop eating meat!—that I hope sticks with my readers.

Why did you write Just Food?

I'm a historian by training. I've written extensively about the history of American agriculture and the intricacies of food production. When the locavore trend began to gather steam, I was struck by the historical rhetoric accompanying the movement—namely, the rhetoric that said "eat local because that's how our self-sufficient forebears used to do it." This appeal to the past struck me as, well, dead wrong. I knew that seventeenth-century farmers in Puritan New England worked relentlessly to send their produce overseas. They also wanted food from England, the West Indies, and the Deep South. The locavore movement's blatant mythologization of the yeoman farmer intent on keeping things local led me to suspect that the emperor might lack clothing.

There's another reason, too. In 2007, I wrote an op-ed for the *New York Times* that questioned the logic of the locavore movement. My piece generated a tremendous amount of discussion, even for an op-ed, and it quickly became clear to me that this topic touched a nerve, and that it deserved a book-length treatment.

Global Meat Eating at a Glance

Here's the rundown on some of the key statistics about meat consumption around the world.*

Meat consumption per capita (kg/year) (2002)

New Zealand	142.1
United States	124.8
Spain	118.6
Germany	82.1
Kuwait	60.2
China	52.4
Honduras	24.7
Cambodia	13.9
Ethiopia	7.9
India	5.2

Chicken stocks (thousand heads) (2006)

China	4,356,968
United States	2,050,000
Indonesia	1,366,132
Algeria	125,000
Hungary	31,902
Zimbabwe	23,000
Panama	14,263

*All data comes from Earthtrends.wri.org. Cited January 29, 2010.

Sweden	6,762
Belize	1,600
Mongolia	30

Calorie supply per capita from meat (calories/day) (2002)

Iceland	1,349.7
United States	1,047
Belarus	786.6
Syria	412
Jamaica	392.7
Bolivia	361.5
Morocco	233.7
Yemen	143.4
Sierra Leone	74.4
Congo	35.3

Total grain production fed to livestock (%) (2007)

Canada	66.9
United States	50.1
Argentina	49
Libya	38.5
Guatemala	35.3
China	28.5
Philippines	25.4
Botswana	11.9
Indonesia	8.4
Ivory Coast	2.2

Questions and Topics for Discussion

1. Throughout *Just Food*, McWilliams suggests that the locavore and organic food movements are, to some extent, elitist. Do you agree?

2. How would you describe McWilliams's stance toward the locavore movement? Do you find him to be conciliatory? Combative? Did the book effectively convince you of his ideas?

3. Discuss some of the facts in *Just Food* that were most surprising to you. What assumptions had you previously held about how food is produced that made the information in the book so unexpected?

4. Do you think that your friends, family, or coworkers are aware of your food choices? Have you ever felt judged by a friend who believes his or her choices are more responsible than yours? Have you ever done the judging?

5. In chapter 2, "Organic Panic," McWilliams quotes Nobel Peace Prize winner Norman Borlaug as saying, "If [environmentalists] lived just one month amid the misery of the developing world…they'd be crying out for tractors and fertilizer and irrigation canals and be outraged that fashionable elitists…were trying to deny them these things" (page 60). Imagine for a moment that you have just launched a nonprofit organization with the goal of helping a developing country create a sustainable agriculture industry. What would your

organization's position be about the use of pesticides, GM seeds, inorganic fertilizers, industrial irrigation, and so forth? Would you encourage farmers to focus on producing staple foods, or on growing cash crops that could be exported for profit?

6. McWilliams argues that, in general, buying food from a supermarket is more energy efficient than visiting your local farmers' market. But many people simply enjoy visiting farmers' markets, and feel good about eating food purchased there. To what extent do you think personal happiness should be factored into our decisions about food? When scientific evidence points against choices that feel intuitively right or desirable to you, how do you decide what to do?

7. In chapter 3, McWilliams provides numerous reasons to support the wider use of genetically modified crops. However, he also states that he is opposed to some of the ways agribusiness currently exploits these crops. Do you agree with McWilliams's positions about GM crops? If so, do you think it more important to support GM crops because of their environmental benefits, or to avoid them because big corporations profit from them?

8. Discuss your reaction to chapter 4, "Meat—The New Caviar." Do you agree with McWilliams that to consider oneself an ethical eater one must give up or drastically reduce meat consumption?

9. What was your response to McWilliams's argument in chapter 5, "The Blue Revolution," that aquaculture has a better chance of becoming a sustainable industry than livestock production does? What do you think would need to change in order for Americans to begin relying on fish, rather than meat and

poultry, for the majority of their protein? Can you imagine yourself making this switch?

10. In chapter 6, "Merging Ecology and Economy," McWilliams argues that perverse subsidies "actively and aggressively work against every proposal offered in this book" (page 190). However, if perverse subsidies are eliminated, some foods may become more expensive. Do you think Americans would be willing to pay higher prices for food? How much more would you be willing to pay for sustainably produced food?

11. Before you read *Just Food*, how did you decide which foods to eat? Did you try to eat mostly local, organic, or GM-free foods? Having read *Just Food*, do you plan to make any changes to your eating choices? If so, what do you expect will be the biggest challenges in making these changes?

James E. McWilliams's Suggestions for Further Reading

Here are six of my favorite books about sustainable eating:

Tomorrow's Table by Pamela Ronald and Raoul Adamchak

The End of Food by Paul Roberts

The Way We Eat by Peter Singer and Jim Mason

Agrarian Dreams by Julie Guthman

Against the Grain by Richard Manning

The End of the Line by Charles Clover

THE TIPPING POINT

How Little Things Can Make a Big Difference
by Malcolm Gladwell

"A fascinating book that makes you see the world in a different way."
—*Fortune*

JULIE AND JULIA

My Year of Cooking Dangerously
by Julie Powell

"Powell shows signs of being one of our better, loopier culinary thinkers, more in the iconoclast mode of M. F. K. Fisher than the rhapsodic, sun-dappled vein of *Saveur* magazine at its most perfect-peach fetishizing."   —David Kamp, *New York Times Book Review*

COLD

Adventures in the World's Frozen Places
by Bill Streever

"A crisp and bracing little book....*Cold* is a striding tour through a disappearing world."   —Dwight Garner, *New York Times*

Back Bay Books
Available wherever books are sold